大学英语应用能力进阶系列教材

# 英语语音训练教程

A Training Course
of English
Pronunciation

主　编：梁　鲜
副主编：郭锦萍
编　者：郝文凤　潘海岸　邱新慧

清华大学出版社
北京

## 内容简介

本书专为进一步提高中国学生英语语音能力而设计，旨在通过对英语语音知识的讲解、常见错误发音的分析以及大量发音实例的操练，纠正学生错误发音或不规范的节律和语调，帮助学生最终实现语言交际的准确性、流畅性及有效性。教材共28课，涵盖元音、辅音、音素组合、语流音变、音律节奏、语调六大部分内容。

本书的突出特色在于理论与实践结合，尤其针对中国学生英语学习中的不规范发音现象进行分析，指出弊病原因，提出纠正办法。此外，教材设计以练习为主、讲解为辅，活动真实、丰富，以帮助学习者实现语音能力质的飞跃。

本教程提供配套的音视频资料。请访问www.tsinghuaelt.com，搜索本书书名后获取音视频下载路径。

版权所有，侵权必究。举报：010-62782989，beiqinquan@tup.tsinghua.edu.cn。

**图书在版编目（CIP）数据**

英语语音训练教程 / 梁鲜等主编. —北京：清华大学出版社，2016（2023.9重印）
（大学英语应用能力进阶系列教材）
ISBN 978-7-302-42716-2

Ⅰ.①英… Ⅱ.①梁… Ⅲ.①英语–语音–高等学校–教材
Ⅳ.①H311

中国版本图书馆CIP数据核字（2016）第020232号

**责任编辑**：曹诗悦
**封面设计**：平　原
**责任校对**：王凤芝
**责任印制**：丛怀宇

出版发行：清华大学出版社
网　　址：http:// www.tup.com.cn，http:// www.wqbook.com
地　　址：北京清华大学学研大厦A座　　邮　编：100084
社 总 机：010-83470000　　邮　购：010-62786544
投稿与读者服务：010-62776969, c-service@tup.tsinghua.edu.cn
质量反馈：010-62772015, zhiliang@tup.tsinghua.edu.cn
印 装 者：三河市春园印刷有限公司
经　　销：全国新华书店
开　　本：185mm×260mm　　印　张：16.5　　字　数：307千字
版　　次：2016年9月第1版　　印　次：2023年9月第6次印刷
定　　价：65.00元

产品编号：058960-02

# 总 序

高等教育改革发展在党的十八大之后，站在了新的历史起点上。就大学英语教学本身而言，我们当前面临的主要任务是如何把大学英语课程建设成大学生真心喜欢、终身受益的优质课程，以便更好地满足大学生接受高质量、多样化大学英语教学的需求，更加适应国家经济社会发展对人才培养的新要求。

近十年来，围绕着提高大学英语教学质量这一目标，海南大学的大学英语教学改革经历了四个阶段：

一、2004年参与教育部启动的大学英语教学改革项目，成为全国180家试点院校之一，推行大学英语网络化教学试点；

二、2007年成为全国65所教育部大学英语教学改革示范点单位之一，承担向周边院校推广辐射大学英语教学改革成果的重任；

三、2010年，全面推行大学英语网络化教学，同年海南大学成为大学英语四、六级网考试点单位，大学英语教学改革全面普及；

四、2012年海南大学启动基于课程改革的新一轮大学英语教学改革。此次改革以课程改革为出发点，改变以往大学英语只有一门课程的局面，通过拓展课程逐步形成新的大学英语课程体系，赋予大学英语新的内涵，以满足学生个性需要和社会需求。

此次出版的"大学英语应用能力进阶系列教材"便是我校多年大学英语教学改革的结晶之作。在出版的过程中，我们得到了学校教务处的大力支持，将该系列教材纳入学校"中西部提升项目——本科教学质量与改革工程"的子项目，予以全额资助，并多次组织专家对立项教材的选题、内容给予指导。同时，该系列教材也倾注了相关任课教师的心血，正是由于这些教师多年的坚持积累和无私付出，才有了这些成果。

在本系列教材即将付梓之际，敬请广大读者和专家斧正，使之日臻完善。同时，谨向关心、支持本系列教材的所有相关人员表示衷心感谢！

是为序。

陈鸣芬

2016年4月

# 前 言

本教材是海南大学"中西部提升项目——本科教学质量与改革工程项目"及"海南大学教育教学研究基金项目（hdjy1343）"的系列成果之一，专为学生在完成大学英语基础课程后欲进一步提升英语语音能力而设计，可作为大学英语拓展课程教材使用，亦可供英语专业基础阶段学生及广大英语学习者使用。

本教材旨在通过对英语语音知识的讲解、常见发音错误的分析以及大量相关发音实例的操练，力促学习者加强语音学习的意识，纠正其错误发音或不规范的节律和语调，最终实现语言交际的准确性、流畅性及有效性。

## 设计思路

本教材分6个单元，共28课。每课均设有"考一考""导入""学习目标""学习内容""常见错误""纠错训练"和"专项训练"共7个部分。

"考一考"设计在每课学习之前，选材内容为简短的英语对话、谚语、谜语、小诗等，旨在通过热身的方式，测试学习者是否具备与该课内容相关的语音知识，调动学习积极性，帮助学习者认识到语音知识并非想象中那么枯燥乏味，而是体现在许多平时不太为人注意的语音现象中。

"导入"概括介绍每课将要学习的语音知识，为学习者搭建相应的理论框架，提高学习者的元认知意识。

"学习目标"明确学生每课语音学习所应达到的目标要求。

"学习内容"是每课的主体部分，着重介绍该课所涉及的语音学概念及知识点。

"常见错误"是本教材的特色。该部分针对中国学习者在英语语音语调学习中经常遇到的难点、常犯错误或不规范的语音语调现象进行分析，指出弊病原因，提出纠正办法。

"纠错训练"是一系列有针对性的纠音正音训练，针对"常见错误"板块中提到的各种问题"对症下药"，帮助学习者纠正不正确或不规范的语音语调。

"专项训练"为综合练习，专门针对每课所涉及的语音知识点进行进一步的巩固和强化训练。

# 教材特色

## 1. 理论实用

语音理论及术语在许多学习者看来都过于"高大上"，艰深晦涩却又于实际无裨益。为此，本教材做了如下设计：一是采用汉语行文，以帮助学习者更好地理解理论；二是避免冗长讲解，力求理论实用、深入浅出、通俗易懂。为此，教材在每课开始之前设计了"考一考"这一环节，还在部分章节里增设了"你知道吗"小知识窗口，譬如将英语语音现象与汉语日常交际中类似的语音现象进行横向对比，在帮助学习者加深理论理解的同时拓展其知识面，丰富其语用认知。

## 2. 纠错针对

"纠错训练"为本教材一大亮点。语言学习和健康体检一样，需定期进行全面系统性检查，发现问题时更应看病问诊、对症下药。制约语音学习的要素有很多，除去年龄、个体学习能力以及学习动机等因素外，中国学习者因受其母语音系的负迁移甚至各地方言影响，语音语调问题既有共性，又存在地区性差异。本教材针对中国学习者存在的各种语音语调"亚健康"状况做了较全面的总结归纳，以求提供一幅较为完整的中国学习者英语语音语调"病灶图"，帮助学习者自行"把脉"，并针对各自存在的实际问题加强纠音正音训练。

## 3. 练习丰富

本教材设计思想为讲练结合，练习为主，讲解为辅。题型设计力求多样化和生动化，主要包括：跟读模仿、听辨音、句子听写、视听说练习等。练习安排由浅入深、循序渐进、难易适当。此外，强调一定数量的多角度的听音、辨音、发音操练，以帮助学习者实现语音能力从量变到质变的飞跃。

## 4. 活动真实

本教材除提供母语为英语人士的标准音频外，还在每课中设计了英音视听说练习。英音视听说练习围绕电影对白中相关的语音语调现象进行设计，将原本索然无味的语音学习可视化、娱乐化，充分调动学习者的兴趣，同时培养学习者实际语言交际能力，使其在今后的交际中具备较为规范的语音语调，发音清晰，语流适度，从而使交际顺利自然。

## 教学建议

本教材共 28 课，建议授课学时 30 学时，课外自学辅导 30 学时。考虑到语音训练的系统性和完备性，本教材在内容设计上力求系统全面，但教师在课堂授课时可根据学生水平及具体情况对教学内容进行适度调整和取舍。原则上，建议"纠错训练"及部分"专项训练"用于课堂练习，大部分"专项训练"用于学生课后练习。

与教材配套的音视频资源，学习者可从清华大学出版社的资源库里下载。请学习者访问 www.tsinghuaelt.com，选取所需的视听资源。

## 编者队伍

本教材编写组成员均为海南大学具有多年教学经验的英语教师。主编梁鲜，负责本教材的整体构思、框架设计、全书审稿和统稿以及编写进程的全程监督；副主编郭锦萍，负责教材部分审稿以及第 4 单元和第 5 单元（15~20 课、23~24 课）的编写；邱新慧负责编写第 2 单元和第 6 单元（6~10 课、25~28 课）；郝文凤负责编写第 1 单元（1~5 课）；潘海岸负责编写第 3 单元和第 5 单元（11~14 课、21~22 课）。

## 致谢

靡不有初，鲜克有终。本教材终能出版，实为不易。从最初的酝酿出书、教材构思、人员确定，到具体编写及修改完善，教材编写组遭遇了诸多困难和突发状况。所幸筚路蓝缕，玉汝于成。为此，特向所有为本书编写提供无私帮助的朋友们表示衷心感谢！此外，本书在编写过程中也参考了国内外专家同行们的优秀著作及教材，也向他们致以衷心谢意！因编者水平有限，错误及纰漏在所难免，敬请广大读者及各位同行批评指正。

《英语语音训练教程》编写组
2016 年 3 月

# 目 录

| 第1单元 | 元音音素 | 1 |
|---|---|---|
| 第 1 课 | 前元音 | 2 |
| 第 2 课 | 后元音 | 10 |
| 第 3 课 | 中元音 | 19 |
| 第 4 课 | 合口双元音 | 25 |
| 第 5 课 | 集中双元音 | 33 |

| 第2单元 | 辅音音素 | 39 |
|---|---|---|
| 第 6 课 | 爆破音 | 40 |
| 第 7 课 | 摩擦音 | 48 |
| 第 8 课 | 破擦音 | 57 |
| 第 9 课 | 鼻音和舌侧音 | 63 |
| 第 10 课 | 延续音 | 69 |

| 第3单元 | 音素组合 | 75 |
|---|---|---|
| 第 11 课 | 音节 | 76 |
| 第 12 课 | 读音规则（一） | 84 |
| 第 13 课 | 读音规则（二） | 96 |
| 第 14 课 | 辅音连缀 | 104 |

| 第4单元 | 语流音变 | 113 |
|---|---|---|
| 第 15 课 | 爆破音变 | 114 |
| 第 16 课 | 同化 | 123 |
| 第 17 课 | 连读 | 133 |

| 第 18 课 | 省音 | 144 |
| 第 19 课 | 缩读 | 153 |

## 第 5 单元　音律节奏 ............................................................................ 161

| 第 20 课 | 单词重音 | 162 |
| 第 21 课 | 句子重音 | 172 |
| 第 22 课 | 强读式和弱读式 | 182 |
| 第 23 课 | 节奏 | 192 |
| 第 24 课 | 停顿 | 201 |

## 第 6 单元　语调 ........................................................................................ 209

| 第 25 课 | 语调简介 | 210 |
| 第 26 课 | 陈述句式的语调模式 | 220 |
| 第 27 课 | 疑问句式的语调模式 | 230 |
| 第 28 课 | 其他句式的语调模式 | 238 |

## 附　　录

| 附录 1 | 英语国际音标总表 | 248 |
| 附录 2 | 常用英语语音术语汉英对照表 | 248 |
| 附录 3 | 常用英语语音符号一览表 | 252 |

# 第 1 单元 元音音素

音素于语言就如同砖瓦于楼房,其重要性不言而喻。要学好一门语言,对音素的准确掌握就显得至关重要。

在英语的音素中,发音时气流在口腔中不受发音器官阻碍而形成的音素被称为元音,它们听起来响亮、饱满、清晰。元音音素共有 20 个,包括 12 个单元音和 8 个双元音。

根据发音时舌位最高点出现的位置,英语的 12 个单元音被分成前元音、后元音和中元音。根据发音时口型的前后变化,5 个双元音又被称为合口双元音,而都以中元音 /ə/ 结尾的另外 3 个双元音被称为集中双元音。

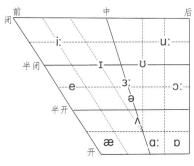

英语元音音素图

如同汉语拼音中有韵母一样,英语音素中有元音音素。二者的相似之处为中国英语学习者提供了一定的便利,然而二者的不同之处也造成了学习者习得英语的某些障碍。有些学习者习惯用一些汉语韵母直接取代英语中的元音音素,从而形成了"独具中式口音的英语发音",一定程度上影响了交流效果。因此,要想说一口流利地道的英语,学习者务必要克服母语负迁移的影响,仔细揣摩英语元音音素的发音特点。

## 第 1 课 前元音

### 考一考

请你和你的同伴大声朗读下面的谚语：
1. A **bad** be**gi**nning **ma**kes a **bad** **e**nding.
2. A **friend** in **need** is a **friend** indeed.
3. A **man** is as old as he **feels**.

请听录音，注意比较黑体单词的发音。这些单词均含有本课将要学习的前元音。你和你的同伴读对了吗？

### 导入

英语前元音音素共有 4 个，包括：/iː/、/ɪ/、/e/ 和 /æ/。该组元音发音时，舌高点都在舌的前部，故称为前元音。根据发音时舌位的高低来排列，/iː/ 的舌位最高，/ɪ/ 次之，/e/ 再次之，/æ/ 的舌位最低。根据发音时开口度的大小来排列，/æ/ 的开口度最大，/e/ 次之，/ɪ/ 再次之，/iː/ 的开口度最小。该组音素在口腔梯形图中的位置详见图 1-1。

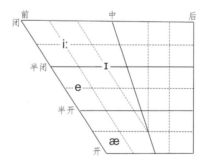

图 1-1　前元音音位图

## 一、学习目标

——了解英语前元音的发音部位及发音要领
——掌握该组元音正确的发音方法和技巧
——纠正该组元音常见的发音错误

## 二、学习内容

### （一）/iː/

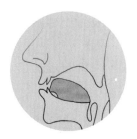

图 1-2　/iː/ 口型图

**发音要领**

1. 舌尖轻抵下牙中部，舌前部向硬腭抬起，但不接触硬腭；
2. 口型接近闭合状，上下齿之间约可放进一根或一根半火柴棍，唇形扁平，呈微笑状；
3. 口腔肌肉紧张，发音较长。

### （二）/ɪ/

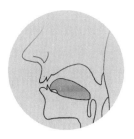

图 1-3　/ɪ/ 口型图

**发音要领**

1. 舌尖轻抵下牙中下部，舌前部向硬腭抬起，但略低于 /iː/ 的舌位，舌高点比 /iː/ 的舌高点略偏后；
2. 口型呈半闭合状，上下齿之间约可放进小指尖，唇形扁平；
3. 口腔肌肉较松弛，发音短促有力。

### （三）/e/

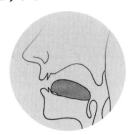

图 1-4　/e/ 口型图

**发音要领**

1. 舌尖轻抵下牙中下部，舌前部稍微抬起，稍低于 /ɪ/ 的舌位；
2. 下颌朝下移动，口型半开半闭，上下齿之间约可放进食指尖，唇形稍扁；
3. 口腔肌肉较松弛，发音短促有力。

### （四）/æ/

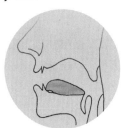

图 1-5　/æ/ 口型图

**发音要领**

1. 舌尖轻抵下齿龈，舌前部微抬起，低于 /e/ 的舌位；
2. 下颌朝下移动，口型接近全开，上下齿之间约可容纳食指和中指叠加的厚度，唇形扁平自然；
3. 口腔肌肉较松弛，发音短促有力。

## 三、常见错误

### （一）单音相混

部分学生对一些单元音的发音技巧和方法掌握不到位，导致发音不准确，听起来变成了另一单元音或其类似音。例如：

| | | | | | | |
|---|---|---|---|---|---|---|
| 1. | 将 /ɪ/ 发成 /i:/ 或其类似音 | eleven | /ɪˈlevn/ | √ | /i:ˈlevən/ | × |
| 2. | 将 /ɪ/ 发成 /e/ 或其类似音 | fix | /fɪks/ | √ | /feks/ | × |
| 3. | 将 /e/ 发成 /æ/ 或其类似音 | excellent | /ˈeksələnt/ | √ | /ˈæksələnt/ | × |
| 4. | 将 /e/ 发成 /ʌ/ 或其类似音 | yet | /jet/ | √ | /jʌt/ | × |
| 5. | 将 /æ/ 发成 /e/ 或其类似音 | bad | /bæd/ | √ | /bed/ | × |
| 6. | 将 /æ/ 发成 /ɑ:/ 或其类似音 | cat | /kæt/ | √ | /kɑ:t/ | × |

**纠正办法**

1. /ɪ/ 和 /i:/：/i:/ 的舌位最高点略前于 /ɪ/ 的舌位最高点，舌位也略高于 /ɪ/ 的舌位。同时，/i:/ 的口型接近闭合，/ɪ/ 的口型则为半闭。同 /ɪ/ 相比，/i:/ 的上下齿之间的距离更小一些。此外，发 /i:/ 时口腔肌肉更紧张一些。
2. /ɪ/ 和 /e/：/ɪ/ 的开口度小于 /e/ 的开口度，且前者发音时的舌位稍高于后者。
3. /e/ 和 /æ/：/e/ 的口型不及 /æ/ 的口型大，而舌位高于 /æ/。
4. /e/ 和 /ʌ/：/e/ 为前元音，舌位最高点在舌的前部，而 /ʌ/ 为中元音，舌位最高点在舌中部，且 /e/ 的开口度不及 /ʌ/ 的大。
5. /æ/ 和 /e/：/æ/ 的口型为自然张大，/e/ 则为半开半闭，/æ/ 的舌位低于 /e/。
6. /æ/ 和 /ɑ:/：/æ/ 为前元音，舌位最高点在舌的前部，/ɑ:/ 为后元音，舌位最高点在舌后部。

### （二）变单为双

一些学生发单元音时，由于前后口型和舌位未能保持一致，从而使发出的音听起来变成了双元音或其类似音。例如：

| | | | | | | |
|---|---|---|---|---|---|---|
| 1. | 将 /i:/ 发成 /eɪ/ 或其类似音 | week | /wi:k/ | √ | /weɪk/ | × |
| 2. | 将 /ɪ/ 发成 /eɪ/ 或其类似音 | kick | /kɪk/ | √ | /keɪk/ | × |
| 3. | 将 /e/ 发成 /aɪ/ 或其类似音 | ahead | /əˈhed/ | √ | /əˈhaɪd/ | × |
| 4. | 将 /e/ 发成 /eɪ/ 或其类似音 | pleasure | /ˈpleʒə/ | √ | /ˈpleɪʒə/ | × |
| 5. | 将 /æ/ 发成 /eɪ/ 或其类似音 | had | /hæd/ | √ | /heɪd/ | × |

6. 将 /æ/ 发成 /aɪ/ 或其类似音　　sad　　　/sæd/　　　√　　/saɪd/　　　×

> **纠正办法**
>
> 1. /iː/ 和 /eɪ/：/iː/ 的舌位高于 /e/ 和 /ɪ/，开口度小于 /e/ 和 /ɪ/，且发音过程中不存在口型和舌位的变化。
> 2. /ɪ/ 和 /eɪ/：/ɪ/ 的舌位高于 /e/，开口度小于 /e/，口型、舌位前后不变。
> 3. /e/ 和 /aɪ/：/e/ 的舌位最高点在舌前部，/ɑ/ 的发音要领同 /ɑː/，但音长不及 /ɑː/，其舌位最高点在舌后部，且 /e/ 开口度不及 /ɑ/ 的大，但大于 /ɪ/ 的开口度，发 /e/ 时，无口型、舌位的变化。
> 4. /e/ 和 /eɪ/：发 /e/ 时，口型、舌位前后无变化，而 /eɪ/ 的口型则由半开半闭到半闭，舌位稍有抬高。
> 5. /æ/ 和 /eɪ/：/æ/ 的开口度大于 /e/ 和 /ɪ/，且舌位低于 /e/ 和 /ɪ/，发 /æ/ 音时，口型和舌位需前后保持一致。
> 6. /æ/ 和 /aɪ/：/æ/ 为前元音，发音时口型、舌位前后无变化；/ɑ/ 的发音要领同 /ɑː/，但音长不及 /ɑː/，发 /aɪ/ 时，从 /ɑ/ 过渡到 /ɪ/，口型由全开过渡到半闭。

## （三）长短不分

以汉语为母语的学习者因受母语负迁移的影响，对长音和短音概念较模糊，往往发音时较随意，因而易将英语元音音素中的长音发得不够长，或拖长部分短音。例如：

1. 将 /iː/ 发成 /ɪ/　　　　meeting　　/ˈmiːtɪŋ/　　√　　/ˈmɪtɪŋ/　　×
2. 将 /ɪ/ 发成 /iː/　　　　rid　　　　/rɪd/　　　　√　　/riːd/　　　×

> **纠正办法**
>
> 牢记英语音素中有长短音之分，长元音音长约为短音音长的两倍；且部分看似成对的长短音，如 /iː/ 和 /ɪ/，实则音质也不同，因而要熟练掌握每个音素的发音技巧和方法。同时，同一元音在浊辅音前往往稍长于其在清辅音之前，如，need 中 /iː/ 的音长要长于 neat 中 /iː/ 的音长。

## （四）汉英混淆

1. 将 /iː/ 用汉语拼音中"yi"(同"一"音)代替　　eat　　/iːt/　　√　　"意特"　×

2. 将 /e/ 用汉语拼音中"e"（同"鹅"音）代替　　pen　/pen/　√　"喷"　×
3. 将 /æ/ 用汉语拼音中"an"（同"安"音）代替　　apple　/ˈæpl/　√　/ˈænpl/　×

**纠正办法**

1. /iː/ 和 "yi"：汉语拼音中，"yi"发音时口腔肌肉的紧张度小于发 /iː/ 的紧张度，嘴角较放松。同时，舌的前部抬起的高度远低于发 /iː/ 时的高度。此外，"yi"的音长短于 /iː/ 的音长。
2. /e/ 和 "e"：英语元音音素 /e/ 的舌位最高点在舌前部，汉语拼音中"e"舌位最高点则在舌中后部，且"e"开口度不及 /e/ 大。同时，发"e"时嘴角不及发 /e/ 时紧张。
3. /æ/ 和 "an"："an"发音时位置靠后，且受"n"的影响有鼻音。而 /æ/ 为前元音，发音时舌前部抬高，且不能出现鼻音。

## 四、纠错训练

**（一）模仿录音，注意区分每组单词中不同的单元音音素。**

**/iː/ 和 /ɪ/**

eat /iːt/　—　it /ɪt/　　　　seat /siːt/　—　sit /sɪt/
leave /liːv/　—　live /lɪv/　　read /riːd/　—　rid /rɪd/

**/ɪ/ 和 /e/**

lit /lɪt/　—　let /let/　　　git /gɪt/　—　get /get/
bid /bɪd/　—　bed /bed/　　wit /wɪt/　—　wet /wet/

**/e/ 和 /æ/**

met /met/　—　mat /mæt/　　head /hed/　—　had /hæd/
end /end/　—　and /ænd/　　pen /pen/　—　pan /pæn/

**/e/ 和 /ʌ/**

get /get/　—　gut /gʌt/　　net /net/　—　nut /nʌt/
shed /ʃed/　—　shut /ʃʌt/　bet /bet/　—　but /bʌt/

### /æ/ 和 /ɑː/

| cat /kæt/ | — | cart /kɑːt/ | chat /tʃæt/ | — | chart /tʃɑːt/ |
| ban /bæn/ | — | barn /bɑːn/ | jam /dʒæm/ | — | jar /dʒɑː/ |

**（二）模仿录音，注意区分每组单词中的单元音和双元音音素。**

### /iː/ 和 /eɪ/

| seem /siːm/ | — | same /seɪm/ | pea /piː/ | — | pay /peɪ/ |
| bee /biː/ | — | bay /beɪ/ | leak /liːk/ | — | lake /leɪk/ |

### /ɪ/ 和 /eɪ/

| did /dɪd/ | — | date /deɪt/ | kick /kɪk/ | — | cake /keɪk/ |
| mid /mɪd/ | — | made /meɪd/ | fix /fɪks/ | — | face /feɪs/ |

### /e/ 和 /aɪ/

| let /let/ | — | light /laɪt/ | bet /bet/ | — | bite /baɪt/ |
| set /set/ | — | sight /saɪt/ | red /red/ | — | ride /raɪd/ |

### /e/ 和 /eɪ/

| met /met/ | — | mate /meɪt/ | rest /rest/ | — | race /reɪs/ |
| shed /ʃed/ | — | shade /ʃeɪd/ | get /get/ | — | gate /geɪt/ |

### /æ/ 和 /eɪ/

| mad /mæd/ | — | made /meɪd/ | lack /læk/ | — | lake /leɪk/ |
| cat /kæt/ | — | Kate /keɪt/ | hat /hæt/ | — | hate /heɪt/ |

### /æ/ 和 /aɪ/

| sat /sæt/ | — | sight /saɪt/ | hat /hæt/ | — | height /haɪt/ |
| bat /bæt/ | — | bite /baɪt/ | tap /tæp/ | — | type /taɪp/ |

## （三）模仿录音，注意单词中前元音音素的音长。

**/iː/**

seat /siːt/ — seed /siːd/    beat /biːt/ — bead /biːd/
leaf /liːf/ — leave /liːv/    neat /niːt/ — need /niːd/

## （四）模仿录音，注意区分单词中的前元音音素和与其相似的汉语拼音。

**/iː/（注意不要将下列单词中的 /iː/ 发成汉语拼音中的"yi"）**

bee /biː/    see /siː/    tree /triː/    key /kiː/

**/e/（注意不要将下列单词中的 /e/ 发成汉语拼音中的"e"）**

pen /pen/    tend /tend/    cent /sent/    mend /mend/

**/æ/（注意不要将下列单词中的 /æ/ 发成汉语拼音中的"安"）**

bad /bæd/    rat /ræt/    apple /'æpl/    at /æt/

## 五、专项训练

### （一）根据录音，完成句子。

1. She _____ him with her _____.
2. It was a real _____ to _____ the Queen.
3. The _____ takes the _____ as his bed.
4. Do not _____ on the _____ floor.
5. A fat _____ sat on a _____.
6. Mary's _____ is very _____.

### （二）比一比，看你和你的同伴谁能读得又快又好？

1. How many sheets could a sheet slitter slit if a sheet slitter could slit sheets?
2. Can you can a can as a canner can can a can?
3. Ann sent Andy ten hens and Andy sent Ann ten pens.

4. A cricket critically cricked his neck at a critical cricket match, and so this cricket quit the cricket match quickly.

5. She sells seashells by the sea shore. The shells she sells are surely seashells, so if she sells shells on the seashore, I'm sure she sells seashore shells.

(三) 英音视听说练习。

欣赏电影《简·爱》(*Jane Eyre*) 片段，并判断以下电影对白中所划出的 8 个单词是否含有本课所学的前元音音素。如果有，请在所标示的横线上写出该音素。

Rochester: You are very quiet this evening. What is on your mind?

　　Jane: Many things, sir. My aunt's 1. <u>death</u>, being 2. <u>back</u> at Thornfield.

Rochester: And?

　　Jane: Adele tells me your 3. <u>sending</u> her away to school.

Rochester: Yes. It's a good idea, don't you think? Paris is her home, after all.

　　Jane: May I ask why, sir?

Rochester: I thought perhaps you might have 4. <u>guessed</u>.

　　Jane: 5. <u>Perhaps</u>, perhaps because you're going to be 6. <u>married</u>?

Rochester: Exactly. 7. <u>Precisely</u>. With your usual acuteness you've hit the nail straight on the head. I am to be married, which means Adele will go away to school. And you will need to find a new situation.

　　Jane: I will 8. <u>advertise</u>… directly.

| 1._____ | 2._____ | 3._____ | 4._____ |
| 5._____ | 6._____ | 7._____ | 8._____ |

# 第 2 课 后元音

### 考一考

请你和你的同伴大声朗读下面的谜语：
1. **What room** has no **walls**, no **doors**, no windows, and no **floors**?
2. **What's too** much **for** one, just right for **two**, but nothing at **all for** three?
3. What **always** travels **on foot**?

请听录音，注意比较黑体单词的发音。这些单词均含有本课将要学习的后元音。你和你的同伴都读对了吗？

### 导入

英语后元音音素共有 5 个，包括 /ɑː/、/ɒ/、/ɔː/、/ʊ/ 和 /uː/。该组元音发音时，舌高点都在舌的后部，故称为后元音。以开口度而言，/ɑː/ 和 /ɒ/ 接近全开，/ɔː/、/ʊ/ 和 /uː/ 的开口度依次变小（详见图 2-1）。

本课所涉及的后元音音素容易同汉语拼音中某些韵母混淆。因此，学习者要注意仔细体会它们的不同。

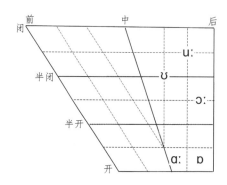

图 2-1 后元音音位图

## 一、学习目标

——了解英语后元音的发音部位及发音要领
——掌握该组元音正确的发音方法和技巧
——纠正该组元音常见的发音错误

## 二、学习内容

### （一）/ɑ:/

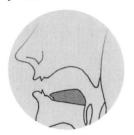

图 2-2 /ɑ:/ 口型图

**发音要领**

1. 舌身放平，稍往后缩，使舌尖不接触下齿龈，舌前部下降，舌高点出现在舌后部；
2. 下颌稍微朝下移动，口型自然张大，唇形自然，略成圆形；
3. 口腔肌肉紧张，发音较长。

### （二）/ɒ/

图 2-3 /ɒ/ 口型图

**发音要领**

1. 舌身放平，稍往后缩，使舌尖不接触下齿龈，舌前部下降，舌高点略高于 /ɑ:/；
2. 下颌朝下移动，口型接近全开，但略微小于 /ɑ:/ 的大小，唇形微圆；
3. 口腔肌肉较松弛，发音较短。

### （三）/ɔ:/

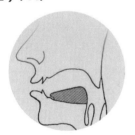

图 2-4 /ɔ:/ 口型图

**发音要领**

1. 舌身放平，稍往后缩，使舌尖不接触下齿龈，舌后部抬起，舌高点略高于 /ɒ/；
2. 下颌朝下移动，口型接近半开，双唇前凸，唇形滚圆；
3. 口腔肌肉紧张，发音较长。

### （四）/ʊ/

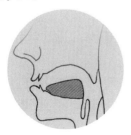

图 2-5 /ʊ/ 口型图

**发音要领**

1. 舌身放平，稍往后缩，使舌尖不接触下齿龈，舌后部抬起，舌高点略高于 /ɔ:/；
2. 下颌略微向上抬高，口型半闭，双唇稍微前凸，唇形自然、较圆，但不及 /u:/ 的唇形圆；
3. 口腔肌肉较松弛，发音较短。

## (五) /uː/

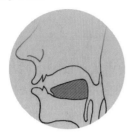

图 2-6 /uː/ 口型图

**发音要领**

1. 舌身放平,稍往后缩,使舌尖不接触下齿龈,舌后部抬起,舌高点略高于 /ʊ/;
2. 下颌向上抬高,口型接近闭合状,双唇前凸,自然圆唇;
3. 口腔肌肉紧张,发音较长。

# 三、常见错误

## (一) 单音相混

| | | | | | | |
|---|---|---|---|---|---|---|
| 1. | 将 /ɑː/ 发成 /ʌ/ 或其类似音 | calm | /kɑːm/ | √ | /kʌm/ | × |
| 2. | 将 /ɑː/ 发成 /ɔː/ 或其类似音 | car | /kɑː/ | √ | /kɔː/ | × |
| 3. | 将 /ɔː/ 发成 /ɜː/ 或其类似音 | war | /wɔː/ | √ | /wɜː/ | × |
| 4. | 将 /ʊ/ 发成 /ɒ/ 或其类似音 | look | /lʊk/ | √ | /lɒk/ | × |
| 5. | 将 /ʊ/ 发成 /uː/ 或其类似音 | cook | /kʊk/ | √ | /kuːk/ | × |
| 6. | 将 /ʊ/ 发成 /ɜː/ 或其类似音 | good | /gʊd/ | √ | /gɜːd/ | × |
| 7. | 将 /uː/ 发成 /ʊ/ 或其类似音 | root | /ruːt/ | √ | /rʊt/ | × |

**纠正办法**

1. /ɑː/ 和 /ʌ/:/ɑː/ 为后元音,发 /ɑː/ 时,舌位最高点出现在舌后部,且口型自然张大。/ʌ/ 为中元音,发 /ʌ/ 时舌位最高点在舌中部,口型不及 /ɑː/ 的口型大。

2. /ɑː/ 和 /ɔː/:/ɑː/ 为后元音,舌高点略前于 /ɔː/ 的舌高点,口型自然张大,唇形自然,略成圆形。/ɔː/ 为后元音,口型接近半开,圆唇音。

3. /ɔː/ 和 /ɜː/:/ɔː/ 为后元音,舌高点在口腔后部,口型为半开,圆唇音。/ɜː/ 为中元音,舌高点在舌中部,口型为半开半闭,唇形扁平。

4. /ʊ/ 和 /ɒ/:/ʊ/ 为后元音,口型半闭,舌位最高点略前于 /ɒ/,圆唇音。/ɒ/ 为后元音,口型接近全开,圆唇音。

5. /ʊ/ 和 /uː/:/ʊ/ 为后元音,舌位最高点稍前于 /uː/,口型为半闭,开口度大于 /uː/,口腔肌肉不及 /uː/ 紧张。/uː/ 为后元音,口型小于半闭,口腔肌肉紧张,音长约为 /ʊ/ 的两倍。

6. /ʊ/ 和 /ɜː/：/ʊ/ 为后元音，口型半闭，圆唇音。/ɜː/ 为中元音，舌位最高点前于 /ʊ/，开口度稍大于 /ʊ/，唇形扁平，音长约为 /ʊ/ 的两倍。

## （二）变单为双

1. 将 /ɒ/ 发成 /əʊ/ 或其类似音　　soft　　/sɒft/　　√　　/səʊft/　　×
2. 将 /ɑː/ 发成 /aɪ/ 或其类似音　　park　　/pɑːk/　　√　　/paɪk/　　×
3. 将 /ʊ/ 发成 /ʊə/ 或其类似音　　look　　/lʊk/　　√　　/lʊək/　　×

**纠正办法**

1. /ɒ/ 和 /əʊ/：/ɒ/ 为单元音、后元音，舌高点在舌后部，口型接近全开，圆唇音。该元音发音时，口型、舌位前后均保持一致。/əʊ/ 为双元音，其中 /ə/ 为中元音，舌高点在舌中部，口型接近半开，为非圆唇音；/ʊ/ 为后元音，舌高点在舌后部，口型半闭，唇形较圆。该双元音发音时要从 /ə/ 的口型和舌位变至 /ʊ/ 的口型和舌位。

2. /ɑː/ 和 /aɪ/：/ɑː/ 为单元音、后元音，舌高点在舌后部，口型自然张大，略成圆形。/aɪ/ 为双元音，其中 /a/ 的发音要领同 /ɑː/ 一致，但音长不及 /ɑː/ 的音长；/ɪ/ 则为前元音，舌高点在舌前部，口型半闭，唇形扁平。发 /aɪ/ 音时要从 /a/ 的口型和舌位变至 /ɪ/ 的口型和舌位。

3. /ʊ/ 和 /ʊə/：/ʊ/ 为单元音、后元音，舌高点在舌后部，口型半闭，圆唇音。/ʊə/ 为双元音，其中 /ʊ/ 的发音要领不变，/ə/ 为中元音，舌高点在舌中部，口型接近半开，为非圆唇音。发 /ʊə/ 时要从 /ʊ/ 的口型和舌位变至 /ə/ 的口型和舌位。

## （三）长短不分

1. 将 /ɔː/ 发成 /ɒ/　　　　　　　　four　　/fɔː/　　√　　/fɒ/　　×
2. 将 /ɒ/ 发成 /ɔː/ 或其类似音　　　not　　 /nɒt/　　√　　/ˈnɔːt/　　×

**纠正办法**

/ɒ/ 和 /ɔː/：/ɒ/ 为后元音，口型接近全开，发音时嘴唇肌肉不及 /ɔː/ 紧张。/ɔː/ 为后元音，口型为半开，音长约为 /ɒ/ 的两倍。

## （四）任意卷舌

很多学生受美式英语卷舌音的影响，习惯任意卷舌。例如：

1. 将 /ɒ/ 发成 /ɒr/     because   /bɪˈkɒz/   √   /bɪˈkɒrz/   ×
2. 将 /ɔː/ 发成 /ɔːr/    sauce     /sɔːs/    √   /sɔːrs/    ×
3. 将 /ɑː/ 发成 /ɑːr/   class     /klɑːs/   √   /klɑːrs/   ×

**纠正办法**

英式发音中，不论单词中的元音后有无"r"，都不卷舌；而美式发音中，有"r"时卷舌，无"r"时不卷舌。

## （五）汉英混淆

1. 将 /ɑː/ 用汉语拼音中"a"代替（同"阿"音）    bar   /bɑː/    √  "爸"   ×
2. 将 /ɒ/ 用汉语拼音中"ao"代替（同"奥"音）   box   /bɒks/   √  "抱 ks" ×
3. 将 /ɒ/ 用汉语拼音中"o"代替（同"窝"音）    dog   /dɒg/    √  "多 g"  ×
4. 将 /ɔː/ 用汉语拼音中"ao"代替（同"奥"音）  door  /dɔː/    √  "道"   ×
5. 将 /ʊ/ 用汉语拼音中"wu"代替（同"乌"音）   book  /bʊk/    √  "不 k"  ×
6. 将 /uː/ 用汉语拼音中"wu"代替（同"乌"音）  moon  /muːn/   √  "木 n"  ×

**纠正办法**

1. /ɑː/ 和"a"：/ɑː/ 发音时位置比"a"靠后，且开口度大于"a"。
2. /ɒ/ 和"ao"：/ɒ/ 发音时，位置更靠后，开口度也大于"ao"。
3. /ɒ/ 和"o"：/ɒ/ 的发音位置更靠后，开口度更大，圆唇程度不及"o"。
4. /ɔː/ 和"ao"：/ɔː/ 比"ao"的发音位置更靠后，开口度不及后者，口腔肌肉比后者紧张。
5. /ʊ/ 和"wu"：/ʊ/ 发音时圆唇程度不及"wu"，口腔肌肉不及后者紧张。
6. /uː/ 和"wu"：/uː/ 比"wu"的发音位置稍靠后，口腔肌肉比后者紧张。

## 四、纠错训练

**（一）模仿录音，注意区分每组单词中不同的单元音音素。**

/ɑː/ 和 /ʌ/

art /ɑːt/ — us /ʌs/   bark /bɑːk/ — but /bʌt/
cart /kɑːt/ — cut /kʌt/   calm /kɑːm/ — come /kʌm/

/ɑː/ 和 /ɔː/

barn /bɑːn/ — born /bɔːn/   far /fɑː/ — four /fɔː/
car /kɑː/ — core /kɔː/   shard /ʃɑːd/ — short /ʃɔːt/

/ɔː/ 和 /ɜː/

reform /rɪˈfɔːm/ — refer /rɪˈfɜː/   court /kɔːt/ — curt /kɜːt/
bought /bɔːt/ — bird /bɜːd/   war /wɔː/ — work /wɜːk/

/ʊ/ 和 /ɒ/

put /pʊt/ — pot /pɒt/   look /lʊk/ — lock /lɒk/
should /ʃʊd/ — shop /ʃɒp/   hook /hʊk/ — hot /hɒt/

/uː/ 和 /ʊ/

cool /kuːl/ — cook /kʊk/   loot /luːt/ — look /lʊk/
pool /puːl/ — put /pʊt/   moon /muːn/ — wool /wʊl/

/ʊ/ 和 /ɜː/

hood /hʊd/ — heard /hɜːd/   look /lʊk/ — lurk /lɜːk/
book /bʊk/ — bird /bɜːd/   should /ʃʊd/ — shirt /ʃɜːt/

**（二）模仿录音，注意区分每组单词中的单元音和双元音音素。**

/ɒ/ 和 /əʊ/

not /nɒt/ — no /nəʊ/   lot /lɒt/ — low /ləʊ/
shot /ʃɒt/ — show /ʃəʊ/   pot /pɒt/ — post /pəʊst/

/ɑː/ 和 /aɪ/

heart /hɑːt/ — height /haɪt/   bar /bɑː/ — buy /baɪ/
hard /hɑːd/ — hide /haɪd/   mark /mɑːk/ — Mike /maɪk/

（三）模仿录音，注意单词中后元音音素的音长。

/ɔː/

door /dɔː/   core /kɔː/   floor /flɔː/   form /fɔːm/
cause /kɔːz/   horse /hɔːs/   short /ʃɔːt/   snore /snɔː/

（四）模仿录音，注意不要在单词中的后元音音素后卷舌。

/ɒ/

box /bɒks/   dot /dɒt/   ox /ɒks/   because /bɪˈkɒz/

/ɔː/

bought /bɔːt/   caught /kɔːt/   cause /kɔːz/   thought /θɔːt/

/ɑː/

fast /fɑːst/   blast /blɑːst/   glass /glɑːs/   task /tɑːsk/

（五）模仿录音，注意区分单词中的后元音音素和与其相似的汉语拼音。

/ɑː/（注意不要将下列单词中的 /ɑː/ 发成汉语拼音中的 "a"）

father /ˈfɑːðə/   ask /ɑːsk/   harvest /ˈhɑːvɪst/   pass /pɑːs/

/ɒ/（注意不要将下列单词中的 /ɒ/ 发成汉语拼音中的 "ao" 或 "o"）

spot /spɒt/   fox /fɒks/   stop /stɒp/   bomb /bɒm/

/ɔː/（注意不要将下列单词中的 /ɔː/ 发成汉语拼音中的 "ao"）

before /bɪˈfɔː/   form /fɔːm/   saw /sɔː/   accord /əˈkɔːd/

## /ʊ/（注意不要将下列单词中的 /ʊ/ 发成汉语拼音中的 "wu"）

woman /ˈwʊmən/    goods /gʊdz/    cookie /ˈkʊkɪ/    football /ˈfʊtbɔːl/

## /uː/（注意不要将下列单词中的 /uː/ 发成汉语拼音中的 "wu"）

blue /bluː/    through /θruː/    root /ruːt/    noon /nuːn/

## 五、专项训练

**（一）根据录音，完成句子。**

1. With a _____ knife, they go out after _____.
2. The _____ and broke.
3. The _____ of the ship was due _____.
4. They are so poor that they cannot _____ a _____.
5. The _____ proves to be _____.
6. She goes there _____ a week.

**（二）比一比，看你和你的同伴谁能读得又快又好？**

1. Give papa a cup of proper coffee in a copper coffee cup.
2. How much dew would a dewdrop drop if a dewdrop could drop dew?
3. Paul called from the hall that he had slipped on the floor and couldn't get to the door.
4. Who washed Washington's white woolen underwear when Washington's washer woman went west?
5. A tutor who tooted a flute tried to tutor two tooters to toot. The two said to their tutor, "Is it harder to toot or to tutor two tooters to toot?"

**（三）英音视听说练习。**

欣赏电影《简·爱》（*Jane Eyre*）片段，并判断以下电影对白中所划出的 8 个单词是否含有本课所学的后元音音素。如果有，请在所标示的横线上写出该音素。

Jane:　　　Adele, 1. <u>watch</u> and listen.

Adele:　　Do you mean like this?

Rochester: I have examined Adele. I've found that you've taken great pains with her. She's not bright. She's no particular talent. Given a very short time, she's made much 2. <u>improvement</u>.

Jane: She has worked hard.

Rochester: I gather you are teaching her to play the piano.

Jane: Yes, sir.

Rochester: Are you 3. <u>fond</u> of music? Do you play well?

Jane: I'm very fond of music. I play a little.

Rochester: A little. Like any other English schoolgirl. Perhaps better than some but not... Well, Adele showed me some sketches. She said they were yours. I don't know if they were entirely of your doing. Perhaps some 4. <u>master</u> helped you?

Jane: No one helped me, sir.

Rochester: Ah. That wounds your pride. These pictures must have taken much time and 5. <u>thought</u>. When did you do them?

Jane: In the last two vacations I spent at Lowood.

Rochester: Did you copy them?

Jane: No, sir. They came out of my head.

Rochester: That head I see now on your 6. <u>shoulders</u>?

Jane: Yes, sir.

Rochester: Has it other furniture of the same kind within?

Jane: I think it may have. Better, I hope.

Rochester: Were you happy when you painted these pictures?

Jane: I didn't have the skill to paint what was in my imagination. I always wanted to achieve more.

Rochester: You may have insufficient technique. But the thoughts are magical. Ah, nine o'clock. Is Adele in bed?

Jane: Not yet, sir.

Rochester: She 7. <u>should</u> be in bed long before this. I don't 8. <u>approve</u> of these late hours. See to it, Miss Eyre.

1. _____   2. _____   3. _____   4. _____
5. _____   6. _____   7. _____   8. _____

第 1 单元　元音音素

## 第 3 课　中元音

### 考一考

请和你的同伴大声朗读下面的对话：

Mom: **Honey**, what do you want for your **birthday**?

Daughter: Mm. I have no idea. Lily's mom gave **her a** pet **bird**. It's cute.

Mom: Then, what **about a** pet dog for you?

Daughter: Great!

请听录音，注意比较黑体单词的发音。这些单词均含有本课将要学习的中元音。你和你的同伴都读对了吗？

### 导入

英语中中元音音素共有 3 个，包括 /ʌ/、/ɜː/ 和 /ə/。该组元音发音时，舌位的最高点出现在舌中部，因此被称为中元音。此外，舌尖均不接触下齿，舌中部抬高，开口度按 /ɜː/、/ə/ 和 /ʌ/ 的顺序依次增大。其中，音素 /ɜː/ 往往出现在重读音节，而音素 /ə/ 则出现在非重读音节，且英语中的很多音最后都弱化为该音（详见本书第 5 单元"音律节奏"部分）。中元音音素在口腔梯形图中的位置详见图 3-1。

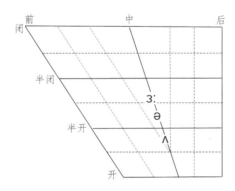

图 3-1　中元音音位图

19

## 一、学习目标

——了解英语中中元音的发音部位及发音要领
——掌握该组元音正确的发音方法和技巧
——纠正该组元音常见的发音错误

## 二、学习内容

### （一）/ʌ/

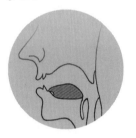

图 3-2　/ʌ/ 口型图

**发音要领**

1. 舌身低平，舌尖轻触下齿龈上方，舌中部稍微抬起，舌高点较 /ɜː/ 和 /ə/ 略微靠后；
2. 下颌朝下移动，口型略大于半开，唇形扁平，大于 /ə/ 的开口度；
3. 口腔肌肉较松弛，发音短促有力。

### （二）/ɜː/

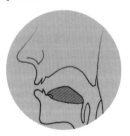

图 3-3　/ɜː/ 口型图

**发音要领**

1. 舌身低平，舌尖轻触下齿龈上方，舌中部稍微抬起；
2. 口型半开半闭，唇形扁平；
3. 口腔肌肉紧张，发音较长。

### （三）/ə/

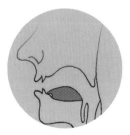

图 3-4　/ə/ 口型图

**发音要领**

1. 舌身低平，舌尖轻触下齿龈上方，舌中部稍微抬起；
2. 口型接近半开，唇形扁平、放松；
3. 口腔肌肉较松弛，发音短而弱。

## 三、常见错误

### （一）单音相混

1. 将 /ʌ/ 发成 /ɑː/ 的短音或其近似音　　touch　/tʌtʃ/　√　/tɑtʃ/　×
2. 将 /ʌ/ 发成 /ɒ/ 或其近似音　　　　　　come　/kʌm/　√　/kɒm/　×
3. 将 /ɜː/ 发成 /ɔː/ 或其近似音　　　　　work　/wɜːk/　√　/wɔːk/　×

**纠正办法**

1. /ʌ/ 和 /ɑː/：/ʌ/ 为中元音，发音时舌位最高点在舌中部，口型不及 /ɑː/ 的口型大。/ɑː/ 为后元音，发音时，舌位最高点出现在舌后部，且口型自然张大。
2. /ʌ/ 和 /ɒ/：/ʌ/ 为中元音，发音时，舌中部稍微抬起，口型略大于半开，不及 /ɒ/ 的开口度大。/ɒ/ 为后元音，发音时，舌后部抬起，口型接近全开，唇形微圆。
3. /ɜː/ 和 /ɔː/：/ɜː/ 为中元音，发音时，舌高点在舌中部，唇形扁平。/ɔː/ 为后元音，发音时，舌高点在舌后部，为圆唇音。

### （二）长短不分

1. 将 /ʌ/ 发成 /ʌː/　　　　　　　love　/lʌv/　√　/lʌːv/　×
2. 将 /ɜː/ 发成 /ɜ/ 或者 /ə/　　　word　/wɜːd/　√　/wəd/　×
3. 将 /ə/ 发成 /əː/　　　　　　　after　/ˈɑːftə/　√　/ˈɑːftəː/　×

**纠正办法**

牢记长音音长约为短音的两倍。

### （三）任意卷舌

将 /ə/ 发成 /ər/　　　　　　　famous　/ˈfeɪməs/　√　/ˈfeɪmərs/　×

**纠正办法**

英式发音，不论单词中的元音后有无"r"，都不卷舌。而美式发音，有"r"时卷舌，无"r"时不卷舌。

## （四）"汉英混淆"

将 /ɜː/ 用汉语拼音中 "e" 代替（同 "饿" 音）　　earth /ɜːθ/　√　"饿θ"　×

**纠正办法**

仔细对比两者发音要领的差异：/ɜː/ 为中元音，发音时，舌的中部稍微抬起；而汉语拼音中的 "e" 发音时，发音位置更靠后。其次，英语中的 /ɜː/ 的唇形比汉语的 "e" 的唇形稍扁，口腔肌肉也更紧张。

## 四、纠错训练

### （一）模仿录音，注意区分每组单词中不同的单元音音素。

**/ʌ/ 和 /ɑː/**

| hut /hʌt/ | — | heart /hɑːt/ | muck /mʌk/ | — | mark /mɑːk/ |
| luck /lʌk/ | — | lark /lɑːk/ | much /mʌtʃ/ | — | march /mɑːtʃ/ |

**/ʌ/ 和 /ɒ/**

| suck /sʌk/ | — | sock /sɒk/ | sun /sʌn/ | — | song /sɒŋ/ |
| nut /nʌt/ | — | not /nɒt/ | cut /kʌt/ | — | cock /kɒk/ |

**/ɜː/ 和 /ɔː/**

| third /θɜːd/ | — | thought /θɔːt/ | shirt /ʃɜːt/ | — | short /ʃɔːt/ |
| nurse /nɜːs/ | — | north /nɔːθ/ | firm /fɜːm/ | — | form /fɔːm/ |

### （二）模仿录音，注意每组单词中中元音音素的音长。

**/ʌ/**

| rough /rʌf/ | button /ˈbʌtn/ | muff /mʌf/ | up /ʌp/ |
| trust /trʌst/ | enough /ɪˈnʌf/ | touch /tʌtʃ/ | drum /drʌm/ |

## /ɜː/

| | | | |
|---|---|---|---|
| murder /ˈmɜːdə/ | further /ˈfɜːðə/ | church /tʃɜːtʃ/ | verb /vɜːb/ |
| person /ˈpɜːsn/ | blur /blɜː/ | nerve /nɜːv/ | shirt /ʃɜːt/ |

## /ə/

| | | | |
|---|---|---|---|
| after /ˈɑːftə/ | luster /ˈlʌstə/ | tender /ˈtendə/ | remember /rɪˈmembə/ |
| lender /ˈlendə/ | butter /ˈbʌtə/ | former /ˈfɔːmə/ | poster /ˈpəʊstə/ |

**（三）模仿录音，注意不要在单词中的中元音音素后卷舌。**

## /ə/

| | | |
|---|---|---|
| custom /ˈkʌstəm/ | position /pəˈzɪʃn/ | famous /ˈfeɪməs/ |
| jealous /ˈdʒeləs/ | dilemma /dɪˈlemə/ | drama /ˈdrɑːmə/ |

**（四）模仿录音，注意区分单词中的中元音音素和与其相似的汉语拼音。**

**/ɜː/（注意不要将下列单词中的 /ɜː/ 发成汉语拼音中的"e"）**

| | | | |
|---|---|---|---|
| urge /ɜːdʒ/ | worth /wɜːθ/ | purse /pɜːs/ | word /wɜːd/ |

# 五、专项训练

## （一）根据录音，完成句子。

1. The _____ about her son.
2. The _____ on the wall.
3. He's just the _____ we need for the _____.
4. If he doesn't stop _____ so hard, he'll _____ himself out.
5. Whenever I was in _____, she would come to _____ me.
6. The _____ was released _____ because of good conduct.

## （二）比一比，看你和你的同伴谁能读得又快又好？

1. A skunk sat on a stump. The skunk thought the stump stunk, and the stump thought the skunk stunk.

2. Never trouble trouble till trouble troubles you.
3. Dust is a disk's worst enemy.
4. Thank the other three brothers of their father's mother's brother's side.
5. To run and play under the sun is fun. When your work is done, come out in the sun and have some fun.

(三) 英音视听说练习。

欣赏电影《简·爱》(*Jane Eyre*) 片段，并判断以下电影对白中所划出的 8 个单词是否含有本课所学的中元音音素。如果有，请在所标示的横线上写出该音素。

Jane: Mrs. Fairfax. 1. <u>Pilot</u>. Hello, Pilot.

Rochester: Pilot. Pilot. No more 2. <u>noise</u>.

Mrs. Fairfax: Miss Eyre.

Rochester: Mrs. Fairfax? Bring me a glass of 3. <u>water</u>. Who's there? Who is it?

Jane: Pilot knows me.

Rochester: My brain will 4. <u>burst</u>. What delusion is this? What sweet madness? Her 5. <u>fingers</u>... her very fingers. Jane Eyre. Jane Eyre. So many times I've dreamed of this 6. <u>moment</u>. Then the dream 7. <u>vanishes</u> and flies away. Just like a dream. Kiss me 8. <u>before</u> you go.

Jane: I shall never leave you.

| 1. _____ | 2. _____ | 3. _____ | 4. _____ |
| 5. _____ | 6. _____ | 7. _____ | 8. _____ |

# 第 4 课 合口双元音

● 考一考

请你和你的同伴大声朗读下面的谚语：

1. A book is the **same today** as it **always** was and it will never **change**.
2. A **road** of a **thousand miles** begins with one step.
3. A **wise** head **makes** a **close mouth**.

请听录音，注意比较黑体单词的发音。这些单词均含有本课将要学习的合口双元音。你和你的同伴都读对了吗？

● 导入

英语中合口双元音音素共有 5 个，包括 /eɪ/、/aɪ/、/ɔɪ/、/əʊ/ 和 /aʊ/。该组音素发音时，均从前一个单元音音素自然、连贯地过渡到第二个音素。其中，第一个音素发音响亮、饱满，而第二个音素发音弱而模糊。该组元音发音时均具备口型从大到小、由张到合的特点，故被称为合口双元音。

## 一、学习目标

——了解英语合口双元音的发音部位及发音要领

——掌握该组元音正确的发音方法和技巧

——纠正该组元音常见的发音错误

## 二、学习内容

### （一）/eɪ/

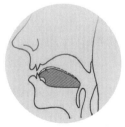

图 4-1　/eɪ/ 口型图

**发音要领**

1. 先清晰、响亮地发出 /e/，再滑至 /ɪ/，舌位由低到高，舌高点均在舌前部；
2. 口型由接近半开到半闭，唇形整体扁平；
3. /e/ 较长，/ɪ/ 弱而模糊，二者前后无停顿，衔接自然、连贯。

## （二）/aɪ/

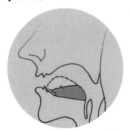

图 4-2　/aɪ/ 口型图

**发音要领**

1. 先清晰、响亮地发出 /a/，再滑至 /ɪ/，舌位由低到高，舌高点由舌后部移至舌前部；
2. 口型由全开到半闭，唇形由自然略圆变为扁平；
3. /a/ 较长，/ɪ/ 弱而模糊，二者前后无停顿，衔接自然、连贯。

## （三）/ɔɪ/

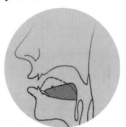

图 4-3　/ɔɪ/ 口型图

**发音要领**

1. 先清晰、响亮地发出 /ɔ/，再滑至 /ɪ/，舌位由低向高，舌高点由舌后部移至舌前部；
2. 口型由接近全开到半闭，唇形由圆唇变为扁平；
3. /ɔ/ 较长，/ɪ/ 弱而模糊，二者前后无停顿，衔接自然、连贯。

## （四）/əʊ/

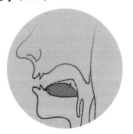

图 4-4　/əʊ/ 口型图

**发音要领**

1. 先清晰、响亮地发出 /ə/，再滑至 /ʊ/，舌位由低到高，舌高点由舌中部移至舌后部；
2. 口型由接近半开到略小于半闭，唇形由扁平变为较圆；
3. /ə/ 较长，/ʊ/ 弱而模糊，二者前后无停顿，衔接自然、连贯。

## （五）/aʊ/

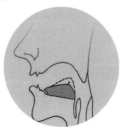

图 4-5　/aʊ/ 口型图

**发音要领**

1. 先清晰、响亮地发出 /a/，再滑至 /ʊ/，舌位由低到高，舌高点在舌后部；
2. 口型由全开变为半闭，唇形由自然略圆变为较圆；
3. /a/ 较长，/ʊ/ 弱而模糊，二者前后无停顿，衔接自然、连贯。

## 三、常见错误

### （一）双音相混

有些学生在发合口双元音时，其中一个音素甚至两个音素发音均不到位，从而使发出的双元音听起来"变了味"，有的甚至变成了一个根本不存在的"双元音"。例如：

将 /ɔɪ/ 发成 /ɔe/ 或其类似音　　boy　　/bɔɪ/　　√　　/bɔe/　　×

**纠正办法**

/ɔɪ/ 和 /ɔe/：/ɪ/ 的口型为半闭合状，/e/ 为半开，且前者发音时的舌位稍高于后者。

### （二）变双为单

汉语拼音中虽然有复韵母，但其发音方式同英语双元音迥然不同，不存在从前一个音素滑至后一个音素。因而，一些中国学生在发英语双元音时，对"从前一音素滑至后一音素"的发音方式缺乏充分的认识，有时直接如同发汉语复韵母一样，没有前后过渡，双元音变成了单元音。

- **变双为短**

有些学生将双元音发成了单元音、短元音。例如：

1. 将 /eɪ/ 发成 /ɪ/ 或其类似音　　contain　　/kənˈteɪn/　　√　　/kənˈtɪn/　　×
2. 将 /aɪ/ 发成 /e/ 或其类似音　　night　　/naɪt/　　√　　/net/　　×
3. 将 /aɪ/ 发成 /æ/ 或其类似音　　time　　/taɪm/　　√　　/tæm/　　×
4. 将 /aɪ/ 发成 /a/ 或其类似音　　bite　　/baɪt/　　√　　/bat/　　×
5. 将 /əʊ/ 发成 /ɒ/ 或其类似音　　tomorrow　　/tʊˈmɒrəʊ/　　√　　/təˈmɒrɒ/　　×

**纠正办法**

1. /eɪ/ 和 /ɪ/：先发 /e/，再滑至 /ɪ/，/e/ 和 /ɪ/ 同为前元音，但前者开口度大于后者，舌高点比后者略微靠前。
2. /aɪ/ 和 /e/：/a/ 的发音要领同 /ɑː/，但音长不及 /ɑː/，其口型自然张大；/e/ 为前元音，开口度小于 /a/。发完 /a/ 之后滑至 /ɪ/。/ɪ/ 和 /e/ 同为前元音，但开口度小于后者，/ɪ/ 的舌位略高于 /e/。
3. /aɪ/ 和 /æ/：/a/ 的发音要领同 /ɑː/，但音长不及 /ɑː/，其口型自然张大；

滑至 /ɪ/ 时，口型为半闭，舌高点由后到前。/æ/ 为前元音，口型接近全开，舌高点在舌前部，前后口型、唇形无变化。

4. /aɪ/ 和 /ɑ/：先发 /a/，再滑至 /ɪ/。/a/ 的发音要领同 /ɑː/，但音长不及 /ɑː/，其口型自然张大；/ɪ/ 为前元音，口型为半闭。

5. /əʊ/ 和 /ɒ/：/ə/ 为中元音，口型接近半开，唇形扁平；/ʊ/ 为后元音，口型为半闭，唇形较圆。/ɒ/ 为后元音，口型接近全开，唇形自然成圆形。

- 变双为长

有些学生将双元音发成了单元音、长元音。例如：

1. 将 /eɪ/ 发成 /eː/ 或其类似音　　name　　/neɪm/　　√　　/neːm/　　×
2. 将 /aʊ/ 发成 /ɑː/ 或其类似音　　proud　　/praʊd/　　√　　/prɑːd/　　×
3. 将 /aʊ/ 发成 /ɔː/ 或其类似音　　outside　　/ˈaʊtsaɪd/　　√　　/ˈɔːtsaɪd/　　×

**纠正办法**

1. /eɪ/ 和 /eː/：前者由 /e/ 滑至 /ɪ/，口型由半开半闭变为半闭，舌位也稍微有抬高；后者是将 /e/ 拖长，前后无口型、舌位的变化。
2. /aʊ/ 和 /ɑː/：前者先发 /a/，再滑至 /ʊ/；后者前后无口型、舌位的变化。
3. /aʊ/ 和 /ɔː/：/aʊ/ 由 /a/ 滑至 /ʊ/，口型由接近半开到半闭，唇形由自然略圆到较圆。/ɔː/ 的口型为接近半开，唇形滚圆。

## （三）汉英混淆

1. 将 /aɪ/ 用汉语拼音中 "ai" 代替（同 "爱" 音）　　why　　/waɪ/　　√　　"外"　　×
2. 将 /ɔɪ/ 发成近似汉语 "ao ei"（同 "奥诶" 的音）　　toy　　/tɔɪ/　　√　　"掏诶"　　×
3. 将 /əʊ/ 用汉语拼音中 "ou" 代替（同 "欧" 音）　　road　　/rəʊd/　　√　　"肉 d"　　×
4. 将 /aʊ/ 用汉语拼音中 "ao" 代替（同 "奥" 音）　　about　　/əˈbaʊt/　　√　　"ə 抱 t"　　×

**纠正办法**

1. /aɪ/ 和 "ai"：/a/ 的发音要领同 /ɑː/，但音长不及 /ɑː/，发音位置比 "ai" 靠后，且口型大于 "ai"；/aɪ/ 发音时要从 /a/ 滑至 /ɪ/，而 "ai" 则无须从前音滑至后音。
2. /ɔɪ/ 和 "ao ei"：/ɔ/ 的发音位置比 "ao" 靠后，开口度大于 "ao"，/ɪ/

的发音位置比"ei"靠前，开口度小于"ei"。

3. /əʊ/ 和"ou"："ou"的发音位置比 /ə/ 靠后，且无须从前音滑至后音，/əʊ/ 则先发 /ə/，再滑至 /ʊ/。

4. /aʊ/ 和"ao"：/aʊ/ 先发 /a/，再发 /ʊ/，"ao" 则无须从前音滑至后音，且 /a/ 的开口度大于"ao"。

## 四、纠错练习

**（一）模仿录音，注意不要将下列单词中的 /ɔɪ/ 读成 /əɪ/。**

/ɔɪ/

| voice /vɔɪs/ | noise /nɔɪz/ | annoy /ə'nɔɪ/ | royal /'rɔɪəl/ |
| avoid /ə'vɔɪd/ | boil /bɔɪl/ | roil /rɔɪl/ | choice /tʃɔɪs/ |

**（二）模仿录音，注意区分每组单词中不同的元音音素。**

/eɪ/ 和 /ɪ/

| take /teɪk/ | — | tick /tɪk/ | lake /leɪk/ | — | lick /lɪk/ |
| sake /seɪk/ | — | sick /sɪk/ | shape /ʃeɪp/ | — | ship /ʃɪp/ |

/aɪ/ 和 /e/

| night /naɪt/ | — | net /net/ | white /waɪt/ | — | wet /wet/ |
| bite /baɪt/ | — | bet /bet/ | find /faɪnd/ | — | fend /fend/ |

/aɪ/ 和 /æ/

| bike /baɪk/ | — | back /bæk/ | site /saɪt/ | — | sat /sæt/ |
| might /maɪt/ | — | mat /mæt/ | pike /paɪk/ | — | pack /pæk/ |

/aɪ/ 和 /ɑː/

| fine /faɪn/ | — | far /fɑː/ | buy /baɪ/ | — | bar /bɑː/ |
| kind /kaɪnd/ | — | card /kɑːd/ | pike /paɪk/ | — | park /pɑːk/ |

### /əʊ/ 和 /ɒ/

| | | | |
|---|---|---|---|
| loaf /ləʊf/ | — loft /lɒft/ | toast /təʊst/ | — toss /tɒs/ |
| dote /dəʊt/ | — dot /dɒt/ | coke /kəʊk/ | — cock /kɒk/ |

### /aʊ/ 和 /ɑː/

| | | | |
|---|---|---|---|
| loud /laʊd/ | — lard /lɑːd/ | shout /ʃaʊt/ | — shark /ʃɑːk/ |
| town /taʊn/ | — tar /tɑː/ | fowl /faʊl/ | — far /fɑː/ |

### /aʊ/ 和 /ɔː/

| | | | |
|---|---|---|---|
| about /əˈbaʊt/ | — bought /bɔːt/ | loud /laʊd/ | — lord /lɔːd/ |
| cow /kaʊ/ | — core /kɔː/ | doubt /daʊt/ | — door /dɔː/ |

**（三）模仿录音，注意区分单词中的合口双元音音素和与其相似的汉语拼音。**

**/aɪ/（注意不要将下列单词中的 /aɪ/ 发成汉语拼音中的"ai"）**

shy /ʃaɪ/    mine /maɪn/    line /laɪn/    sign /saɪn/

**/ɔɪ/（注意不要将下列单词中的 /ɔɪ/ 发成汉语拼音中的"ao ei"）**

Troy /trɔɪ/    coin /kɔɪn/    enjoy /ɪnˈdʒɔɪ/    soy /sɔɪ/

**/əʊ/（注意不要将下列单词中的 /əʊ/ 发成汉语拼音中的"ou"）**

boat /bəʊt/    coat /kəʊt/    sold /səʊld/    note /nəʊt/

**/aʊ/（注意不要将下列单词中的 /aʊ/ 发成汉语拼音中的"ao"）**

loud /laʊd/    mouse /maʊs/    shout /ʃaʊt/    cow /kaʊ/

## 五、专项练习

**（一）根据录音，完成句子。**

1. We were left _____ in the _____ for two hours.
2. He _____ me a box wrapped in _____ brown _____.

3. Please _____ on both _____ of the paper.
4. There is a _____ on her face.
5. The naughty _____ made a lot of _____.
6. The flowers grow well in the _____.

### （二）比一比，看你和你的同伴谁能读得又快又好？

1. A noise annoys an oyster, but a noisy noise annoys an oyster more!
2. Ripe white wheat reapers reap ripe white wheat right.
3. The great Greek grape growers grow great Greek grapes.
4. Nine nice night nurses nurse nicely.
5. A bloke's back bike brake block broke.

### （三）英音视听说练习。

欣赏电影《爱玛》（*Emma*）片段，并判断以下电影对白中所划出的 8 个单词是否含有本课所学的合口双元音音素。如果有，请在所标示的横线上写出该音素。

Mrs. Elton: Oh, you know, your home 1. <u>reminds</u> me of Maple Grove, which is the seat of my brother, Mr. Suckling.

Mr. Elton: Suckling.

Mrs. Elton: The hall? And the size of the rooms? I'm really quite struck by it. I 2. <u>almost</u> fancy myself there.

Emma: I'm glad you can feel so at ease.

Mrs. Elton: My brother and sister will be 3. <u>enchanted</u> with this place. People who have extensive 4. <u>grounds</u> are always pleased to meet other people with… extensive grounds.

Emma: I'm 5. <u>afraid</u> you overrate Hartfield. Surrey is full of beauties.

Mrs. Elton: Don't tell me 6. <u>about</u> Surrey! I always say it is "the garden of England".

Emma: Yes, but many counties are called that.

Mrs. Elton: Oh? I fancy not. I never heard any county but Surrey called so. Oh! Ah.

Emma: Well, I know little of other places. We are… a quiet set of people. More 7. <u>disposed</u> to stay at home.

Mrs. Elton: Yes. Well, your father's health must be a great drawback to your seeing the country. Why does he not try Bath? It would do him a world of good!

Emma: He has... tried it before without receiving any benefit.

Mrs. Elton: Oh, it will do him good if only to improve his spirits, which, I understand, are sometimes much 8. <u>depressed</u>. You must take him! A line from me and... you would have some of the best society in the place. And my particular friend there, Mrs. Partridge...

Emma: Thank you, but our going to Bath is out of the question.

1. _____   2. _____   3. _____   4. _____
5. _____   6. _____   7. _____   8. _____

# 第 5 课 集中双元音

### ● 考一考

请你和你的同伴大声朗读下面的谜语：
1. What has **ears** but can not **hear**?
2. What **wears** a cap but has no head?

请听录音，注意比较黑体单词的发音。这些单词均含有本课将要学习的集中双元音。你和你的同伴都读对了吗？

### ● 导入

英语中集中双元音音素共有 3 个，即 /ɪə/、/eə/ 和 /ʊə/。该组音素的发音同合口双元音音素有相似之处，即从前一个单元音音素自然、连贯地过渡到第二个单元音音素。第一个单元音音素发音响亮、饱满，而第二个单元音音素弱而模糊。同时，该组元音音素发音时均以中元音音素 /ə/ 结尾，舌高点有从前到中，或从后到中的变化过程，故称为集中双元音。

## 一、学习目标

——了解英语集中双元音的发音部位及发音要领
——掌握该组元音正确的发音方法和技巧
——纠正该组元音常见的发音错误

## 二、学习内容

### （一）/ɪə/

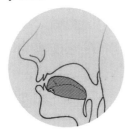

图 5-1  /ɪə/ 口型图

**发音要领**

1. 先清晰、响亮地发出 /ɪ/，再滑至 /ə/，舌位由高到低，舌高点由前到中；
2. 口型由半闭到接近半开，唇形由扁平到略大，呈自然状态；
3. /ɪ/ 较长，/ə/ 弱而模糊，二者衔接自然、连贯。

## （二）/eə/

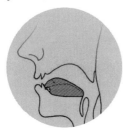

图 5-2　/eə/ 口型图

**发音要领**

1. 先清晰、响亮地发出 /e/，进而滑至 /ə/，舌位由高到低，舌高点由前到中；
2. 口型由半开半闭到略小于半开，唇形由扁平到扁平、放松；
3. /e/ 较长，/ə/ 弱而模糊，前后过渡自然、连贯。

## （三）/ʊə/

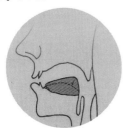

图 5-3　/ʊə/ 口型图

**发音要领**

1. 先清晰、响亮地发出 /ʊ/，再滑至 /ə/，舌位由高到低，舌高点由后到中；
2. 口型由半闭到接近半开，唇形由较圆到扁平；
3. /ʊ/ 较长，/ə/ 弱而模糊，前后衔接自然、连贯。

# 三、常见错误

## （一）双音相混

| | | | | |
|---|---|---|---|---|
| 1. 将 /ɪə/ 发成 /iə/ 或其类似音 | ear | /ɪə/ √ | /iə/ × |
| 2. 将 /ɪə/ 发成 /eə/ 或其类似音 | here | /hɪə/ √ | /heə/ × |
| 3. 将 /eə/ 发成 /ɪə/ 或其类似音 | hair | /heə/ √ | /hɪə/ × |
| 4. 将 /eə/ 发成 /el/ 或其类似音 | air | /eə/ √ | /el/ × |

**纠正办法**

1. /ɪə/ 和 /iə/：/iə/ 中的 /i/ 发音要领同 /iː/，但音长不及 /iː/。/ɪ/ 的口型为半闭，开口度略大于 /i/，且舌高点比 /i/ 略靠后，口腔肌肉不及 /i/ 紧张。
2. /ɪə/ 和 /eə/：/ɪ/ 和 /e/ 同为前元音，但 /ɪ/ 的口型为半闭，/e/ 的口型为半开半闭，/ɪ/ 的开口度略小于 /e/，舌高点比 /e/ 略靠后。
3. /eə/ 和 /el/：/ə/ 为中元音音素，口型接近半开，唇形扁平，而 /l/ 则为辅音音素（其发音要领详见本书第 9 课舌侧音部分）。

## （二）变双为单

该组双元音的发音要求从前一个单元音自然、无停顿地滑至第二个单元音，但有些学生无法做到这一点，而在两个单元音之间有短暂停顿，过渡不自然，生硬，致使一个双元音听起来变成了两个单元音。例如：

1. 将 /ɪə/ 发成 /ɪ-ə/　　　fear　　/fɪə/　　√　　/fɪ-ə/　　×
2. 将 /eə/ 发成 /e-ə/　　　pair　　/peə/　　√　　/pe-ə/　　×
3. 将 /ʊə/ 发成 /ʊ-ə/　　　tour　　/tʊə/　　√　　/tʊ-ə/　　×

**纠正办法**

发英语双元音时，要从前一个单元音自然、连贯地滑至第二个单元音，中间无任何停顿，整体一气呵成。

## （三）汉英混淆

将 /ʊə/ 用汉语拼音中 "o" 代替（同"窝"音）　sure　/ʃʊə/　√　"说"　×

**纠正办法**

/ʊə/ 和 "o"：/ʊə/ 先发 /ʊ/，再发 /ə/。/ʊ/ 为后元音，发音位置比 "o" 略微靠后，滑至 /ə/ 时，舌高点移至舌中部，口型变为扁平。"o" 则为圆唇音，且无须从一个音滑至另一个音。

# 四、纠错训练

## （一）模仿录音，注意区分每组单词中不同的双元音音素。

**/ɪə/ 和 /eə/**

| ear /ɪə/ | — | air /eə/ | fear /fɪə/ | — | fair /feə/ |
| here /hɪə/ | — | hair /heə/ | beer /bɪə/ | — | bear /beə/ |

## （二）模仿录音，注意单词中的集中双元音音素的发音要领。

**/ɪə/（注意不要将下列单词中的 /ɪə/ 读成 /iə/）**

ear /ɪə/　　beer /bɪə/　　idea /aɪˈdɪə/　　rear /rɪə/

### /eə/（注意不要将下列单词中的 /eə/ 读成 /eɪ/）

dare /deə/    bear /beə/    care /keə/    chair /tʃeə/

**（三）模仿录音，注意单词中集中双元音音素发音时中间无停顿。**

### /ɪə/

beer /bɪə/    dear /dɪə/    near /nɪə/    clear /klɪə/

### /eə/

bear /beə/    pair /peə/    fair /feə/    share /ʃeə/

### /ʊə/

tour /tʊə/    poor /pʊə/    sure /ʃʊə/    assure /əˈʃʊə/

**（四）模仿录音，注意区分单词中的集中双元音音素和与其相似的汉语拼音。**

### /ʊə/（注意不要将下列单词中的 /ʊə/ 发成汉语拼音中的 "o"）

rural /ˈrʊərəl/    bureau /ˈbjʊərəʊ/    furious /ˈfjʊərɪəs/
during /ˈdjʊərɪŋ/    gourd /gʊəd/    sure /ʃʊə/

## 五、专项训练

**（一）根据录音，完成句子。**

1. He realized that his acting _____ was over.
2. A really _____ thing happened last night.
3. There is a garden at the _____ of the house.
4. The _____ over dinner was warm and friendly.
5. Please make your meaning _____.
6. All we are asking for is a _____ wage.

**（二）比一比，看你和你的同伴谁能读得又快又好？**

1. Real weird rear wheels.

2. A weary warrior will rarely worry why we rule.
3. If you notice this notice, you will notice that this notice is not worth noticing.
4. Bright blows the broom on the brook's bare brown banks.
5. I cannot bear to see a bear bearing down upon a hare. When the bear strips the hare bare of hair, right there I cry, "Forbear!"

**（三）英音视听说练习。**

欣赏电影《爱玛》（*Emma*）片段，并判断以下电影对白中所划出的 6 个单词是否含有本课所学的集中双元音音素。如果有，请在所标示的横线上写出该音素。

Knightley: Emma! Forgive me. Uh, I was, uh… I was lost in my thoughts.
Emma: And how are you? Happy?
Knightley: W-Well, I'm… happy to see you, as always.
Emma: Ah. I didn't, uh, know that you were back.
Knightley: Just.
Emma: Oh.
Knightley: Yes, just.
Emma: Oh. Yes. I'm on my way home.
Knightley: I was just 1. there. May I join you?
Emma: Of course. … Oh, 2. dear.
Knightley: What?
Emma: What? Oh. Oh! Something about the 3. deer we need for the venison 4. stew.
Knightley: Uh-huh. Emma. There's… There's something I have to ask.
Emma: Oh, wait. Now that you are back, there is some news that will surprise you.
Knightley: Of what nature is this news?
Emma: The very best. It is a wedding between two people…
Knightley: Oh, yes, between Jane and Mr. Churchill. Mr. Weston wrote to me.
Emma: Undoubtedly you were not surprised.
Knightley: Well.
Emma: But I seem doomed to blindness.
Knightley: Time will heal your wound.

Emma: My wound?

Knightley: I know you must've been cruelly disappointed by his secret. He's a scoundrel.

Emma: You are kind. But I must tell you that I quickly saw that Frank lacked qualities, honesty being one of them, which are 5. <u>essential</u> to me in any kind of friend.

Knightley: Emma, uh, is that true?

Emma: He imposed on me, but he has not injured me.

Knightley: Yes. He got everything he wanted at great expense to others and at no cost to himself. He offends me deeply. Yet, there is, there's something in his situation that I envy.

Emma: Did I mention that we are having a new drain installed?

Knightley: You will not ask me the point of my envy? Well, perhaps you are wise. But I... I cannot be wise. Emma, I must tell you what you will not ask, though I may wish it unsaid the next moment.

Emma: Then do not speak it. Do not commit yourself to something which may 6. <u>injure</u> us both to have said.

Knightley: Very well. Very well... Good day.

1._____    2._____    3._____    4._____
5._____    6._____

# 第 2 单元 辅音音素

在英语的音素中，发音时气流在口腔中受到限制或阻碍后形成的音素被称为辅音。辅音音素共有 28 个，其分类可根据发音方式、发音部位及清浊音进行归类。根据发音方式，英语辅音可分为：爆破音、摩擦音、破擦音、鼻音、舌侧音和延续音；根据发音部位，英语辅音可分为：双唇音、唇齿音、齿间音、齿龈音、齿龈后音、腭龈音、硬腭音、软腭音以及声门音；最后，辅音还可分为清辅音和浊辅音（具体分类请参考附录 1）。

中国学生在学习辅音音素时，常常对辅音的发音部位或发音方法把握不准，造成发音偏差；或者是受汉语拼音或方言影响，导致发音失误。本单元将在介绍辅音音素的发音要领的同时，详尽地分析辅音音素的常见发音错误，并为学习者提供错误发音的纠正方法。

# 第 6 课 爆破音

● **考一考**

请你和你的同伴大声朗读下面的对话：

Dad: **Peter**, **did** you **do** your **homework** yesterday?

Peter: I **didn't**, **dad**.

Dad: Why **not**?

Peter: **Because** I **played computer games**. **Don't** worry **about it**, I will **do it today**.

请听录音，注意比较黑体单词的发音。这些单词均含有本课将要学习的爆破音。你和你的同伴都读对了吗？

● **导入**

　　英语辅音音素中有 6 个爆破音，分别是 3 对清浊相对的 /p/ 和 /b/、/t/ 和 /d/ 以及 /k/ 和 /g/。它们发音的共同特点是：首先让气流在口腔中的某个地方受到完全的限制或阻碍，然后让气流冲破阻碍，实现爆破，完成发音。简而言之，我们可以把爆破音发音的整个过程简化为 3 个步骤：1）成阻；2）持阻；3）除阻。

　　第 1 对爆破音 /p/ 和 /b/ 的发音字母分别为 p 和 b。第 2 对爆破音 /t/ 和 /d/ 的发音字母分别为 t 和 d，动词过去式词尾 -ed 在清辅音结尾的动词后和在浊辅音结尾的动词后也发 /t/ 和 /d/（这一点将在本书第 15 课谈及）。第 3 对爆破音 /k/ 和 /g/ 的发音字母分别为 k 和 g，发 /k/ 音的还有字母 c 和字母组合 ch、ck 和 qu。

　　英语学习者读到爆破音时常常会出现一些问题，有些是由于对爆破音的发音方法掌握不够引起的，如混淆清辅音和浊辅音、分不清送气强弱和声带振动程度等；有些是由于母语或方言的影响，如在音素 /p/、/k/ 后加上类似 /ɛ:/ 的音，或者用类似汉语拼音来代替爆破音音素。对于这些错误，本课将逐一列举分析。

## 一、学习目标

——了解英语爆破音的发音部位及发音要领

——掌握该组爆破音正确的发音方法和技巧

——纠正该组爆破音常见的发音错误

## 二、学习内容

### （一）双唇爆破音 /p/ 和 /b/

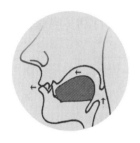

图 6-1　/p/ 和 /b/ 口型图

**发音要领**

1. 双唇闭合形成阻碍，气流受阻于口腔中；
2. 气流冲破双唇形成的阻碍，爆破成音；
3. /p/ 是清辅音，发音时声带不振动，而 /b/ 是浊辅音，发音时声带振动。

### （二）齿龈爆破音 /t/ 和 /d/

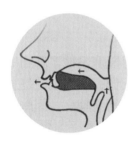

图 6-2　/t/ 和 /d/ 口型图

**发音要领**

1. 口腔自然半开，舌尖抵住上齿龈形成阻碍，气流受阻于口腔内；
2. 气流冲破舌齿形成的阻碍，爆破成音；
3. /t/ 是清辅音，发音时声带不振动，而 /d/ 是浊辅音，发音时声带振动。

### （三）软腭爆破音 /k/ 和 /g/

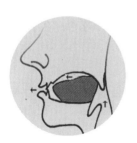

图 6-3　/k/ 和 /g/ 口型图

**发音要领**

1. 舌后部抬高，与软腭接触形成阻碍，气流受阻于咽喉部。
2. 气流冲破舌后与软腭形成的阻碍，爆破成音；
3. /k/ 是清辅音，发音时声带不振动，而 /g/ 是浊辅音，发音时声带振动。

## 三、常见错误

### （一）清浊不分

许多学生对爆破音的发音要领掌握不好，常常清浊音不分，特别是当爆破音出现在词首时，常把清浊音混为一谈。例如：

1. /p/ 和 /b/　　　　pill　　/pɪl/　　√　　/bɪl/　　×
　　　　　　　　　　pad　　/pæd/　　√　　/bæd/　　×
2. /t/ 和 /d/　　　　too　　/tu:/　　√　　/du:/　　×
　　　　　　　　　　ton　　/tʌn/　　√　　/dʌn/　　×
3. /k/ 和 /g/　　　　Kate　/keɪt/　　√　　/geɪt/　　×
　　　　　　　　　　card　/kɑ:d/　　√　　/gɑ:d/　　×

**纠正办法**

> 根据本课中爆破音的发音图和发音要领的介绍，我们可以清楚地了解到每组爆破音中的两个音素的发音部位和发音方法都是一样的，它们的区别主要是发音时是否引起声带振动：声带振动的是浊辅音，声带不振动的是清辅音。因此，要正确区别每组爆破音，尤其是当它们出现在词首时，就必须注意声带是否振动。

### （二）忽略送气强弱

很多学生都注意到清辅音 /p/、/t/ 和 /k/ 发音时常需送气，然而他们会忽略这些清辅音的送气强弱变化，误认为不管什么时候这些音素的送气强度都是保持不变的。实际上当它们出现在词中重读元音前、非重读元音前，或出现在词尾、在 /s/ 音后，其送气强度都会发生细微变化。请参考表 2-1：

表 2-1　/p/、/t/ 和 /k/ 送气变化

| 清辅音＼送气强弱 | 送气较强（在重读元音前） | 送气较弱（在非重读元音前） | 送气最弱（在词尾） | 不送气（在 /s/ 后） |
| --- | --- | --- | --- | --- |
| /p/ | pig /pɪg/ | upper /ˈʌpə/ | beep /bi:p/ | sport /spɔ:t/ |
| /t/ | tube /tju:b/ | better /ˈbetə/ | soft /sɒft/ | stock /stɒk/ |
| /k/ | locate /ləʊˈkeɪt/ | career /kəˈrɪə/ | work /wɜ:k/ | skate /skeɪt/ |

**纠正办法**

认真掌握清辅音 /p/、/t/ 和 /k/ 发音时送气强度的变化规律，注意区别这些清辅音送气强度变化。

## （三）忽略声带振动强弱

许多学生常常误以为浊辅音 /b/、/d/ 和 /g/ 的声带振动强度是固定不变的，忽略了在某些情况下它们的声带振动会有强弱变化，甚至有时完全不需振动声带。例如：当前后都有元音时，读这些浊辅音需充分振动声带；当它们在词首时，声带部分振动；当它们在词尾时，声带不振动。请参考表 2-2：

表 2-2  /b/、/d/ 和 /g/ 发音声带振动情况

| 浊辅音 | 声带振动强弱 | 声带充分振动（前后都有元音） | 声带部分振动（在词首） | 声带不振动（在词尾） |
|---|---|---|---|---|
| /b/ | | rubber /ˈrʌbə/ | best /best/ | rob /rɒb/ |
| /d/ | | leader /ˈliːdə/ | dust /dʌst/ | bread /bred/ |
| /g/ | | regular /ˈregjələ/ | get /get/ | log /lɒg/ |

**纠正办法**

认真掌握浊辅音 /b/、/d/ 和 /g/ 发音时声带振动强度的变化规律，注意区别这些浊辅音发音时的声带振动强度变化。

## （四）词尾添音

当爆破音出现在词尾时，受汉语发音习惯影响，许多学生往往在其后加上类似 /ɜː/ 的音，结果 /-p/ 同"坡"、/-b/ 同"波"、/-t/ 同"特"、/-d/ 同"德"、/-k/ 同"克"、/-g/ 同"哥"。例如：

| | | | | | |
|---|---|---|---|---|---|
| /-p/ 和 /-b/： | lamp | /læmp/ | √ | /læmpɜː/ | × |
| | cab | /kæb/ | √ | /kæbɜː/ | × |
| /-t/ 和 /-d/： | late | /leɪt/ | √ | /leɪtɜː/ | × |
| | speed | /spiːd/ | √ | /spiːdɜː/ | × |
| /-k/ 和 /-g/： | back | /bæk/ | √ | /bækɜː/ | × |
| | bag | /bæg/ | √ | /bægɜː/ | × |

**纠正办法**

当爆破音出现在词尾时，可在完成发音后，将舌位、唇形及口型立刻恢复到发音前的自然状态。

## （五）方言影响

某些方言中没有类似这些爆破音的发音，来自这些地区的学生很难准确发出这些音素，常常把一些爆破音误发成其他音素。例如：

1. 来自华南地区的部分学生常常把 /t/ 发成 /d/ 或者 /k/。

    | | | | | |
    |---|---|---|---|---|
    | tear | /tɪə/ | √ | /dɪə/ | × |
    | take | /teɪk/ | √ | /keɪk/ | × |

2. 闽南方言区的部分学生常常把 /k/ 误发成 /h/。

    | | | | | |
    |---|---|---|---|---|
    | Kate | /keɪt/ | √ | /heɪt/ | × |
    | kind | /kaɪnd/ | √ | /haɪnd/ | × |

**纠正办法**

参照 /t/ 和 /k/ 的发音要领，认真操练，努力克服方言影响。

## 四、纠错训练

### （一）模仿录音，注意区分每组单词中不同的词首辅音音素。

**/p/ 和 /b/**

pea /piː/　—　bee /biː/　　　　pig /pɪg/　—　big /bɪg/
pay /peɪ/　—　bay /beɪ/　　　　pack /pæk/　—　back /bæk/

**/t/ 和 /d/**

tall /tɔːl/　—　doll /dɒl/　　　　tear /tɪə/　—　dear /dɪə/
team /tiːm/　—　deem /diːm/　　till /tɪl/　—　deal /diːl/

### /k/ 和 /g/

| clue /klu:/ | — | glue /glu:/ | coast /kəʊst/ | — | ghost /gəʊst/ |
| curl /kɜ:l/ | — | girl /gɜ:l/ | card /ka:d/ | — | guard /ga:d/ |

**（二）模仿录音，注意爆破音的送气强弱和声带振动程度的变化。**

1. pencil /ˈpensl/    super /ˈsu:pə/    rope /rəʊp/    spill /spɪl/
2. labor /ˈleɪbə/    bell /bel/    nib /nɪb/
3. talk /tɔ:k/    tattoo /təˈtu:/    lest /lest/    still /stɪl/
4. reader /ˈri:də/    deal /di:l/    lord /lɔ:d/
5. cargo /ˈka:gəʊ/    walker /ˈwɔ:kə/    mark /ma:k/    skull /skʌl/
6. argue /ˈa:gju:/    goal /gəʊl/    flag /flæg/

**（三）模仿录音，注意区分单词词尾辅音音素和与其相似的汉语拼音。**

### /-p/ 和 /-b/（注意不要把音素 /p/ 和 /b/ 发成 / 汉语里的"坡"或"波"）

| cap /kæp/ | — | cab /kæb/ | cup /kʌp/ | — | cub /kʌb/ |
| rip /rɪp/ | — | rib /rɪb/ | rope /rəʊp/ | — | robe /rəʊb/ |

### /-t/ 和 /-d/（注意不要把音素 /t/ 和 /d/ 发成汉语里的"特"和"德"）

| bent /bent/ | — | bend /bend/ | bright /braɪt/ | — | bride /braɪd/ |
| great /greɪt/ | — | grade /greɪd/ | lent /lent/ | — | lend /lend/ |

### /-k/ 和 /-g/（注意不要把音素 /k/ 和 /g/ 发成汉语里的"克"或"哥"）

| lock /lɒk/ | — | log /lɒg/ | pick /pɪk/ | — | pig /pɪg/ |
| block /blɒk/ | — | blog /blɒg/ | dick /dɪk/ | — | dig /dɪg/ |

**（四）根据听到的发音给下列每组音标按顺序标号。模仿录音，注意比较词首音素。**

1. (　) /pi:/    (　) /bi:/    (　) /fi:/
2. (　) /tæt/    (　) /dæt/    (　) /kæt/
3. (　) /təʊst/    (　) /dəʊst/    (　) /kəʊst/
4. (　) /kæt/    (　) /gæt/    (　) /hæt/

5. （　）/kaɪ/　　　　　（　）/gaɪ/　　　　　（　）/haɪ/
6. （　）/kɒst/　　　　（　）/gɒst/　　　　（　）/hɒst/

## 五、专项训练

### （一）根据录音，完成句子。

1. _____ met each other in the park.
2. Setting up this business is _____.
3. I know that James is _____ of person.
4. A repetition of practices is the resort of _____.
5. The cook is in charge of _____.
6. _____ are meat and drink to him.

### （二）比一比，看你和你的同伴谁能读得又快又好？

1. A pleasant peasant keeps a pleasant pheasant and both the peasant and the pheasant have a pleasant time together.
2. Double bubble gum bubbles double.
3. Betty beat a bit of butter to make a better batter.
4. Bill's big brother is building a beautiful building between two big brick blocks.
5. A tiger tied a tie tighter to tidy its tiny tail.

### （三）英音视听说练习。

欣赏英剧《克兰弗德》（*Cranford*）第二季的片段，并把你所听到的单词写在文后所标示的空格上。

Doctor Harrison: Hello, Walter. Hello, Miss Hutton.

Walter: We've come for whitening 1. (paste / baste) for my sisters' shoes.

Sophy Hutton: 2. (Hid / Kid) is such a 3. (trial / dryer) to keep clean.

Doctor Harrison: And where will you be going looking so spotless?

Sophy Hutton: Oh, the garden party at Hanbury 4. (Gout / Court).

Walter: We all are. Are you going?

Doctor Harrison: Most certainly.

Sophy Hutton: On the day itself, all 5. (writers / riders) and carriages meet by the heath at noon. It is always done so, and I am sure you'd be welcome to follow the <u>6.</u> (party / buddy). If you didn't want to <u>7.</u> (ride / write) there alone, that is...

Doctor Harrison: Noon it is, then!
Shop woman: Miss Hutton.
Sophy Hutton: Thank you.
Shop woman: What can I get for you, Doctor?
Doctor Harrison: A... <u>8.</u> (rush / brush).
Shop woman: Pastry, yard, hearth, scrubbing or hair? If you want hair, they're in Fancy Goods.

1._____    2._____    3._____    4._____
5._____    6._____    7._____    8._____

# 第 7 课 摩擦音

## 考一考

请你和你的同伴大声朗读下面的对话：

Celine: **Fred**, what time **should** we meet tomorrow?

Fred: **The usual** time. **Six** o'clock in **the afternoon**.

Celine: Will you come **with Henry**?

Fred: No, he **is busy with his pictures**. He **must send the pictures** to **Martha's father** in **five weeks**.

请听录音，注意比较黑体单词的发音。这些单词均含有本课将要学习的摩擦音。你和你的同伴都读对了吗？

## 导入

英语音素中摩擦音一共有 9 个：前 8 个是 4 对清浊对应的摩擦音，即 /f/ 和 /v/、/θ/ 和 /ð/、/s/ 和 /z/、/ʃ/ 和 /ʒ/，最后一个是 /h/。它们发音的共同特点是：首先让气流在口腔中的某个部位受到部分的限制或阻碍，然后通过口腔中的缝隙流出，形成一定程度的摩擦，完成发音。

各个摩擦音的发音字母或字母组合分别如下：

表 7-1 摩擦音音素

| 摩擦音 | 字母或字母组合 | 摩擦音 | 字母或字母组合 |
| --- | --- | --- | --- |
| /f/ | f, ff, gh, ph | /v/ | v, f, ph |
| /θ/ | th | /ð/ | th |
| /s/ | s, c, ss | /z/ | z, s, x, ss, zz |
| /ʃ/ | s, ch, sh, sch, ss | /ʒ/ | s, z, si |
| /h/ | h, wh | | |

学习摩擦音时，不少学生可能出现混淆清浊音等的错误。值得注意的是，个别摩擦音发音方式特殊，常常被某些学生用其他音素替代。本课将列出这些常见错误及其纠正办法，帮助学生更准确地发好摩擦音。

## 一、学习目标

——了解英语摩擦音的发音部位及发音要领
——掌握该组摩擦音的发音方法
——纠正该组摩擦音的常见发音错误

## 二、学习内容

### （一）唇齿摩擦音 /f/ 和 /v/

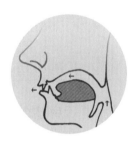

图 7-1 /f/ 和 /v/ 口型图

**发音要领**

1. 上齿轻咬住下唇，唇形扁平，气流受阻于口腔中；
2. 气流从上齿与下唇间的缝隙泻出，摩擦成音；
3. /f/ 是清辅音，发音时声带不振动，而 /v/ 是浊辅音，发音时声带振动。

### （二）齿间摩擦音 /θ/ 和 /ð/

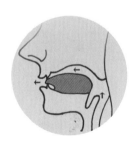

图 7-2 /θ/ 和 /ð/ 口型图

**发音要领**

1. 舌尖接触上齿，唇形扁平，气流受阻于口腔中；
2. 气流通过舌尖和上齿之间的缝隙泻出，摩擦成音；
3. /θ/ 是清辅音，发音时声带不振动，而 /ð/ 是浊辅音，发音时声带振动。

### （三）齿龈摩擦音 /s/ 和 /z/

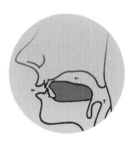

图 7-3 /s/ 和 /z/ 口型图

**发音要领**

1. 舌尖靠近上齿龈，唇形扁平，气流受阻于口腔中；
2. 气流从舌尖和上齿龈的缝隙泻出，摩擦成音；
3. /s/ 是清辅音，发音时声带不振动，而 /z/ 是浊辅音，发音时声带振动。

## （四）齿龈后摩擦音 /ʃ/ 和 /ʒ/

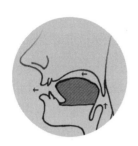

图 7-4 /ʃ/ 和 /ʒ/ 口型图

**发音要领**

1. 舌前部抬高，靠近上齿龈；舌后部向硬腭抬高，气流受阻于口腔中；
2. 气流从舌和硬腭以及齿槽间的隙缝中穿过，摩擦成音；
3. /ʃ/ 是清辅音，发音时声带不振动，而 /ʒ/ 是浊辅音，发音时声带振动。

## （五）声门摩擦音 /h/

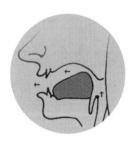

图 7-5 /h/ 口型图

**发音要领**

1. 口腔自然半开，声门肌肉紧张，舌后部抬高，气流受阻于口腔中；
2. 气流从声门通过，摩擦成音；
3. /h/ 是清辅音，发音时声带不振动。

# 三、常见错误

## （一）清浊不分

| | | | | | |
|---|---|---|---|---|---|
| 1. | /f/ 和 /v/ | fine | /faɪn/ | √ | /vaɪn/ × |
| | | staff | /stɑːf/ | √ | /stɑːv/ × |
| 2. | /s/ 和 /z/ | bus | /bʌs/ | √ | /bʌz/ × |
| | | zoo | /zuː/ | √ | /suː/ × |

**纠正办法**

　　同爆破音一样，摩擦音中的两个音素的发音部位和发音方法也是一样的，它们的区别主要是发音时是否引起声带振动：声带振动的是浊辅音，声带不振动的是清辅音。因此，要正确区别每组摩擦音，尤其是当它们出现在词首时，必须注意声带是否振动。

## （二）音素混淆

由于忽视摩擦音的发音要领，有些学生常把较为相似的摩擦音相混淆。例如：

1. /ʃ/ 和 /s/　　shoe　　/ʃuː/　　√　　/su/　　×
　　　　　　　sell　　/sel/　　√　　/ʃel/　　×
2. /h/ 和 /f/　　hit　　/hɪt/　　√　　/fɪt/　　×
　　　　　　　fat　　/fæt/　　√　　/hæt/　　×

**纠正办法**

参照 /ʃ/ 和 /s/ 以及 /h/ 和 /f/ 的发音要领，认真操练，注意区分它们的发音。

## （三）难发音素

由于汉语拼音和各地方言中几乎没有任何类似发音，很多学生很难准确发出摩擦音 /θ/ 和 /ð/，因此常常出现 /θ/ 和 /ð/ 不分，或是用 /t/ 或 /s/ 代替 /θ/，或是用 /d/ 或 /z/ 代替 /ð/ 等情况。除此以外，摩擦音 /ʒ/ 也是中国英语学习者的发音难点之一。例如：

1. think　　/θɪŋk/ √　　/ðɪŋk/ ×　　/tɪŋk/ ×　　/sɪŋk/ ×
2. casual　　/ˈkæʒʊəl/ √　　/ˈkæzʊəl/ ×　　/ˈkæsʊəl/ ×　　/ˈkædʒʊəl/ ×

**纠正办法**

发 /θ/ 和 /ð/ 时，注意舌尖应放在上下齿之间；发 /ʒ/ 时，注意舌后部向硬腭抬高。同时参照这些音素的发音要领，认真操练。

## （四）拼音影响

常见错误如下：

1. 发 /f/ 时，常常带上 /u/ 音，使 /f/ 听起来像汉语里的"福"；
2. 发 /v/ 时，上齿没有咬住下唇，使 /v/ 听起来像汉语里的"五"；
3. 发 /s/ 时，把音拉长，误发成汉语的"丝"；
4. 发 /ð/ 时，把音拉长，误发成汉语的"滋"；
5. 发 /ʒ/ 时，摩擦太轻，把 /ʒ/ 误发成汉语的"乙"；
6. 发 /h/ 时，摩擦太重，把 /h/ 误发成汉语的"喝"。

**纠正办法**

参照 /f/、/v/、/s/、/ð/、/ʒ/ 和 /h/ 的发音要领，认真操练，努力克服汉语拼音影响。

## （五）方言影响

由于很多方言中没有类似英语音素的某些发音，来自这些地区的学生很难准确发出这些英语音素，常常混淆某些发音相近的音素。常见问题如下：

1. 在吴方言（即江浙话或江南话）和闽南方言地区，有些学生常常把 /f/ 和 /h/、/v/ 和 /w/ 混同。例如：

    | five | /faɪv/ | √ | /hwaɪv/ | × |
    | very | /ˈverɪ/ | √ | /ˈwerɪ/ | × |

2. 有些南方地区的学生受方言影响，常常把 /θ/ 和 /ð/ 与其方言中的 /s/ 和 /z/ 混淆。例如：

    | thin | /θɪn/ | √ | /sɪn/ | × |
    | breathe | /briːð/ | √ | /briːz/ | × |

3. 常将汉字"花"和"发"的发音混淆的学生也会出现 /h/ 和 /f/ 混淆的错误。例如：

    | hell | /hel/ | √ | /fel/ | × |
    | hill | /hɪl/ | √ | /fɪl/ | × |

**纠正办法**

参照音素发音要领，认真操练，努力克服方音影响。

## 四、纠错训练

### （一）模仿录音，注意区分每组单词中的摩擦音。

**/f/ 和 /v/**

face /feɪs/ — vase /vɑːz/　　　fan /fæn/ — van /væn/
fast /fɑːst/ — vast /vɑːst/　　 feel /fiːl/ — veal /viːl/

### /s/ 和 /z/

| | | | |
|---|---|---|---|
| sad /sæd/ | — Zed /zed/ | sink /sɪŋk/ | — zinc /zɪŋk/ |
| sip /sɪp/ | — zip /zɪp/ | lacer /ˈleɪsə/ | — laser /ˈleɪzə/ |

### /ʃ/ 和 /s/

| | | | |
|---|---|---|---|
| shame /ʃeɪm/ | — same /seɪm/ | shelf /ʃelf/ | — self /self/ |
| shark /ʃɑːk/ | — suck /sʌk/ | clash /klæʃ/ | — class /klɑːs/ |

（二）模仿录音，注意区分每组单词词首、词尾的摩擦音音素。

### /θ/ 和 /ð/

| | | | |
|---|---|---|---|
| bath /bɑːθ/ | — bathe /beɪð/ | breath /breθ/ | — breathe /briːð/ |
| cloth /klɔθ/ | — clothe /kləʊð/ | forth /fɔːθ/ | — further /ˈfɜːðə/ |

### /θ/ 和 /t/

| | | | |
|---|---|---|---|
| thank /θæŋk/ | — tank /tæŋk/ | three /θriː/ | — tree /triː/ |
| thin /θɪn/ | — tin /tɪn/ | thought /θɔːt/ | — taught /tɔːt/ |

### /θ/ 和 /s/

| | | | |
|---|---|---|---|
| thank /θæŋk/ | — sank /sæŋk/ | thick /θɪk/ | — sick /sɪk/ |
| theme /θiːm/ | — seem /siːm/ | thief /θiːf/ | — sleeve /sliːv/ |

### /ð/ 和 /d/

| | | | |
|---|---|---|---|
| then /ðen/ | — den /den/ | thee /ðiː/ | — deed /diːd/ |
| they /ðeɪ/ | — day /deɪ/ | leather /ˈleðə/ | — ladder /ˈlædə/ |

### /ð/ 和 /z/

| | | | |
|---|---|---|---|
| bathe /beɪð/ | — blaze /bleɪz/ | lathe /leɪð/ | — laze /leɪz/ |
| breathe /briːð/ | — breeze /briːz/ | clothe /kləʊð/ | — close /kləʊz/ |

### /ʒ/、/z/ 和 /s/

| beige /beɪʒ/ | — | bays /beɪz/ | — | base /beɪs/ |
| erasure /ɪˈreɪʒə/ | — | razor /reɪzə/ | — | racer /reɪsə/ |

**（三）模仿录音，注意区分摩擦音和与其相似的汉语拼音。**

### /f/ 和 /v/（注意不要把词尾音素 /f/ 和 /v/ 发成汉语里的"福"或"五"）

| half | if | cuff | knife |
| carve | dive | starve | prove |

### /s/ 和 /z/（注意不要把词尾音素 /s/ 和 /z/ 发成汉语里的"丝"或"滋"）

| police | place | loose | prince |
| cause | noise | praise | please |

### /ʒ/（注意不要把音素 /ʒ/ 发成汉语里的"乙"）

| garage | prestige | massage | decision |
| measure | revision | division | invasion |

### /h/（注意不要把 /h/ 发成汉语里的"喝"）

| hole | handle | history | holiday |
| hair | horrible | hacker | harsh |

**（四）根据听到的发音给下列音标按顺序标号。模仿录音，注意区分音素 /h/、/f/ 和 /g/。**

1. (　) /heɪt/　　(　) /feɪt/　　(　) /geɪt/
2. (　) /hæl/　　(　) /fæl/　　(　) /gæl/
3. (　) /haɪd/　　(　) /faɪd/　　(　) /gaɪd/
4. (　) /hɑːm/　　(　) /fɑːm/　　(　) /gɑːm/
5. (　) /haʊ/　　(　) /faʊ/　　(　) /gaʊ/

## 五、专项训练

### （一）根据录音，完成句子。

1. I'll never _____ about the trifles with him.
2. _____ were injured as fighting flared up.
3. She _____ of what she was saying.
4. In time of adversity, those _____ are real friends.
5. There was not a star to twinkle _____ to him.
6. _____ of success would help produce real success.

### （二）比一比，看你和你的同伴谁能读得又快又好？

1. Flee from frog to fight flu fast.
2. How high His Highness holds his haughty head!
3. A snow-white swan swam swiftly to catch a slowly swimming snake in a lake.
4. The brave diver dived into the river to save the villager.
5. This shop sells the latest fashion of shorts and shirts.

### （三）英音视听说练习。

欣赏英剧《克兰弗德》（*Cranford*）第二季的片段，并为画线部分音节选择正确发音，将其写在横线上。

Dad: Happy Bir<u>th</u>day (1. A. /θ/ B. /ð/), Harry.

Harry: Dadda! Do you like the new baby?

Dad: He looks like a Greg<u>s</u>on (2. A. /s/ B. /z/). He'll do me. Open it.

Harry: Boo<u>ts</u> (3. A. /ts/ B. /z/)!

Mom: You're ten-year-old. A growing boy.

Dad: You've been doing a man's job, looking after this lot. I reckon you deserve (4. A. /s/ B. /z/) some de<u>c</u>ent (5. A. /s/ B. /z/) lea<u>th</u>er (6. A. /θ/ B. /ð/) on your feet.

Harry: Thank you.

Dad: What are you looking at?

Harry: The letters. I know this word. It says "Jame<u>s</u>" (7. A. /s/ B. /z/). That's the baby's name.

Dad: Don't you go dallying around with that! Learning's not for everyone.

We do all right without (8. A. /θ/ B. /ð/) it. Now, go and do the rabbit traps, go on.

1._____    2._____    3._____    4._____
5._____    6._____    7._____    8._____

## 第 8 课 破擦音

● 考一考

请你和你的同伴一起朗读下面的对话:

Jack: **Jane**, you know what? **Jim** will come to our city by **train**!

Jane: Oh, really? Maybe we should **drive** to the station to pick him up?

Jack: Great idea. Then we can take him to one of the best **restaurants** to have a dinner.

Jane: Exactly. But first of all, I need to get my dirty clothes **changed**.

Jack: Hurry up, or there will be traffic jams on the **roads**.

请听录音,注意比较黑体单词的发音。这些单词均含有本课将要学习的破擦音。你和你的同伴都读对了吗?

● 导入

　　本课主要介绍英语辅音中的 3 对破擦音:/tʃ/ 和 /dʒ/、/tr/ 和 /dr/ 以及 /ts/ 和 /dz/。顾名思义,破擦音融合了爆破音和摩擦音的特点,其发音方法是:先做好发前面爆破音的准备,然后发后面的摩擦音,两个发音部位不完全分离,前面爆破音不出声,后面摩擦音发音响亮。简单地讲,发音时前两个步骤是与发爆破音一样的,即先完成"成阻"和"持阻"两个步骤,然后做第三个步骤"除阻"。所不同的是,爆破音的"除阻"是爆破成音,而破擦音的"除阻"是摩擦成音。

　　第一对和第二对破擦音是由一些字母或字母组合发出。发 /tʃ/ 的字母组合是 ch、tch 和 ture;发 /dʒ/ 的字母和字母组合是 j、g、ge 和 dge;发 /tr/ 和 /dr/ 的字母组合分别是 tr 和 dr。第三对破擦音比较特殊,仅出现在词尾,且这类单词很少,仅有 quartz 和 waltz 等几个单词,更多的情况是在以 t 或 d 结尾的单词后加 -s 或 -es 发出 /ts/ 或 /dz/。

　　在学习破擦音时,许多学生因为舌位错误,很难准确发出这几个破擦音;还有一些学生用相近的汉语拼音替代破擦音。

## 一、学习目标

——了解英语破擦音的发音部位及发音要领

——掌握破擦音正确的发音方法和技巧

——纠正破擦音常见的发音错误

## 二、学习内容

### （一）齿龈硬腭破擦音 /tʃ/ 和 /dʒ/

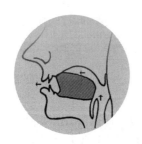

图 8-1 /tʃ/ 和 /dʒ/ 口型图

**发音要领**

1. 双唇略微突出，舌尖顶住上齿龈后部，舌前部抵住硬腭，气流受阻于口腔中；
2. 气流冲破舌尖和上齿龈形成的阻碍，几乎同时发出 /t/ 和 /ʃ/，摩擦形成 /tʃ/ 音；
3. 气流冲破舌尖和上齿龈形成的阻碍，几乎同时发出 /d/ 和 /ʒ/，摩擦形成 /dʒ/ 音；
4. /tʃ/ 是清辅音，发音时声带不振动，而 /dʒ/ 是浊辅音，发音时声带振动。

### （二）齿龈后破擦音 /tr/ 和 /dr/

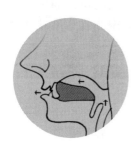

图 8-2 /tr/ 和 /dr/ 口型图

**发音要领**

1. 双唇略突出，软腭上升，堵住鼻腔通道，舌中心凹陷，舌尖顶住上齿龈后部，气流受阻于口腔中；
2. 气流冲破舌尖和上齿龈形成的阻碍，几乎同时发出 /t/ 和 /r/，摩擦形成 /tr/ 音；
3. 气流冲破舌尖和上齿龈形成的阻碍，几乎同时发出 /d/ 和 /r/，摩擦形成 /dr/ 音；
4. /tr/ 是清辅音，发音时声带不振动，而 /dr/ 是浊辅音，发音时声带振动。

## （三）齿龈前破擦音 /ts/ 和 /dz/

图 8-3 /ts/ 和 /dz/ 口型图

**发音要领**

1. 舌前部贴近上齿龈，气流受阻于口腔中；
2. 气流冲破舌前部和上齿龈形成的阻碍，几乎同时发出 /t/ 和 /s/，摩擦形成 /ts/ 音；
3. 气流冲破舌前部和上齿龈形成的阻碍，几乎同时发出 /d/ 和 /z/，摩擦形成 /dz/ 音；
4. /ts/ 是清辅音，发音时声带不振动，而 /dz/ 是浊辅音，发音时声带振动。

## 三、常见错误

### （一）舌位错误

发 /tr/ 和 /dr/ 时，舌中部没有凹陷，没有卷舌，使 /tr/ 和 /dr/ 听起来像是 /tʃw/ 或 /tsw/、/dʒw/ 或 /dzw/。例如：

| truck | /trʌk/ | √ | /tʃwʌk/ 或 /tswʌk/ | × |
| drop | /drɒp/ | √ | /dʒwɒp/ 或 /dzwɒp/ | × |

**纠正办法**

发 /tr/ 和 /dr/ 时，注意舌位靠后，可先发 /tʃ/ 和 /dʒ/，然后加上后面的 /r/ 音，即可完成 /tr/ 和 /dr/ 的正确发音。

### （二）拼音影响

许多学生在发破擦音时受汉语拼音影响严重也是较为常见的现象。例如：

1. 发 /tʃ/ 时，舌尖没有顶住上颚，而是卷起舌头，把 /tʃ/ 错发成汉语的"吃"，或者直接用平舌，把 /tʃ/ 错发成汉语的"期"；
2. 发 /dʒ/ 时，舌尖没有顶住上颚，而是卷起舌头，把 /dʒ/ 错发成汉语里的"知"，或者直接用平舌，把 /dʒ/ 错发成汉语的"机"；
3. 发 /ts/ 时，没有先做好发 /t/ 的准备，常常直接发成汉语里的"刺"；
4. 发 /dz/ 时，没有先做好发 /d/ 的准备，常常直接发成汉语里的"字"。

**纠正办法**

发 /tʃ/ 和 /dʒ/ 时，注意双唇收圆，舌前端不能卷曲；发 /ts/ 和 /dz/ 时，注意用舌尖抵住上齿龈，先摆好发 /t/ 和 /d/ 的舌位，然后舌尖缓缓下降，改发 /s/ 和 /z/。

## 四、纠错训练

**（一）根据听到的发音给下列每组单词按顺序标号。模仿录音，注意不要把词首的 /tʃ/ 和 /dʒ/ 发成汉语里的"吃"和"知"。**

1. (　　) choose /tʃu:z/          (　　) juice /dʒu:s/
2. (　　) charge /tʃɑ:dʒ/         (　　) judge /dʒʌdʒ/
3. (　　) chains /tʃeɪnz/         (　　) James /dʒeɪmz/
4. (　　) cherry /ˈtʃerɪ/         (　　) jelly /ˈdʒelɪ/
5. (　　) choke /tʃəuk/           (　　) joke /dʒəuk/
6. (　　) chin /tʃɪn/             (　　) gin /dʒɪn/

**（二）根据听到的发音给下列每组单词按顺序标号。模仿录音，注意不要把词尾的 /tʃ/ 和 /dʒ/ 发成汉语里的"吃"和"知"。**

1. (　　) catch /kætʃ/            (　　) cage /keɪdʒ/
2. (　　) ranch /rɑ:ntʃ/          (　　) range /reɪndʒ/
3. (　　) lunch /lʌntʃ/           (　　) lunge /lʌndʒ/
4. (　　) preach /pri:tʃ/         (　　) bridge /brɪdʒ/
5. (　　) branch /brɑ:ntʃ/        (　　) bandage /ˈbændɪdʒ/
6. (　　) larch /lɑ:tʃ/           (　　) large /lɑ:dʒ/

**（三）模仿录音，注意不要把 /tr/ 发成 /tʃw/ 或 /tsw/。**

  tree /tri:/　　　trick /trɪk/　　　track /træk/
  entry /ˈentrɪ/　　trend /trend/　　intrude /ɪnˈtru:d/

**（四）模仿录音，注意不要把 /dr/ 发成 /dʒw/ 或 /dzw/。**

  address /əˈdres/　　drum /drʌm/　　drive /draɪv/
  drill /drɪl/　　laundry /ˈlɔ:ndrɪ/　　dress /dres/

## （五）模仿录音，注意比较 /tr/ 和 /dr/、/tr/ 和 /tʃ/ 以及 /dr/ 和 /dʒ/。

tram /træm/ — dram /dræm/      trunk /trʌŋk/ — drunk /drʌŋk/
train /treɪn/ — chain /tʃeɪn/      trip /trɪp/ — chip /tʃɪp/
Drury /ˈdrʊərɪ/ — jury /ˈdʒʊərɪ/    draw /drɔː/ — jaw /dʒɔː/

## （六）模仿录音，注意不要把 /ts/ 发成汉语里的"刺"。

cats /kæts/      rats /ræts/      jackets /ˈdʒækɪts/
kites /kaɪts/    lets /lets/      rockets /ˈrɒkɪts/

## （七）模仿录音，注意不要把 /dz/ 发成汉语里的"滋"。

birds /bɜːdz/    reads /riːdz/    gods /gɒdz/
fades /feɪdz/    beds /bedz/      words /wɜːdz/

# 五、专项训练

## （一）根据录音，完成句子。

1. I came here to earn the right to _____.
2. Judge other people _____.
3. He had _____ and triumphed.
4. We chased the rabbits out of the _____.
5. _____ stamp him as a man of honor.
6. How important is it to pray to _____?

## （二）比一比，看你和你的同伴谁能读得又快又好？

1. Charles chose cheap cheese and cherries.
2. The seizure of the treasure is a pleasure.
3. The cheerful children are chanting charming tunes.
4. I had a strange dream in the train.
5. There are hundreds and hundreds of arts and crafts in the huts.

## （三）英音视听说练习。

欣赏英剧《克兰弗德》（*Cranford*）第二季的片段，并给画线部分音节选择正确发音，将其写在横线上。

Smith Mary: I do not encourage (1. A. /dʒ/  B. /ʒ/) her behavior, Dr. Harrison.

I am sure you would be the first to know there is not the smallest spark of attrac<u>t</u>ion (2. A. /tʃ/ B. /ʃ/) between us.

Dr. Harrison: Miss Smith, I'm dismayed that you feel you must apologize.

Smith Mary: I am constantly forced to make light of it. But it is so hard to be reminded that my absence from home is desired so very earnestly!

Dr. Harrison: I am so sorry.

Smith Mary: Do not even think to take my hand! She has the eyes of a hawk and will ima<u>g</u>ine (3. A. /dʒ/ B. /ʒ/) an en<u>g</u>agement (4. A. /dʒ/ B. /ʒ/)!

Smith Mary: Do you think you will settle in Cranford, Dr. Harrison? There is no dark purpose to my ques<u>t</u>ion (5. A. /tʃ/ B. /ʃ/). I am only being polite.

Dr. Harrison: It is a town unlike any other I have known before.

Smith Mary: It attracted me at first because it was my mother's home. But I find I love it for its own sake now. All around us, England shif<u>ts</u> (6. A. /ts/ B. /s/) and chan<u>g</u>es (7. A. /dʒ/ B. /ʃ/), but Cranford stan<u>ds</u> (8. A. /dz/ B. /ʒ/) fast. Its women are like Amazons, and to those that live here, it is the world entire.

Dr. Harrison: And it has one great attraction I could never find elsewhere!

Smith Mary: Now, that is what I call an intriguing remark. Are you a man in love?

Dr. Harrison: Perhaps.

Smith Mary: With Sophy Hutton?

Dr. Harrison: Is it very plain?

Smith Mary: Only to me, I think.

Dr. Harrison: Do you suppose I have a <u>ch</u>ance (9. A. /tʃ/ B. /ʃ/)?

Smith Mary: I have not known her long, but I think you will find her quite kindly disposed. And I wi<u>sh</u> (10. A. /tʃ/ B. /ʃ/) you well.

1. _____  2. _____  3. _____  4. _____
5. _____  6. _____  7. _____  8. _____
9. _____  10. _____

## 第 9 课 鼻音和舌侧音

● 考一考
● 请你和你的同伴大声朗读下面的对话：
● Mum: **Lily**, what **time** it is now?
● Lily: It is **nine** o'clock, **mum**.
● Mum: What is **Nina** doing in her **room**?
● Lily: She is **singing** a **song**,
● Mum: **Tell** her to stop **singing** and get ready to go to **sleep**.
● 请听录音，注意比较黑体单词的发音。这些单词均含有本课将要学习的鼻音或舌侧音。你和你的同伴都读对了吗？

● 导入

英语辅音中有 3 个鼻音：/m/、/n/ 和 /ŋ/。它们发音的共同特点：发音时，气流从肺部到达口腔时，受到完全阻碍，同时软腭下降，气流终从鼻腔流出。英语中只有一个舌侧音：/l/，但它有两个重要音位变体——清晰 /l/ 和含糊 /l/。

发鼻音的字母和字母组合如下：

/m/　　　　m, mb, mm

/n/　　　　n, nn, kn

/ŋ/　　　　ng, nk

发舌侧音的字母是 l，字母组合是 ll。

在学习英语鼻音 /m/、/n/ 和 /ŋ/ 以及舌侧音 /l/ 时，部分学生受汉语拼音影响比较明显。这些音素与汉语拼音中的声母 m、n 和 l 虽有相似之处，但也有明显区别。例如，发音时，辅音 /m/ 和 /n/ 和拼音 m 和 n 都是气流通过鼻腔，但是辅音 /m/ 和 /n/ 在气流通过鼻腔后即完成发音，而拼音 m 和 n 在气流通过鼻腔后仍有类似英语元音音素的 /ə/ 音才完成发音。另外，舌侧音 /l/ 也能在汉语拼音中找到类似发音 l，所以也常常出现混淆。来自中国西南地区很多学生受方言影响，不能区分汉语拼音中的 n 和 l，遇到英语辅音 /n/ 和 /l/ 也常常分不清楚。本课将详细介绍鼻音和舌侧音的发音方法，配以大量练习，希望借此帮助学生摆脱母语困扰，正确发音。

## 一、学习目标

——了解英语鼻音和舌侧音的发音部位及发音要领
——掌握鼻音和舌侧音的发音方法和技巧
——纠正鼻音和舌侧音的常见发音错误

## 二、学习内容

### （一）双唇鼻音 /m/

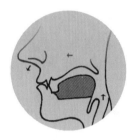

图 9-1 /m/ 口型图

**发音要领**

1. 双唇自然闭拢，形成阻碍，舌位自然；
2. 气流从鼻腔通过；
3. /m/ 是浊辅音，发音时声带振动。

### （二）齿槽鼻音 /n/

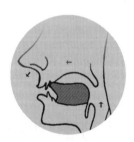

图 9-2 /n/ 口型图

**发音要领**

1. 口腔微张，舌前部抵住上齿龈，形成阻碍；
2. 气流从鼻腔冲出；
3. /n/ 是浊辅音，发音时声带振动。

### （三）软腭鼻音 /ŋ/

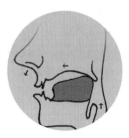

图 9-3 /ŋ/ 口型图

**发音要领**

1. 口腔自然半开，舌后部抬高贴住软腭，形成阻碍；
2. 气流从鼻腔流出；
3. /ŋ/ 是浊辅音，发音时声带振动。

## （四）舌侧音 /l/

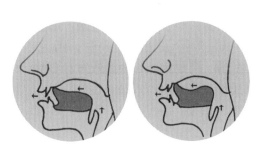

图 9-4　清晰 /l/ 口型图和模糊 /l/ 口型图

**发音要领**

1. 舌侧音 /l/ 在词首或元音前发清晰 /l/，在词末或词末辅音前发模糊 /l/；
2. 发清晰 /l/ 时，舌尖抵住上齿龈，舌身平直，气流从舌的两侧流出，声音清晰；
3. 发含糊 /l/ 时，舌尖抵住上齿龈，舌身形成凹槽，舌后部抬高，气流从舌的两侧流出，声音模糊；
4. /l/ 是浊辅音，发音时声带振动。

## 三、常见错误

### （一）音素混淆

不少中国学生由于对鼻音的发音要领掌握不清，常常混淆 3 个鼻音的发音方法。同样，由于发音方法不准确，有些学生也会把舌侧音错发成其他英语辅音音素。

1. /m/ 出现在词尾时，有些学生没有闭紧双唇，把 /m/ 错发成 /n/。例如：

   | same | /seɪm/ | √ | /seɪn/ | × |
   | lime | /laɪm/ | √ | /laɪn/ | × |

2. /n/ 出现在词尾时，闭拢双唇，把 /n/ 和 /m/ 混为一谈。例如：

   | chin | /tʃɪn/ | √ | /tʃɪm/ | × |
   | line | /laɪn/ | √ | /laɪm/ | × |

3. 发 /ŋ/ 时，没有把舌后部抬高，使 /ŋ/ 和 /n/ 混淆不清。例如：

   | sing | /sɪŋ/ | √ | /sɪn/ | × |
   | sun | /sʌn/ | √ | /sʌŋ/ | × |

4. 发清晰 /l/ 时，舌尖没有抵住上齿龈，把 /l/ 错发成 /r/。例如：

   | loud | /laʊd/ | √ | /raʊd/ | × |
   | blow | /bləʊ/ | √ | /brəʊ/ | × |

**纠正办法**

当词尾出现 /m/ 或 /n/ 时，需要记住其正确的口型：发 /m/ 时，双唇紧闭；发 /n/ 时，嘴巴微张。当词尾出现 /n/ 或 /ŋ/ 时，需要把握正确的发音部位：/n/ 的发音部位是舌尖和齿龈，舌尖抵住上齿龈，形成阻碍，软腭下垂，气流通过鼻腔；/ŋ/ 的发音部位是舌后部和软腭，舌后部抬高，抵住软腭。发清晰 /l/ 时，舌尖应该抵住上齿龈，气流由舌两侧流出。要纠正这些错误，需要我们参考音素发音要领，认真操练，并通过大量模仿练习，直至熟练、正确发音。

## （二）拼音影响

由于受普通话影响，很多学生常常把英语辅音音素 /m/ 和 /n/ 等同于汉语拼音中 m 和 n；而汉语拼音中没有 l 放在最后的情况，很多学生也会把出现在词尾的舌侧音 /l/ 忽略。

1. 当 /m/ 音出现在词尾时，错发成汉语的"木"；
2. 当 /n/ 音出现在词尾时，错发成汉语的"呢"；
3. 发模糊 /l/ 时，有些学生常常将模糊 /l/ 错发成 /əʊ/，若后面有辅音，则把模糊 /l/ 忽略不读。例如：

| table | /ˈteɪbl/ | √ | /ˈteɪbəʊ/ | × |
| world | /wɜːld/ | √ | /wɜːd/ | × |

**纠正办法**

参照 /m/、/n/ 和 /l/ 的发音要领，认真操练，努力克服汉语拼音影响。

## （三）方言影响

有些来自西南地区的学生受方言的影响，就像不分普通话里的 n 和 l 一样，英语里的鼻音 n 和舌侧音 l 也混淆不分。例如：

| no | /nəʊ/ | √ | /ləʊ/ | × |
| light | /laɪt/ | √ | /naɪt/ | × |

**纠正办法**

参照 /n/ 和 /l/ 的发音要领，认真操练，注意摆脱方言干扰。

## 四、纠错训练

**（一）模仿录音，注意比较音素 /m/ 和 /n/。**

moon /muːn/ — noon /nuːn/          meat /miːt/ — neat /niːt/
mine /maɪn/ — nine /naɪn/          shim /ʃɪm/ — shin /ʃɪn/
comb /kəʊm/ — cone /kəʊn/          some /sʌm/ — sun /sʌn/

**（二）模仿录音，注意比较音素 /ŋ/ 和 /n/、/ŋ/ 和 /ŋk/。**

thing /θɪŋ/ — thin /θɪn/          ring /rɪŋ/ — rain /reɪn/
wing /wɪŋ/ — win /wɪn/            ring /rɪŋ/ — rink /rɪŋk/
wing /wɪŋ/ — wink /wɪŋk/          sing /sɪŋ/ — sink /sɪŋk/

**（三）模仿录音，注意区别音素 /l/ 和 /n/、/l/ 和 /r/。**

lame /leɪm/ — name /neɪm/         light /laɪt/ — night /naɪt/
lest /lest/ — nest /nest/         light /laɪt/ — right /raɪt/
lock /lɒk/ — rock /rɒk/           bin /bɪn/ — bill /bɪl/

## 五、专项训练

**（一）根据录音，完成句子。**

1. The tailor _____ for a new suit.
2. _____ frightened the birds to take wing.
3. We sat down to a wonderful meal _____.
4. Don't _____ of what you read in the papers.
5. They did their best to _____.
6. There's been _____ in temperature recently.

**（二）比一比，看你和你的同伴谁能读得又快又好？**

1. Cheryl's chilly cheap chip shop sells cheap chilly chips.
2. The dame hath a lame tame crane.
3. Nancy's number is neither ninety nor nineteen.
4. The monkey's fingers were clinging to the hanging rock.
5. Let the sleeping dog lie.

## （三）英音视听说练习。

欣赏电影《国王的演讲》（*The King's Speech*）片段，并把你所听到的单词填在所标示的空格上。

Doctor Logue: Ah, Mrs. Johnson, there you are. I'm sorry, I don't have a receptionist. I like to keep <u>1.</u> (things / tins) simple. "Poor and content is rich and rich enough."

Mrs. Johnson: Sorry?

Doctor Logue: Shakespeare. How are you?

Mrs. Johnson: How do you do?

Doctor Logue: Oh, chuffing <u>2.</u> (along / a none). Um, this is <u>3.</u> (lightly / slightly) awkward, but I'm afraid you're late.

Mrs. Johnson: Yes. I'm afraid I am.

Doctor Logue: Where's Mr. Johnson?

Mrs. Johnson: Ah… He doesn't know I'm here.

Doctor Logue: Well, that's not a very <u>4.</u> (processing / promising) start.

Mrs. Johnson: No. No, look, my husband has seen everyone to no avail. I'm awfully afraid he's given up <u>5.</u> (lope / hope).

Doctor Logue: He hasn't <u>6.</u> (seen / seam) me.

Mrs. Johnson: Awfully sure of yourself.

Doctor Logue: Well, I'm sure of anyone who wants to be cured.

Mrs. Johnson: Of course he wants to be cured. My husband is, um… Well, he's required to speak <u>7.</u> (publicity / publicly).

Doctor Logue: Perhaps he should change jobs.

Mrs. Johnson: He can't.

Doctor Logue: Indentured servitude?

Mrs. Johnson: Something of that <u>8.</u> (mature / nature), yes.

| 1._____ | 2._____ | 3._____ | 4._____ |
| 5._____ | 6._____ | 7._____ | 8._____ |

## 第10课 延续音

● **考一考**

请你和你的同伴大声朗读下面的对话：

Joe: **Rudy**, **where** is the **water wagon**?

Rudy: **where's what wagon**?

Joe: The **water wagon**!

Rudy: I've **returned** it to **Robert**.

请听录音，注意比较黑体单词的发音。这些单词均含有本课将要学习的延续音。你和你的同伴都读对了吗？

● **导入**

  英语辅音中的延续音在发音方法上与元音很相似，即在发音时不产生摩擦，但要振动声带；但其功能又与辅音相同，也就是说，它们不能像元音那样单独构成音节或与辅音一起构成音节，必须和元音一起构成音节。因此，语言学家们更倾向把它们归于辅音音素。有些语音学家把延续音称为滑动音。

  延续音 /r/、/w/ 和 /j/ 的发音字母分别为 r、w 和 u、y 和 u。此外，字母组合 wh- 也发 /w/。当延续音与其后面的元音一起构成音节时，其发音应该从延续音迅速滑向后面的元音。例如，读 "we" 这个单词时，我们应该从延续音 /w/ 迅速地滑向其后的元音 /ɪ/；当我们读单词 "yes" 时，也是用同样的方法，由延续音 /j/ 迅速地滑向后面的 /es/，构成一个完整的音节。需注意：延续音是前置辅音，即只能与其后的元音一起构成音节，永不出现在元音之后。

  在通常情况下，字母 r 在词尾时是不发音的，通常被称为哑音 r。但当哑音 r 之后紧接以元音字母开头的单词时，字母 r 就会恢复其延续音的功能，与后面的元音一起发音，但此时的 /r/ 音读音不再如以往那样充分响亮，而是弱且含糊。这种读音状况属于连读现象，将在本书第 17 课做重点介绍。

## 一、学习目标

——了解英语延续音的发音部位及发音要领

——掌握延续音的发音方法和技巧

——纠正延续音的常见发音错误

## 二、学习内容

### （一）齿龈延续音 /r/

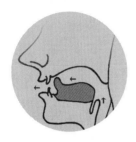

图10-1　/r/ 口型图

**发音要领**

1. 舌尖抬高，向上齿龈硬腭后部弯曲，形成凹形，双唇略突出，气流受阻于口腔中；
2. 气流经由舌中部通过，不产生摩擦；
3. /r/ 是浊辅音，发音时声带振动。

### （二）双唇延续音 /w/

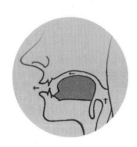

图10-2　/w/ 口型图

**发音要领**

1. 舌后部抬高，双唇收圆，稍微突出，气流受阻于口腔中；
2. 气流通过嘴唇，摩擦成音；
3. /w/ 音极短，一旦发出，即向元音过渡；
4. /w/ 是浊辅音，发音时声带振动。

### （三）硬腭延续音 /j/

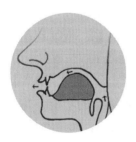

图10-3　/j/ 口型图

**发音要领**

1. 发音部位与 /i:/ 相似，舌尖抵住下齿，舌身抬高，气流受阻于口腔中；
2. 气流通过舌身和硬腭形成的阻碍，摩擦成音；
3. /j/ 发音短促，快速向元音过渡；
4. /j/ 是浊辅音，发音时声带振动。

## 三、常见错误

### （一）发音失误

由于不熟悉发音要领，某些学生把握不准延续音的发音部位、口型或舌位，造成发音失误，甚至出现忽略音素发音的现象。

1. 发 /w/ 时，双唇没有收圆，且上齿接触下唇，把 /w/ 错发成 /v/。例如：

    west /west/ √ /vest/ ×
    well /wel/ √ /vel/ ×

2. /w/ 音在词首时，部分学生容易把 /w/ 省略。例如：

    wood /wuːd/ √ /uːd/ ×
    war /wɔː/ √ /ɔː/ ×

3. /j/ 音在词首时，部分学生会把 /j/ 音省略。例如：

    year /jɪə/ √ /ɪə/ ×
    yell /jel/ √ /el/ ×

4. 发 /r/ 音时，卷舌不够，使 /r/ 音趋向于 /zw/ 音。例如：

    rain /reɪn/ √ /zweɪn/ ×
    rock /rɒk/ √ /zwɒk/ ×

**纠正办法**

> 发 /w/ 时，需注意收圆双唇，即可避免把 /w/ 错发成 /v/；当 /w/ 后紧跟圆唇元音时，需注意唇形应由接近全合的圆唇迅速扩大到半开圆唇，这样就可纠正 /w/ 在圆唇元音前被省略的现象。/j/ 音微弱且短暂，但不能忽略。发 /r/ 音时，舌尖向上齿龈后部卷起。总之，要想准确发音，必须严格按照发音要领的提示步骤，每个动作都要到位才行。

## （二）忽略清辅音化

延续音出现在清辅音后面时，常常清辅音化。但许多学生会忽略这一规律。例如：

1. /r/ 出现在清辅音后

    proud /praʊd/    cry /kraɪ/    grin /grɪn/
    friend /frend/    throw /θrəʊ/    shrink /ʃrɪŋk/

2. /w/ 出现在清辅音 /t/ 和 /k/ 后

    twin /twɪn/    queen /kwiːn/

3. /j/ 在清辅音 /p/、/t/、/k/ 和 /h/ 后

    pure /pjʊə/    tune /tjuːn/    cure /kjʊə/
    huge /hjuːdʒ/

> **纠正办法**
>
> 谨记发音规律，认真操练，直至熟练、正确发音。

## （三）方言影响

我国南方各种方言中没有类似的 /r/ 音，因此来自南方地区的部分学生容易把 /r/ 误发为 /l/。例如：

| red | /red/ | √ | /led/ | × |
| read | /ri:d/ | √ | /li:d/ | × |

> **纠正办法**
>
> 认真区别两者的发音要领：发 /r/ 时，舌尖卷起，舌尖和齿龈后部间留有缝隙；发 /l/ 时，舌尖轻抵住上齿龈后部，气流经舌两侧流出。只要多加操练，我们就能正确发音。

## 四、纠错训练

### （一）模仿录音，注意区别词首音素。

**/w/ 和 /v/**

| went /went/ | — vent /vent/ | wane /weɪn/ | — vane /veɪn/ |
| wise /waɪz/ | — vise /vaɪs/ | wile /waɪl/ | — vile /vaɪl/ |
| west /west/ | — vest /vest/ | well /wel/ | — vell /vel/ |

**/r/ 和 /l/**

| rate /reɪt/ | — late /leɪt/ | rip /rɪp/ | — lip /lɪp/ |
| rat /ræt/ | — let /let/ | rock /rɒk/ | — lock /lɒk/ |
| fright /fraɪt/ | — flight /flaɪt/ | right /raɪt/ | — light /laɪt/ |

### （二）模仿录音，注意延续音清辅音化。

1. pray　　　　bright　　　　crawl　　　　grow
   Frank　　　　thrill　　　　shrug

2. twice      twister     twelve     twenty
   quest      quiet       quick      quality
3. purity     tutor       secure     accuse

**（三）模仿录音，注意区别有音素 /j/ 和没有音素 /j/ 的发音。**

/ji:st/ — /i:st/          /ji:/ — /i:/
/juə/ — /ʊə/              /jɔ:k/ — /ɔ:k/
/jel/ — /el/              /jʌn/ — /ʌn/

## 五、专项训练

**（一）根据录音，完成句子。**

1. It's _____ of time waiting any longer.
2. It is better to die of repletion than to _____.
3. _____ of wheat is higher than ever before.
4. _____ and water, crops won't grow well.
5. These comments are not directly _____ this enquiry.
6. She was still gloating over her _____.

**（二）比一比，看你和你的同伴谁能读得又快又好？**

1. Will you wait a while for some warm wine to keep you warm?
2. His wise wife whistles while weaving his worsted waistcoat.
3. The young lawyer is reading yesterday's newspaper at his beautiful yard.
4. Robert rode a rawboned racer.
5. The young musicians played the music beautifully.

**（三）英音视听说练习。**

欣赏电影《国王的演讲》(*The King's Speech*) 片段，并为画线部分选择正确音标，将其字母序号写在文后所示的横线上。

Doctor Logue:  Now is the 1. (A. /ˈwɪntə(r)/  B. /ˈvɪntə(r)/) of our discontent, made glorious summer by this sun of 2. (A. /ɔ:k/  B. /jɔ:k/). And all the clouds that 3. (A. /lʊə(r)d/  B. /ljʊə(r)d/) upon our house in the deep bosom of the ocean 4. (A. /ˈbelɪd/  B. /ˈberɪd/). Now are our brows bound with 5. (A. /vɪkˈtɔ:rɪəs/  B. /vɪkˈtɔ:lɪəs/)...

Judge: Thank you. Lovely diction, Mr...
Doctor Logue: Logue. Lionel Logue.
Judge: Well, Mr. Logue, I'm not hearing the cries of a deformed creature 6. (A. /ɜːnɪŋ/ B. /jɜːnɪŋ/) to be king. Nor did I realize Richard III was King of the Colonies.
Doctor Logue: I do know all the lines. I've played the role before.
Judge: Sydney?
Doctor Logue: Perth.
Judge: Major theater town, is it?
Doctor Logue: 7. (A. /ɪnˌθuːzɪˈæstɪk/ B. /ɪnˌθjuːzɪˈæstjk/).
Judge: Ah.
Doctor Logue: I was well 8. (A. /rɪˈvjuːd/ B. /rɪˈvuːd/).
Judge: Yes. Well, Lionel, I think our dramatic society is looking for someone slightly 9. (A. /ˈjʌŋə(r)/ B. /ˈʌŋə(r)/). And a... little more 10. (A. /ˈliːgl/ B. /ˈriːgl/).

| 1. | 2. | 3. | 4. |
| 5. | 6. | 7. | 8. |
| 9. | 10. | | |

# 第3单元 音素组合

　　第1单元、第2单元主要讲解并练习单个音素的发音。音素是英语语音的基础，但仅仅掌握单个音素的发音是不够的，因为音素通常以组合的形式出现。为了使我们说出来的英语更加自然、准确，收到良好的交际效果，我们必须学习英语语音中的音素组合。本单元主要就音素组合进行操练，内容包括音节、读音规则和辅音连缀。

# 第 11 课 音节

● 考一考

请你和你的同伴模仿录音，朗读下面的对话，并指出画线单词的音节数：

A: Your new low-cut <u>dress</u> is wonderful.　　a. 1　b. 2　c. 3　d. 4
B: Thank you, Nancy. I just bought it on sale.
　　It was <u>marked</u> down 50%.　　　　　　a. 1　b. 2　c. 3　d. 4
A: <u>Where</u> did you get it?　　　　　　　　a. 1　b. 2　c. 3　d. 4
B. Lane Crawford. They had a year-end
　　<u>sale</u> that was too good to pass up.　　　a. 1　b. 2　c. 3　d. 4
A: I heard <u>about</u> this store. They have　　　a. 1　b. 2　c. 3　d. 4
　　all the high-end stuff.

● 导入

　　音节是词的构成要素。汉语普通话中，除个别情况外，一个汉字就是一个音节。普通话音节由声母、韵母和声调三个部分构成。与汉语普通话不同，英语音节是以元音为主体构成的发音单位。英语的单词最多可包含十个以上的音节，如：antidisestablishmentmentarianism（"反对废除国教主义"，该词含有 12 个音节）。这么长的一个单词，如果要一口气读完会让人窒息，但如果把它分解成若干个音节，即 an·ti·dis·es·tab·lish·ment·men·ta·ria·ni·sm，并在音节上调整轻重音，不仅读起来更有节奏感、更轻松，也更方便我们记忆该单词的拼写，同时也可以避免书写英语时因错误划分音节而把单词随意换行。

　　拼音音节与英语单词音节概念不同。许多英语学习者用拼音音节的概念来界定或划分单词音节是错误的，甚至可能会引起发音、拼写错误等问题。本课将具体介绍英语单词音节的有关知识。

## 一、学习目标

　　——了解音节的基本概念及类型
　　——掌握音节的划分和移行规则
　　——纠正常见的音划分和移行时的错误

## 二、学习内容

### （一）音节的概念与构成

1. 音节的概念

音节是以元音为主体构成的发音单位。任何单词的读音都可以分解为一个个的音节。一个元音（vowel，简写为 V）可构成一个音节，例如：I /aɪ/、ah /ɑ:/ 和 oar /ɔ:/。一个元音加上一个或数个辅音（consonant，简写为 C）也可构成一个音节。辅音可以在元音前，也可在元音后，也可元音前后都有辅音，例如：fee /fi:/、add /æd/、chest /tʃest/。一个英语单词可以有一个或多个音节，例如：rest /rest/（1 个音节）、author /ˈɔ:θə/（2 个音节）、salary /ˈsælərɪ/（3 个音节）和 university /ˌju:nɪˈvɜ:sətɪ/（5 个音节）。

本课将介绍音节的构成、类型、划分和移行规则。

2. 音节的构成

音节的构成一般有以下 10 种类型：

(1) V（1 个元音）

　　or /ɔ:/　　　　　　　oar /ɔ:/　　　　　　　are /ɑ:/

(2) C V（1 个辅音 + 1 个元音）

　　bay /beɪ/　　　　　　fur /fɜ:/　　　　　　　buy /baɪ/

(3) V C（1 个元音 + 1 个辅音）

　　ace /eɪs/　　　　　　ache /eɪk/　　　　　　up /ʌp/

(4) C V C（辅音 + 元音 + 辅音）

　　good /gʊd/　　　　　gorge /gɔ:dʒ/　　　　　tide /taɪd/

(5) C C V（辅音 + 辅音 + 元音）

　　snow /snəʊ/　　　　　slow /sləʊ/　　　　　　flow /fləʊ/

(6) C V C C（辅音 + 元音 + 辅音 + 辅音）

　　film /fɪlm/　　　　　shift /ʃɪft/　　　　　　rest /rest/

(7) C V C C C（辅音 + 元音 + 辅音 + 辅音 + 辅音）

　　thanks /θæŋks/　　　 films /fɪlmz/　　　　　lands /lændz/

(8) C C C V C（辅音 + 辅音 + 辅音 + 元音 + 辅音）

　　spring /sprɪŋ/　　　　screen /skri:n/　　　　splash /splæʃ/

(9) C + /m, n, l/

　　reason /ˈri:zn/　　　　double /ˈdʌbl/　　　　rhythm /ˈrɪðəm/

（10）-r/-re 音节

shore /ʃɔː/　　　　　　hare /heə/　　　　　　here /hɪə/

一般说来，元音响亮，可以单独构成音节。辅音不响亮，不能构成音节。但英语中有 3 个辅音 /m/、/n/ 和 /l/ 比较响亮，可以和其他辅音音素结合构成音节。这种由辅音加 /m/、/n/ 或 /l/ 构成的音节被称为成音节，通常出现在词尾，一般不重读。

-r 音节是指元音字母或元音字母组合后面有辅音字母 r 构成的音节，包括：-ar、-er、-ir、-or、-ur、-air、-ear、-eer、-eir、-oar、-oor 和 -our。-re 音节是指元音字母或元音字母组合加辅音字母 r 和元音字母 e 构成的音节，包括：-ore、-are、-ere、-ire/-yre 和 -ure。

注意：英语音节的划分是以音标而不是以单词的拼写为依据。例如：单词 place /pleɪs/，只包含一个元音，那么这个单词就只有一个而不是两个音节。另外，双元音算一个元音，由一个双元音和辅音构成的音节也只能算一个音节。例如：单词 aid /eɪd/，字母组合 ai 发 /eɪ/ 是个双元音，所以这个单词只有一个而不是两个音节。

## （二）音节的类型

根据一个音节是以元音还是辅音结尾，音节可以分为开音节和闭音节；根据一个音节在单词读音中是否重读，音节可以分为重读音节和非重读音节。元音字母在音节里读什么音，主要取决于该音节是开音节还是闭音节，也取决于该音节是重读音节还是非重读音节。

1. 开音节和闭音节

（1）开音节

以发音的元音字母结尾的音节及以辅音字母（r 除外）+ 不发音的字母 e 结尾的音节叫开音节，例如：her /hɜː/、mute /mjuːt/。开音节又分为绝对开音节和相对开音节。绝对开音节是指单个元音字母后面没有辅音字母而构成的音节，例如：I /aɪ/、he /hiː/；相对开音节是指单个元音字母后面加单个辅音字母（r 除外），再如一个不发音的字母 e 构成的音节，例如：male /meɪl/、acute /əˈkjuːt/。

在重读开音节中，元音字母通常读字母本音，即 a 读 /eɪ/、e 读 /iː/、i(y) 读 /aɪ/、o 读 /əʊ/、u 读 /əʊ/。

（2）闭音节

以辅音字母结尾（r 除外）的音节叫闭音节，例如：pat /pæt/、cast /kɑːst/。在重读闭音节中，元音字母发相应的短音，即 a 发 /æ/，e 发 /e/，i(y) 发 /ɪ/，o 发 /ɒ/，u 发 /ʌ/。

2. 重读音节和非重读音节

根据在单词读音中是否重读，音节可以分为重读音节和非重读音节。重读音节是指在双音节或多音节词中发音特别响亮的音节，用重音符号"ˈ"标于相应位置，例如：

contact /'kɒntækt/、pardon /'pɑ:dn/。重读音节声音响亮，延续时间较长，音调较高。

除了重读音节，多音节词中还会有次重音音节，用次重音符号"ˌ"表示，例如：preparation /ˌprepə'reɪʃn/、reputation /ˌrepjʊ'teɪʃn/。重读音节比次重读音节读得重，次重读音节比非重读音节读得重。

没有重音的音节叫非重读音节。非重读音节声音不响亮，延续时间较短，音调较低，例如：perfect /'pɜ:fɪkt/、engineer /ˌendʒɪ'nɪə/。

## （三）音节的划分

常见的划分音节的方法是：在两个音节间加符号"·""/"或"-"，例如：in·form，mo/tor，bit-ter。本书用"·"来划分单词音节，在音标中用"-"表示。

音节的划分对于习惯于汉语中只有单音节的人来说是比较困难的。关于音节的概念和划分存在很多争议，不同的字典也会有不同的划分方法。但总体上，音节的划分还是有一定的规律可循的。元音是构成音节的主体，辅音是音节的分界线。一般来说，一个单词有几个元音（不是元音字母）就有几个音节，即一个单词的音节数是由该单词含有的元音音素数量决定的。音节的划分是以其语音形式而非书写形式为依据的。音节的划分有以下规则：

1. 一个音节中必须有且只有一个元音音素（成音节除外），例如：

   aim /eɪm/　　　　　　dive /daɪv/　　　　　　cell /sel/

2. 当两个元音音素之间只有一个辅音字母时，这个辅音字母一般划归到后一个音节，例如：

   ci·gar /sɪ-'gɑ:/　　　de·sert /'de-zət/　　　me·ter /'mi:-tə/

3. 当两个元音音素之间有两个发音不同的辅音字母时，可将这两个辅音字母分别划归到前后两个音节里，例如：

   pos·ter /'pəʊs-tə/　　man·go /'mæŋ-gəʊ/　　sel·dom /'sel-dəm/

4. 当两个元音之间有两个相同的辅音字母时，第一个辅音字母划归前面的音节，使其变为闭音节，辅音字母不发音；第二个辅音字母划归后面的音节，该辅音字母须延长发音，例如：

   fos·sil /'fɒ-səl/　　rot·ten /'rɒ-tn/　　sil·ly /'sɪ-lɪ/

5. 当两个元音音素之间有辅音字母组合时，这个辅音字母组合应划归到后面的音节，字母组合 ck 除外，例如：

   mo·ther /'mʌ-ðə/　　pur·chase /'pɜ:-tʃəs/　　po·cket /'pɒ-kɪt/

6. 当两个元音音素相连但又不构成一个双元音时，应分属前后两个音节，例如：

   bi·o·lo·gy /baɪ-'ɒ-lə-dʒɪ/　　　　ge·o·me·try /dʒɪ-'ɒ-mɪ-trɪ/

7. 当两个元音音素之间有辅音字母 x 时，x 应属前面的音节，例如：

sex·ual /ˈsekʃ-ʊəl/     ex·ile /ˈeks-aɪl/     ex·ert /ɪɡˈz-ɜːt/

8. 前缀、后缀单独划分为一个音节，例如：

   re·print /ˌriːˈprɪnt/     un·load /ʌnˈləʊd/     fall·en /ˈfɔːl-ən/

9. 由两个或两个以上的词组成的合成词，一般按原词分音节，例如：

   base·ball /ˈbeɪs-bɔːl/     hand·bag /ˈhænd-bæɡ/

## （四）移行规则

任何一个英语单词，我们只要能按照音节正确读出来，基本上就能正确拼写出这个单词。掌握划分音节的方法，可以帮助我们掌握读音规则和单词拼写，也可以避免书写英语时对单词的随意换行。英语中单词在需要移行时一般用 "-" 表示，例如：Eng-land /ˈɪŋɡlənd/、na-tion /ˈneɪʃn/ 和 lob-by /ˈlɒbɪ/。总的来说，音节的划分规则和书写移行规则是一致的。具体规则如下：

1. 单音节词不可移行，例如：

   bill /bɪl/     chat /tʃæt/     craft /krɑːft/

2. 双音节词移行时可保留第一个音节，把第二个音节移至下一行，例如：

   pil·low /ˈpɪ-ləʊ/     mo·ral /ˈmɒ-rəl/     pow·der /ˈpaʊ-də/

3. 三音节词及多音节词移行时，根据情况保留一个或两个音节，其他音节移至下一行，例如：

   ca·pi·tals /ˈkæ-pɪ-tlz/     par·ti·cu·lar /pəˈtɪ-kjʊ-lə/

4. 加前缀或后缀的派生词，移行时需按照构词法进行，例如：

   im·pos·si·ble /ɪmˈpɒ-sə-bl/     de·ve·lop·ment /dɪˈve-ləp-mənt/

# 三、常见错误

## （一）规则不清

1. 当两个元音音素之间只有一个辅音字母时，有些学生会随意地把这个辅音字母归至前面的音节，例如：

   | rumor | rum·or | × | ru·mor | √ |
   | forum | for·um | × | fo·rum | √ |

2. 当两个元音音素相连但又不构成一个双元音时，有些学生误将其当作字母组合，把这两个相连的元音音素一起归至前一个或后一个音节，例如：

   | enthusiasm | en·thu·sia·sm | × | en·thus·ia·sm | × | en·thu·si·a·sm | √ |
   | appropriate | ap·pro·pria·te | × | ap·pro·pr·iate | × | ap·pro·pri·ate | √ |

3. 当两个元音音素之间是辅音字母组合时，有些学生会把连在一起的辅音字母分别归为前后不同的音节，例如：

| machine | mac·hine | × | ma·chine | √ |
| fashion | fas·hion | × | fa·shion | √ |

## （二）母语迁移

由于受到汉语母语的影响，很多学生根据拼写而不是根据音标来划分音节，误认为一个音节必须是由一个辅音加一个元音组成，例如：

| code | co·de | × | code | √ |
| side | si·de | × | side | √ |

## 四、纠错训练

（一）下列单词两个元音音素之间有一个辅音字母，给这些单词划分音节，如：jour·nal。

person _____　　column _____　　deduct _____
study _____　　global _____　　legal _____
manual _____　　nature _____　　plural _____

（二）下列单词中含有的两个元音音素相连但又不构成一个双元音，给这些单词划分音节，如：ge·o·me·try。

biology _____　　physiology _____　　creative _____
curiosity _____　　dioxide _____　　geometry _____
priority _____　　periodic _____　　ideology _____

（三）下列单词的元音音素之间有一个辅音字母组合，给这些单词划分音节，如：en·thral。

bachelor _____　　achieve _____　　method _____
father _____　　aphorism _____　　marshal _____
fashion _____　　machine _____　　author _____

（四）给下列单词划分音节，注意根据音标而不是根据拼写来划分音节。

chaos _____　　screw _____　　urge _____
blood _____　　spread _____　　couch _____
shadow _____　　seldom _____　　matter _____

## 五、专项训练

**（一）模仿录音，并给单词标出重读或次重读符号，如：'reason、ˌqualifi'cation。**

| dental | favor | giggle | hero |
| fatality | historical | impossible | legitimate |
| international | metropolitan | possibility | specification |

**（二）模仿录音，注意下列由成音节、-r 音节和 -re 音节构成的单词的读音。**

| marble | riddle | cotton | symbolism |
| circular | scatter | flirt | minor |
| ignore | fare | sphere | admire |

**（三）模仿录音，并标注音节数，如：outstanding(3)。**

| repetition ( ) | stable ( ) | linger ( ) | spill ( ) |
| fundamental ( ) | economy ( ) | illegal ( ) | import ( ) |
| handshake ( ) | feature ( ) | extreme ( ) | fierce ( ) |

**（四）模仿录音，并按规则移行，如：mo·ral。**

| mosque _____ | ancient _____ | bewilder _____ |
| enforcement _____ | indifferent _____ | immigrant _____ |
| cooperate _____ | dismiss _____ | deepen _____ |
| comparable _____ | indicator _____ | prayer _____ |

**（五）英音视听说练习。**

以下是电影《南与北》（*The North and South*）的节选片段，请欣赏，并写出画线单词的音节数，填在文后所示的横线上。

Margaret Hale: I cannot persuade 1. <u>father</u> to join me. He has been very cast down since mother's death. He keeps to the house and his own 2. <u>company</u> and he has very few visitors to disturb him.

Servant: That man Higgins is here.

Margaret Hale: Show him up, Dixon.

Servant: If you saw his shoes you'd say the kitchen were a better place!

Richard Hale: He can 3. <u>wipe</u> them, surely.

Nicholas Higgins: I've been looking for work. Been keeping a civil 4. <u>tongue</u> in my head and not minding who says what back to me. I'm doing it for him, of course, not me. Boucher. Well, not for him. He doesn't need my help where he is, but his children. But I need your help, Master, if you'll give it.

Richard Hale: 5. <u>Gladly</u>. But what can I do?

Nicholas Higgins: Well, Miss here has often talked about the South. I don't 6. <u>know</u> how far it is. But I've been thinking if I can get down there, where food is cheap and wages are good and people are friendly... Maybe you can help me get work there.

Richard Hale: What kind of work?

Nicholas Higgins: I think I am good with a spade.

Margaret Hale: You mustn't leave Milton for the South. You couldn't bear the 7. <u>dullness</u> of life. It would eat away at you like rust. Think no more of it, Nicholas, I beg you! Nicholas, have you been to Marlborough Mills for work?

Nicholas Higgins: Aye, I've been to Thornton's. The 8. <u>overlooker</u> told me to be off and... told me to go away, sharpish.

Margaret Hale: Would you try again? I... I should be so glad if you would.

1. _____  2. _____  3. _____  4. _____
5. _____  6. _____  7. _____  8. _____

# 第12课 读音规则（一）

● **考一考**

给画线字母或字母组合选择正确的读音，并和你的同伴分角色朗读下列对话：

A: I'm so excited about finally seeing this mov<u>ie</u>.　　a. /iː/　　b. /ɪ/

B: Me too. I'm crazy about Harry Potter. Have you heard that J. K. Rowling has added another b<u>oo</u>k to the series?　　a. /uː/　　b. /ʊ/

A: She's already wri<u>t</u>ten Book Seven? I'm still waiting for Book Five…
　　　　　　　　　　　　　　　　　　　　　　　　a. /aɪ/　　b. /ɪ/

B: I know. Who isn't? At least we have the movies to w<u>a</u>tch in the meantime.
　　　　　　　　　　　　　　　　　　　　　　　　a. /ɒ/　　b. /ɑː/

A: By the way, have you seen the tr<u>ai</u>ler yet?　　a. /eɪ/　　b. /e/

B: Yeah. It was great! I think the movie itself will be r<u>ea</u>lly scary.
　　　　　　　　　　　　　　　　　　　　　　　　a. /iː/　　b. /ɪə/

● **导入**

　　在英语的 26 个字母中，有 5 个字母发元音，即 a、e、i(y)、o 和 u，被称为元音字母；其余的 21 个字母都发辅音，被称为辅音字母。

　　无论是元音字母还是辅音字母，组合在一起发一个音，并形成一种固定的搭配，就构成了字母组合。由元音字母组合而成的搭配被称为元音字母组合；由辅音字母组合而成的搭配被称为辅音字母组合。

　　本课主要介绍元音字母和元音字母组合的一般读音规则和一些特例。

## 一、学习目标

　　——了解元音字母和元音字母组合的基本概念

　　——掌握元音字母和元音字母组合的一般读音规则

　　——纠正元音字母及元音字母组合的常见发音错误

## 二、学习内容

### （一）元音字母的读音规则

元音字母（a、e、i(y)、o、u）是英语中发音最为响亮的字母，也是英语语音学习的关键，能否正确读好元音是评价英语学习者语音好坏的主要标准之一。

元音字母在重读音节和非重读音节中的读音不同，在开音节和闭音节中的读音也不同。但多数元音字母和字母组合的发音是有规律可循的。

1. 元音字母在重读音节中的读音

   一般规则：

| 元音字母 | 读音 | | 例　　词 | |
|---|---|---|---|---|
| a | 在重读开音节中 | /eɪ/ | bake /beɪk/ | cage /keɪdʒ/ | hateful /ˈheɪtfl/ |
| | 在重读闭音节中 | /æ/ | bat /bæt/ | sand /sænd/ | mad /mæd/ |
| e | 在重读开音节中 | /iː/ | be /biː/ | peke /piːk/ | Chinese /ˌtʃaɪˈniːz/ |
| | 在重读闭音节中 | /e/ | pest /pest/ | section /ˈsekʃn/ | mellow /ˈmeləʊ/ |
| i(y) | 在重读开音节中 | /aɪ/ | I /aɪ/ | cite /saɪt/ | my /maɪ/ |
| | 在重读闭音节中 | /ɪ/ | wit /wɪt/ | silk /sɪlk/ | typical /ˈtɪpɪkl/ |
| o | 在重读开音节中 | /əʊ/ | go /gəʊ/ | mode /məʊd/ | sole /səʊl/ |
| | 在重读闭音节中 | /ɒ/ | mop /mɒp/ | block /blɒk/ | shop /ʃɒp/ |
| u | 在重读开音节中 | /juː/ | mule /mjuːl/ | tube /tjuːb/ | dude /djuːd/ |
| | 在重读闭音节中 | /ʌ/ | fuss /fʌs/ | suffix /ˈsʌfɪks/ | summary /ˈsʌmərɪ/ |
| | | /ʊ/ | push /pʊʃ/ | bull /bʊl/ | bulletin /ˈbʊlɪtɪn/ |

例外情况：

（1）字母 a 在下列重读开音节词中例外，例如：

　　have /hæv/　　　water /ˈwɔːtə/　　　rather /ˈrɑːðə/

（2）字母 o 在下列重读开音节词中读作 /uː/，例如：

　　too /tuː/　　　　do /duː/　　　　who /huː/
　　move /muːv/　　shoe /ʃuː/　　　whose /huːz/

（3）字母 o 在重读开音节词中，在 m、n、v 和 th 前面时，读 /ʌ/，例如：

　　some /sʌm/　　　one /wʌn/　　　dove /dʌv/

　　（注：单词 gone 和 begone 除外：gone /gɒn/　　begone /bɪˈgɒn/）

（4）字母 e 在下列重读开音节词中读作 /ɪə/，例如：

　　zero /ˈzɪərəu/　　　hero /ˈhɪərəu/　　　serious /ˈsɪərɪəs/　　　period /ˈpɪərɪəd/

（5）字母 i 在下列重读开音节词中读作 /ɪ/ 或 /iː/，例如：

　　give /gɪv/　　　live /lɪv/　　　policeman /pəˈliːsmən/

（6）字母 u 在重读开音节词中，在辅音字母 l、r 和 j 后面读 /uː/，在个别重读开音节词中读 /ɪ/，例如：

　　blue /bluː/　　　June /dʒuːn/　　　busy /ˈbɪzɪ/

2. 元音字母在非重读音节中的读音

　　双音节或多音节词中，通常包含一个重读音节和若干个非重读音节。重读音节中的元音字母按其在重读音节中的读音规则发音。非重读音节中的元音要读得短而轻，如果掌握不好会影响弱读式、节奏和语调等发音技巧的掌握。注意：所有元音字母（字母 o 除外）通常弱化为 /ə/ 或 /ɪ/，其中弱化为 /ə/ 最为常见。元音字母在非重读音节中的读音规则如下：

　　一般规则：

| 元音字母 | 读音 | 例 词 | | 备 注 |
|---|---|---|---|---|
| a | /ə/ | comma /ˈkɒmə/ | avoid /əˈvɒɪd/ | |
| | /ɪ/ | mortgage /ˈmɔːgɪdʒ/ | drainage /ˈdreɪnɪdʒ/ | 通常是当元音字母 a 接一个辅音字母和不发音 e 时 |
| | /eɪ/ | celebrate /ˈselɪbreɪt/ | generate /ˈdʒenəreɪt/ | 动词中的 a 如果处在开音节位置，a 读 /eɪ/ |
| | /æ/ | contrast /ˈkɒntræst/ | acrobat /ˈækrəbæt/ | 分解音节时，当 a 处于闭音节中，a 读 /æ/ |
| e | /ə/ | silent /ˈsaɪlənt/ | item /ˈaɪtəm/ | 例外：content /ˈkɒntent/、comment /ˈkɒment/ |
| | /ɪ/ | relief /rɪˈliːf/ | behave /bɪˈheɪv/ | 主要在前缀和后缀中 |
| | /e/ | index /ˈɪndeks/ | content /ˈkɒntent/ | 分解音节时，e 处于闭音节中，e 读 /e/ |
| i(y) | /ə/ | impossible /ɪmˈpɒsəbl/ | locality /ləuˈkælətɪ/ | |
| | /ɪ/ | indelible /ɪnˈdeləbl/ | animal /ˈænɪml/ | |
| | /aɪ/ | exercise /ˈeksəsaɪz/ apologize /əˈpɒlədʒaɪz/ | simplify /ˈsɪmplɪfaɪ/ clarify /ˈklærɪfaɪ/ | 当 y 或 i 处在开音节中时读 /aɪ/，例外：study /ˈstʌdɪ/、remedy /ˈremədɪ/、practise /ˈpræktɪs/ |

| 元音字母 | 读音 | 例词 | | 备注 |
|---|---|---|---|---|
| o | /ə/ | agony /ˈægənɪ/ | bosom /ˈbɒzəm/ | |
| | /əʊ/ | cargo /ˈkɑːgəʊ/ | hero /ˈhɪərəʊ/ | 当 o 处在开音节中时读 /əʊ/ |
| | /ɒ/ | hostility /hɒˈstɪlətɪ/ | cocotte /kɒˈkɒt/ | 当 o 处在闭音节中时读 /ɒ/ |
| u | /ə/ | autumn /ˈɔːtəm/ | support /səˈpɔːt/ | |
| | /juː(ː)/ | institute /ˈɪnstɪtjuːt/ attitude /ˈætɪtjuːd/ | occupy /ˈɒkjʊpaɪ/ united /jʊˈnaɪtɪd/ | 当 u 处在开音节中时读 /juː/ 或 /jʊ/ |
| | /uː(ː)/ | issue /ˈɪʃuː/ | influence /ˈɪnflʊəns/ | u 处在开音节位置，又在辅音字母 j、l、r、s 后面时 |

注：在非重读音节中，许多单词中的元音字母 a、e、i 既可读 /ɪ/，也可读 /ə/，例如：compliment /ˈkɒmplɪmənt, ˈkɒmpləmənt/、dignity /ˈdɪgnɪtɪ, ˈdɪgnətɪ/。

## （二）元音字母组合的读音规则

1. -r 音节元音字母组合的读音

-r 音节元音字母组合包括 -ar、-er、-ir、-or、-ur、-air、-ear、-eer、-eir、-oar、-oor、-our 等。-r 音节元音字母组合 -ar、-er、-ir、-or、-ur 的读音在非重读音节中通常弱化为 /ə/，例如：cellar /ˈselə/、effort /ˈefət/、martyr /ˈmɑːtə/。这里主要介绍 -r 音节元音字母组合在重读音节中的读音：

| -r 音节元音字母组合 | 读音 | 例词 | | 备注 |
|---|---|---|---|---|
| ar | /ɑː/ | bark /bɑːk/ | charge /tʃɑːdʒ/ charm /tʃɑːm/ | |
| | /ɔː/ | warm /wɔːm/ | towards /təˈwɔːdz/ | ar 在 /w/ 音后面时 |
| air | /eə/ | stair /steə/ | airport /ˈeəpɔːt/ hair /heə/ | |
| ear | /ɪə/ | dear /dɪə/ | fear /fɪə/ clear /klɪə/ | 仅在个别单词中发 /ɑː/，例如：heart /hɑːt/ |
| | /eə/ | bear /beə/ | pear /peə/ wear /weə/ | |
| | /ɜː/ | pearl /pɜːl/ | search /sɜːtʃ/ earn /ɜːn/ | |
| eer | /ɪə/ | cheer /tʃɪə/ | beer /bɪə/ career /kəˈrɪə/ | |
| or | /ɔː/ | absorb /əbˈsɔːb/ | distort /dɪˈstɔːt/ | |
| | /ɜː/ | word /wɜːd/ | work /wɜːk/ worse /wɜːs/ | or 在 /w/ 音后面时 |
| oar/oor | /ɔː/ | roar /rɔː/ | door /dɔː/ floor /flɔː/ | 在个别单词中发 /ʊə/，例如：moor /mʊə/、poor /pʊə/ |

| -r 音节元音字母组合 | 读音 | 例 词 | | | 备 注 |
|---|---|---|---|---|---|
| our | /ɔ:/ /aʊə/ | four /fɔ:/ course /kɔ:s/ | court /kɔ:t/ hour /ˈaʊə/ | sour /ˈsaʊə/ flour /ˈflaʊə/ | 在个别单词中发 /ɜ:/，例如：journey /ˈdʒɜ:nɪ/ |
| er、ir/yr 和 ur | /ɜ:/ | term /tɜ:m/ | virtue /ˈvɜ:tʃu:/ | hurt /hɜ:t/ | |

注：辅音字母 r 双写时，前面的元音字母不能与 r 构成 -r 音节，而是按重读闭音节的拼读规则发音，例如：carry /ˈkærɪ/、sorry /ˈsɒrɪ/、hurry /ˈhʌrɪ/；但双写 r 的派生词仍保持原词根中的 -r 音节的读音，例如：fur—furry /ˈfɜ:rɪ/、tar—tarry /ˈtærɪ/。

2. -re 音节元音字母组合的读音

-re 音节元音字母组合包括：-are、-ere、-ire/-yre、-ore 和 -ure 等。-re 音节元音字母组合 (-ure 除外) 很少出现在非重读音节中。-ure 在非重读音节中通常读 /ə/，例如：picture /ˈpɪktʃə/、pleasure /ˈpleʒə/。这里主要介绍 -re 音节元音字母组合在重读音节中的读音：

| -re 音节元音字母组合 | 读音 | 例 词 | | | 例 外 |
|---|---|---|---|---|---|
| are | /eə/ | dare /deə/ | stare /steə/ | bare /beə/ | are /ɑ:/ |
| ere | /ɪə/ | mere /mɪə/ | interfere /ˌɪntəˈfɪə/ | | were /wə/ |
| | /eə/ | where /weə/ | there /ðeə/ | therefore /ˈðeəfɔ:/ | |
| ire/yre | /aɪə/ | fire /ˈfaɪə/ | hire /ˈhaɪə/ | tyre /ˈtaɪə/ | |
| ore | /ɔ:/ | wore /wɔ:/ | store /stɔ:/ | sore /sɔ:/ | |
| ure | /jʊə/ | pure /pjʊə/ | cure /kjʊə/ | lure /ljʊə/ | |
| | /ʊə/ | sure /ʃʊə/ | insure /ɪnˈʃʊə/ | ensure /ɪnˈʃʊə/ | |

3. 常见普通元音字母组合的读音

| 元音字母组合 | 读音 | 例 词 | 备 注 |
|---|---|---|---|
| ai/ay | 在重读音节中 | /eɪ/ | laid /leɪd/   raid /reɪd/ tray /treɪ/ | |
| ai/ay | 在非重读音节中 | /ɪ/、/ə/、/eɪ/ | captain /ˈkæptɪn/ mountain /ˈmaʊntən/ Friday /ˈfraɪdeɪ/ | |

| 元音字母组合 | | 读音 | 例 词 | 备 注 |
|---|---|---|---|---|
| au/<br>aw | 在重读<br>音节中 | /ɔː/ | fault /fɔːlt/　　launch /lɔːntʃ/<br>claw /klɔː/ | 例外：aunt /ɑːnt/<br>注：组合 au 通常出现<br>在辅音前，很少出现在<br>词尾，aw 则通常出现<br>在词尾。 |
| | 在非重<br>读音节中 | /ɔː/ 或<br>/ɒ/ | authority /ɔːˈθɒrətɪ/<br>Australia /ɒˈstreɪlɪə/ | |
| ea | 在重读<br>音节中 | /iː/ | peace /piːs/　　beat /biːt/<br>beach /biːtʃ/ | |
| | | /e/ | weapon /ˈwepən/<br>treasure /ˈtreʒə/ | |
| | | /eɪ/ | great /greɪt/　　break /breɪk/<br>steak /steɪk/ | |
| | | /ɪə/ | idea /aɪˈdɪə/　　theatre /ˈθɪətə/<br>real /rɪəl/ | |
| | 在非重读<br>音节中 | /ɪ/ | forehead /ˈfɒrɪd/ | |
| ee | 在重读<br>音节中 | /iː/ | steel /stiːl/　peel /piːl/　flee /fliː/ | |
| | 在非重读<br>音节中 | /ɪ/ | coffee /ˈkɒfɪ/<br>committee /kəˈmɪtɪ/ | |
| ei/ey | 在重读<br>音节中 | /eɪ/ | eight /eɪt/　　neighbour /ˈneɪbə/<br>obey /əˈbeɪ/ | 例外：<br>leisure /ˈleʒə/<br>either /ˈaɪðə/<br>height /haɪt/ |
| | | /iː/ | receipt /rɪˈsiːt/　deceive /dɪˈsiːv/<br>key /kiː/ | |
| | 在非重读<br>音节中 | /ɪ/ | foreign /ˈfɒrɪn/ | |
| eu/ew | 在重读<br>音节中 | /juː/ | neutral /ˈnjuːtrəl/　feudal /ˈfjuːdl/<br>few /fjuː/ | 例外：<br>Europe /ˈjʊərəp/ |
| | | /uː/ | blew /bluː/　　crew /kruː/<br>flew /fluː/ | |
| | 在非重读<br>音节中 | | | |
| ie | 在重读<br>音节中 | /iː/ | thief /θiːf/　　field /fiːld/<br>achieve /əˈtʃiːv/ | 注：字母组合 ie 出<br>现在单词的词尾时读<br>/aɪ/，出现在词中间时<br>读 /iː/。<br>例外：friend /frend/ |
| | | /aɪ/ | tie /taɪ/　　die /daɪ/　　lie /laɪ/ | |
| | | /aɪə/ | quiet /ˈkwaɪət/　society /səˈsaɪətɪ/ | |
| | 在非重读<br>音节中 | /ɪ/ | auntie /ˈɑːntɪ/　　Barbie /ˈbɑːbɪ/ | |

| 元音字母组合 | | 读音 | 例 词 | 备 注 |
|---|---|---|---|---|
| oa | 在重读音节中 | /əʊ/ | soap /səʊp/  float /fləʊt/<br>goal /gəʊl/ | |
| | | /ɔː/ | broad /brɔːd/ | |
| | 在非重读音节中 | /əʊ/ | raincoat /ˈreɪnkəʊt/ | |
| oi/oy | 在重读音节中 | /ɔɪ/ | point /pɔɪnt/  boy /bɔɪ/<br>joy /dʒɔɪ/ | 字母组合 oi 只出现在辅音前，oy 只出现在词尾 |
| | 在非重读音节中 | /ɔɪ/ | ovoid /ˈəʊvɔɪd/  alloy /ˈælɔɪ/<br>envoy /ˈenvɔɪ/ | 例外：tortoise /ˈtɔːtəs/ |
| oo | 在重读音节中 | /uː/ | food /fuːd/  tooth /tuːθ/<br>spoon /spuːn/ | |
| | | /ʊ/ | foot /fʊt/  good /gʊd/<br>stood /stʊd/ | |
| | | /ʌ/ | blood /blʌd/  flood /flʌd/ | |
| | 在非重读音节中 | /uː/ | cuckoo /ˈkʊkuː/ | |
| ou/ow | 在重读音节中 | /aʊ/ | shout /ʃaʊt/  couch /kaʊtʃ/<br>flower /ˈflaʊə/ | 在个别单词中发 /ʊ/ 音，例如：could /kʊd/、should /ʃʊd/、would /wʊd/ |
| | | /əʊ/ | soul /səʊl/  mould /məʊld/<br>show /ʃəʊ/ | |
| | | /ʌ/ | tough /tʌf/  county /ˈkʌntri/<br>trouble /ˈtrʌbl/ | |
| | | /uː/ | group /gruːp/  soup /suːp/<br>route /ruːt/ | |
| | 在非重读音节中 | /ə/ | famous /ˈfeɪməs/<br>glorious /ˈglɔːrɪəs/ | |
| ui | 在重读音节中 | /(j)uː/ | juice /dʒuːs/  cruise /kruːz/<br>nuisance /ˈnjuːsns/ | |
| | | /(j)uːɪ/ | fluid /ˈfluːɪd/  suicide /ˈsuːɪsaɪd/ | |
| | | /ɪ/ | build /bɪld/  guild /gɪld/  quit /kwɪt/ | |
| | 在非重读音节中 | /ɪ/ | biscuit /ˈbɪskɪt/  circuit /ˈsɜːkɪt/ | |
| ue | 在重读音节中 | /uː/ | true /truː/  glue /gluː/  rue /ruː/ | |
| | | /juː/ | due /djuː/  cue /kjuː/<br>Tuesday /ˈtjuːzdeɪ/ | |
| | 在非重读音节中 | /juː/ | value /ˈvæljuː/  residue /ˈrezɪdjuː/ | |
| | | /uː/ | issue /ˈɪʃuː/  statue /ˈstætʃuː/ | |

| 元音字母组合 | | 读音 | 例词 | 备注 |
|---|---|---|---|---|
| uy | 在重读音节中 | /aɪ/ | buy /baɪ/ guy /gaɪ/ | |
| | 在非重读音节中 | | | |

## 三、常见错误

### （一）规则不清

1. 不管是重读开音节还是重读闭音节，有些学生只会念一个音，特别是遇到字母 a 和 o 时，通通念 /æ/ 或 /əʊ/，例如：

    | male | /mæl/ | × | /meɪl/ | √ |
    |---|---|---|---|---|
    | doll | /dəʊl/ | × | /dɒl/ | √ |

2. 字母组合 al 在重读音节中通常读 /ɔː/、/ɑː/ 或 /ɔːl/，但很多学生通常会把本应念 /ɔːl/ 的音念成 /ɔː/，例如：

    | also | /ˈɔːsəʊ/ | × | /ˈɔːlsəʊ/ | √ |
    |---|---|---|---|---|
    | almost | /ˈɔːməʊst/ | × | /ˈɔːlməʊst/ | √ |

3. 字母组合 ea 在重读音节中通常读 /iː/、/e/、/eɪ/ 或 /ɪə/，但很多学生通常会把本应念 /ɪə/ 的音念成 /iː/，例如：

    | ideal | /aɪˈdiːl/ | × | /aɪˈdɪəl/ | √ |
    |---|---|---|---|---|
    | realize | /ˈriːlaɪz/ | × | /ˈrɪəlaɪz/ | √ |

4. 字母组合 ie 在重读音节中通常读 /iː/、/aɪ/ 或 /aɪə/，但很多学生通常会把本应念 /aɪə/ 的音念成 /aɪ/，例如：

    | diet | /ˈdaɪt/ | × | /ˈdaɪət/ | √ |
    |---|---|---|---|---|
    | science | /ˈsaɪns/ | × | /ˈsaɪəns/ | √ |

### （二）过分依赖规则

掌握一定的读音规则不但有助于我们正确发音，对我们记忆单词也起着很大的作用。但是，过分地依赖规则，难免会出现这样那样的错误。由于过分依赖读音规则，学生往往会犯以下错误：

1. 字母 a 在重读音节中通常读 /eɪ/ 或 /æ/，但当后面是 -ss、-st、-sp、-sk、-th、-ph、-f、-n、-lf 和 -lm 时通常念 /ɑː/。有些学生会按照一般规则，依然把 a 读成 /eɪ/，例如：

| | | | | | |
|---|---|---|---|---|---|
| plant | /pleɪnt/ | × | /plɑ:nt/ | √ | |
| mask | /meɪsk/ | × | /mɑ:sk/ | √ | |

2. 字母 e 在重读开音节中通常读 /i:/，但在个别重读开音节词中读 /ɪə/。有些学生会按照一般规则，把所有字母 e 读成 /i:/ 而不是 /ɪə/，例如：

| | | | | | |
|---|---|---|---|---|---|
| serious | /ˈsi:rɪəs/ | × | /ˈsɪərɪəs/ | √ | |
| period | /ˈpi:rɪəd/ | × | /ˈpɪərɪəd/ | √ | |

3. 字母组合 oo 在重读音节中通常读 /u:/、/ʊ/ 或 /ʌ/，许多学生通常无法辨别，例如：

| | | | | | |
|---|---|---|---|---|---|
| book | /bu:k/ | × | /bʊk/ | √ | |
| food | /fʊd/ | × | /fu:d/ | √ | |

**纠正办法**

总而言之，英语元音字母和元音字母组合的读音是有规律可循的，掌握这些规律有助于我们正确朗读、辨认和记忆单词。但同时，我们不可过分依赖发音规则，因为英语词汇的词源很复杂，许多单词的发音保有原词源的发音，如果我们一味按照规则来读，很容易犯"过度概括"的发音错误，甚至造成误解或笑话。所以，我们建议学习者要勤查词典以确认单词的发音。

## 四、纠错训练

**（一）模仿录音，注意字母 a 和 o 在重读开音节和重读闭音节中的不同读法。**

| salvation | status | amaze | baggage |
|---|---|---|---|
| adapt | album | component | focus |
| motion | cotton | involve | knot |

**（二）模仿录音，并在字母组合 al 发 /ɔ:l/ 的单词旁画"√"。**

| almost (　) | altogether (　) | alter (　) | always (　) |
|---|---|---|---|
| already (　) | also (　) | salt (　) | ball (　) |
| talk (　) | half (　) | calm (　) | wall (　) |

**（三）模仿录音，并在字母组合 ea 发 /ɪə/ 的单词旁画"√"。**

| deal (　) | jeans (　) | measure (　) | realm (　) |
|---|---|---|---|
| break (　) | tease (　) | leash (　) | ideally (　) |
| heal (　) | spread (　) | seal (　) | theatre (　) |

**（四）模仿录音，注意字母 a 在重读音节中的不同读法。**

| sad | travel | valley | pass |
| past | grasp | mask | staff |
| graph | ask | glass | path |

**（五）模仿录音，并在字母 e 发 /ɪə/ 的单词旁画"√"。**

| menu ( ) | metal ( ) | heroism ( ) | direct ( ) |
| edge ( ) | zero ( ) | electric ( ) | engine ( ) |
| period ( ) | serious ( ) | delete ( ) | fever ( ) |

**（六）模仿录音，并按要求分类。**

| cook | root | spoon | cool |
| good | stood | look | foot |
| book | boost | fool | goose |

字母组合 oo 发 /uː/ 的单词:

_____  _____  _____  _____  _____  _____

字母组合 oo 发 /ʊ/ 的单词:

_____  _____  _____  _____  _____  _____

# 五、专项训练

**（一）模仿录音，注意以下重读开音节词和重读闭音节词的读音。**

| cane | frame | scale | gene | theme |
| confine | refine | pipe | bribe | bride |
| nest | depth | dress | event | expect |
| finger | fish | gym | inch | ill |

**（二）模仿录音，注意 -r 音节在重读音节和非重读音节中的读法。**

| ar | farce | farm | pillar | cellar |
| or | sort | fork | favor | effort |
| er | verb | serve | tiger | voter |
| ur | curve | surface | hurt | surgeon |
|  | surprise | survival | pursue | Saturday |

### （三）模仿录音，注意字母组合在重读音节中的读法。

| ea | /iː/ | teach | easy | cheap | please |
|---|---|---|---|---|---|
| | /e/ | heavy | bread | sweater | weather |
| | /eɪ/ | break | great | steak | |
| | /ɪə/ | idea | theater | real | realistic |
| ear | /ɪə/ | hear | ear | near | clear |
| | /eə/ | bear | pear | wear | swear |
| | /ɜː/ | earth | learn | early | earn |
| ou (ow) | | | | | |
| | /aʊ/ | flower | house | count | down |
| | /ʌ/ | young | country | enough | tough |
| | /uː/ | group | you | soup | route |
| | /əʊ/ | know | row | throw | though |

### （四）英音视听说练习。

欣赏电影《音乐之声》（*The Sound of Music*）片段，给画线处选择正确的音标，并将其字母标号和相应的单词写在文后所示的横线上。这些单词都含有一个元音或元音字母组合。

Captain: Hello. I thought... I... just might find you here.

Maria: Was... was there something you wanted?

Captain: Um? No, no, no, sit down, please. Please. Ah... May I... ha, ha. You know... I... uh... was thinking... I was <u>1</u>. (A. /ˈwʌndərɪŋ/ B. /ˈwɒndərɪŋ/) two things. Why did you run away to the <u>2</u>. (A. /ˈæbɪ/ B. /ˈæbeɪ/)? And what was it that made you come back?

Maria: Well, I... I had an obligation to <u>3</u>. (A. /fʊlˈfɪl/ B. /fuːlˈfɪl/) and I... I came back to fulfill it.

Captain: Is that all?

Maria: And I missed the children.

Captain: Yes, only the children?

Maria: No. Yes. Isn't it right I should have missed them?

Captain: Oh, yes. Yes, of course. I was... only hoping, that <u>4</u>. (A. /pəˈhəps/ B. /pəˈhæps/) you... perhaps you might... ah...

Maria: Yes?

Captain: Well... ah... nothing was the same when you were away and... it'll be all wrong again after you 5. (A. /lɪv/ B. /liːv/). And I just thought that perhaps you might... uh... change your mind?

Maria: I'm sure the Baroness will be able to make things fine for you.

Captain: Maria, there isn't going to be 6. (A. /ˈenɪ/ B. /ˈænɪ/) Baroness.

Maria: There isn't?

Captain: No.

Maria: I don't 7. (A. /ˌʌndəˈstænd/ B. /ˌʌndəˈstənd/).

Captain: Well, we've uh... called off our 8. (A. /ɪnˈɡeɪdʒmənt/ B. /ɪnˈɡeɪdʒment/), you see... and...

Maria: Oh, I'm sorry.

Captain: Yes. You are?

Maria: Umm. You did?

Captain: Yes, well you can't... marry someone when you're... in love with someone else, can you?

1._____  2._____  3._____  4._____
5._____  6._____  7._____  8._____

# 第13课 读音规则(二)

● **考一考**

你知道英语中哪些字母是辅音字母吗？你了解辅音字母组合的发音吗？请给下列单词选择正确的读音：

| | | | |
|---|---|---|---|
| fasten | a. /ˈfɑːsn/ | | b. /ˈfɑːstn/ |
| champagne | a. /ʃæmˈpeɪn/ | | b. /tʃæmˈpeɪn/ |
| breathe | a. /briːθ/ | | b. /briːð/ |

● **导入**

大家已经知道，英文26个字母中，除5个元音字母以外，其他21个都是辅音字母。这些辅音字母都发辅音，只有w和y有时发元音时，可被当作元音字母。辅音字母组合是由两个或三个辅音字母组合而成的，共同发一个辅音。

本课主要介绍辅音字母和辅音字母组合的一般读音规则和一些特例。

## 一、学习目标

——了解辅音字母和辅音字母组合的基本概念
——掌握辅音字母和辅音字母组合的一般读音规则
——纠正辅音字母和辅音字母组合的常见发音错误

## 二、学习内容

### （一）辅音字母的读音规则

| 辅音字母 | 读音 | 例词 | | | 备注 |
|---|---|---|---|---|---|
| b | /b/ | bite /baɪt/ | board /bɔːd/ | boil /bɔɪl/ | |
| | / / | dumb /dʌm/ | thumb /θʌm/ | debt /det/ | b在词尾，前面有m或后面跟t时不发音 |

| 辅音字母 | 读音 | 例词 | | | 备注 |
|---|---|---|---|---|---|
| c | /k/ | calm /kɑ:m/<br>curse /kɜ:s/ | commune /ˈkɒmju:n/<br>clay /kleɪ/ | crane /kreɪn/ | c 在元音字母 a、o、u 及辅音字母 l 和 r 前读作 /k/ |
| | /s/ | certify /ˈsɜ:tɪfaɪ/ | circuit /ˈsɜ:kɪt/ | cyber /ˈsaɪbə/ | c 在元音字母 e 和 i(y) 前读作 /s/ |
| | /ʃ/ | technician /tekˈnɪʃn/ | efficient /ɪˈfɪʃnt/ | | c 在元音字母组合 ia、ie、io 前读作 /ʃ/ |
| d | /d/ | dig /dɪg/ | dish /dɪʃ/ | dine /daɪn/ | |
| f | /f/ | fee /fi:/ | fever /ˈfi:və/ | fill /fɪl/ | 例外：of /əv/ |
| g | /g/ | gamble /ˈgæmbl/<br>glance /glɑ:ns/ | govern /ˈgʌvn/<br>glide /glaɪd/ | guy /gaɪ/<br>gross /grəʊs/ | g 在元音字母 a、o、u 及辅音字母 l 和 r 前读 /g/ |
| | /dʒ/ | gene /dʒi:n/ | gist /dʒɪst/ | gym /dʒɪm/ | |
| h | /h/ | help /help/ | health /helθ/ | hell /hel/ | |
| | / / | hour /ˈaʊə/ | honest /ˈɒnɪst/ | heir /eə/ | |
| j | /dʒ/ | job /dʒɒb/ | join /dʒɔɪn/ | joke /dʒəʊk/ | |
| k | /k/ | kettle /ˈketl/ | like /laɪk/ | Kate /keɪt/ | |
| | / / | kneel /ni:l/ | knell /nel/ | knight /naɪt/ | k 在词首且后面跟 n 时不发音 |
| l | /l/ | life /laɪf/ | milk /mɪlk/ | liberal /ˈlɪbərəl/ | |
| | / / | folk /fəʊk/ | stalk /stɔ:k/ | calm /kɑ:m/ | l 在词尾 k 或 m 前有时不发音；在下列词中也不发音，例如：<br>could /kʊd/<br>should /ʃʊd/<br>would /wʊd/ |
| m | /m/ | music /ˈmju:zɪk/ | come /kʌm/ | mess /mes/ | |
| n | /n/ | money /ˈmʌnɪ/ | opinion /əˈpɪnjən/ | | |
| | /ŋ/ | function /ˈfʌŋkʃn/ | hank /hæŋk/ | link /lɪŋk/ | n 在 /k/ 前读 /ŋ/ |

| 辅音字母 | 读音 | 例词 | | | 备注 |
|---|---|---|---|---|---|
| p | /p/ | panda /ˈpændə/ | paper /ˈpeɪpə/ | pond /pɒnd/ | |
| | / / | pneumonia /njuːˈməʊnɪə/ | psychiatrist /saɪˈkaɪətrɪst/ | | p 在词首且后面跟 n 或 sy 时不发音 |
| q | /k/ | Iraq /ɪˈrɑːk/ | quick /kwɪk/ | quiet /ˈkwaɪət/ | |
| r | /r/ | rely /rɪˈlaɪ/ | remain /rɪˈmeɪn/ | rent /rent/ | |
| s | /s/ | seal /siːl/ | ancestor /ˈænsestə/ | arrest /əˈrest/ | s 在词首时，读 /s/; s 在词中，后面接清辅音时读 /s/ |
| | /z/ | closet /ˈklɒzɪt/ | deposit /dɪˈpɒzɪt/ | desert /ˈdezət/ | s 在元音之间读 /z/; s 在词中浊辅音前也读 /z/，例如: husband /ˈhʌzbənd/ |
| | /ʃ/ 或 /ʒ/ | Asia /ˈeɪʃə/ | pension /ˈpenʃn/ | treasure /ˈtreʒə/ | s 后面接 -ia、-ion、-ure 时多读 /ʃ/ 或 /ʒ/ |
| t | /t/ | notify /ˈnəʊtɪfaɪ/ | object /ˈɒbdʒɪkt/ | omit /əˈmɪt/ | |
| | /ʃ/ | initial /ɪˈnɪʃl/ | dictation /dɪkˈteɪʃn/ | | t 在字母组合 -ial、-ion 前读 /ʃ/ |
| | / / | soften /ˈsɒfn/ | fasten /ˈfɑːsn/ | nestle /ˈnesl/ | t 在字母组合 -ften、-sten 和 -stle 中通常不发音，例外: often /ɒfn, ɒftn/ 有两个读音，t 可发音，也可不发音。 |
| v | /v/ | vote /vəʊt/ | vow /vaʊ/ | love /lʌv/ | |
| w | /w/ | win /wɪn/ | wake /weɪk/ | sweet /swiːt/ | |
| | / / | answer /ˈɑːnsə/ | wrap /ræp/ | sword /sɔːd/ | |
| x | /ks/ | excuse /ɪkˈskjuːz/ | exclude /ɪkˈskluːd/ | | |
| | /gz/ | exact /ɪɡˈzækt/ | exist /ɪɡˈzɪst/ | exhibit /ɪɡˈzɪbɪt/ | x 后面接重读元音时，读 /gz/ |
| y | /j/ | yes /jes/ | yard /jɑːd/ | yellow /ˈjeləʊ/ | |
| z | /z/ | puzzle /ˈpʌzl/ | zero /ˈzɪərəʊ/ | zoo /zuː/ | |

## （二）辅音字母组合的读音规则

| 辅音字母字合 | 读音 | 例 词 | | | 例 外 |
|---|---|---|---|---|---|
| ch | /tʃ/ | rich /rɪtʃ/ | search /sɜːtʃ/ | charity /ˈtʃærəti/ | |
| | /k/ | school /skuːl/ | headache /ˈhedeɪk/ | character /ˈkærəktə/ | |
| | /ʃ/ | machine /məˈʃiːn/ | brochure /ˈbrəʊʃə/ | | |
| ck | /k/ | black /blæk/ | sack /sæk/ | sick /sɪk/ | |
| dj | /dʒ/ | adjust /əˈdʒʌst/ | adjective /ˈædʒɪktɪv/ | | |
| gh | /f/ | enough /ɪˈnʌf/ | rough /rʌf/ | tough /tʌf/ | ghost /gəʊst/ ghetto /ˈgetəʊ/ |
| | / / | light /laɪt/ | daughter /ˈdɔːtə/ | high /haɪ/ | |
| gn | /n/ | sign /saɪn/ | foreign /ˈfɒrən/ | design /dɪˈzaɪn/ | |
| kn | /n/ | kneel /niːl/ | knell /nel/ | knight /naɪt/ | |
| mn | /m/ | autumn /ˈɔːtəm/ | column /ˈkɒləm/ | solemn /ˈsɒləm/ | |
| ng | /ŋ/ | morning /ˈmɔːnɪŋ/ | young /jʌŋ/ | wrong /rɒŋ/ | |
| ph | /f/ | photo /ˈfəʊtəʊ/ | phrase /freɪz/ | phase /feɪz/ | |
| sc | /sk/ | scarlet /ˈskɑːlət/ | scare /skeə/ | scatter /ˈskætə/ | |
| | /s/ | muscle /ˈmʌsl/ | science /ˈsaɪəns/ | scene /siːn/ | |
| sh | /ʃ/ | wash /wɒʃ/ | shame /ʃeɪm/ | shade /ʃeɪd/ | |
| tch | /tʃ/ | watch /wɒtʃ/ | crutch /krʌtʃ/ | witch /wɪtʃ/ | |
| th | /θ/ | method /ˈmeθəd/ | through /θruː/ | theme /θiːm/ | |
| | /ð/ | with /wɪð/ | than /ðæn/ | breathe /briːð/ | |
| wh | /w/ | what /wɒt/ | whale /weɪl/ | wheat /wiːt/ | |
| | /h/ | whose /huːz/ | who /huː/ | whole /həʊl/ | |
| wr | /r/ | write /raɪt/ | wrinkle /ˈrɪŋkl/ | wrist /rɪst/ | |

注：双写辅音字母一般只读一个读音，例如：luggage /ˈlʌgɪdʒ/、mirror /ˈmɪrə/、middle /ˈmɪdl/。例外：cc 在元音字母 e 和 i 之前读 /ks/，如 accident /ˈæksɪdənt/、success /səkˈses/。

## 三、常见错误

### （一）规则不清

1. 字母 b 在词尾，前面有字母 m 或后面跟字母 t 时不发音，但有些学生不了解这个规则，认为必须把所有字母全读出来才标准，因此会把 /b/ 也读出来，例如：

   | debt | /debt/ | × | /det/ | √ |
   | doubt | /daʊbt/ | × | /daʊt/ | √ |

2. 字母 c 的通常读音为 /k/ 和 /s/，但在元音字母组合 ia、ie、io 前读 /ʃ/，很多学生不了解这个规则，遇到这种情况时通常会把 /ʃ/ 念成 /s/，例如：

   | crucial | /ˈkruːsl/ | × | /ˈkruːʃl/ | √ |
   | proficient | /prəˈfɪsnt/ | × | /prəˈfɪʃnt/ | √ |

3. 字母 l 在词尾 k 或 m 前有时不发音，但有些学生会把 /l/ 音清楚地读出来，例如：

   | walk | /wɔːlk/ | × | /wɔːk/ | √ |
   | balm | /bɑːlm/ | × | /bɑːm/ | √ |

4. 字母 s 在元音之间时读 /z/，后面接字母组合 ia、ion 和 ure 时通常读 /ʃ/ 或 /ʒ/，很多学生不了解这个规则，会把字母 s 一律念成 /s/ 音，例如：

   | closet | /ˈklɒsɪt/ | × | /ˈklɒzɪt/ | √ |
   | pleasure | /ˈplesə/ | × | /ˈpleʒə/ | √ |

5. 字母 t 在字母组合 -ften、-sten 和 -stle 中通常不发音，有些学生不了解这个规则，会把 /t/ 音也响亮地读出来，例如：

   | soften | /ˈsɒftn/ | × | /ˈsɒfn/ | √ |
   | castle | /ˈkɑːstl/ | × | /ˈkɑːsl/ | √ |

6. 字母组合 th 通常读为 /θ/ 和 /ð/。英语中，个别名词词尾加字母 e 变成了动词，此时元音或元音字母组合读音有变化，辅音读音同样发生变化，由清音变为浊音，但很多学生往往是不论名词、动词都读清音，例如：

   | breath n. /breθ/ | breathe v. /breθ/ × | /briːð/ | √ |
   | bath n. /bɑːθ/ | bathe v. /bɑːθ/ × | /beɪð/ | √ |

### （二）拼音影响

1. 字母 g 的发音有两种：/g/ 和 /dʒ/，但汉语拼音中 g 只有一种发音，因此很多学生看到字母 g，会按汉语拼音习惯一律读 /g/，例如：

   | gesture | /ˈgestʃə/ | × | /ˈdʒestʃə/ | √ |
   | gym | /gɪm/ | × | /dʒɪm/ | √ |

2. 字母 n 的发音有两种: /n/ 和 /ŋ/, 但汉语拼音中 n 只有一种发音, 因此很多学生看到字母 n, 会按汉语拼音习惯一律读 /n/, 例如:

| uncle | /ˈʌnkl/ | × | /ˈʌŋkl/ | √ |
| hungry | /ˈhʌngrɪ/ | × | /ˈhʌŋgrɪ/ | √ |

3. 汉语中没有 /v/, 但有 /w/, 很多学生会把 /v/ 念成 /w/, 例如:

| victor | /ˈwɪktə/ | × | /ˈvɪktə/ | √ |
| view | /wjuː/ | × | /vjuː/ | √ |

## 四、纠错训练

**(一) 模仿录音, 并将字母 b 不发音的单词写在横线上。**

obtain  thumb  doubt  substance  climb
comb  subscribe  observe  debt  dumb

_____   _____   _____   _____   _____

**(二) 模仿录音, 并将字母 c 发 /ʃ/ 的单词写在横线上。**

affection  cancel  concept  crucial  commercial
facial  recycle  procedure  technician  special

_____   _____   _____   _____   _____

**(三) 模仿录音, 并将字母 l 不发音的单词写在横线上。**

cancel  calk  calculate  profile  calm  stalk
talk  folk  trial  walk  fulfill  melt

_____   _____   _____   _____   _____

**(四) 模仿录音, 并在字母 s 发 /z/、/ʃ/ 或 /ʒ/ 音的单词旁分别写上相应的音标, 如 sugar (/ʃ/)。**

exposure ( )  deserve ( )  deposit ( )  pension ( )
because ( )  Asia ( )  desert ( )  poison ( )
autism ( )  treasure ( )  design ( )  pleasure ( )

**（五）模仿录音，并将字母 t 不发音的单词写在横线上。**

| fasten | nestle | potential | hasten | entail |
|---|---|---|---|---|
| castle | bustle | whistle | nasty | ultimately |

_____   _____   _____   _____   _____

**（六）模仿录音，注意字母和字母组合在不同词性的单词中的不同读音。**

| breath | bath | cloth | wreath | sheath |
|---|---|---|---|---|
| breathe | bathe | clothe | wreathe | sheathe |

**（七）模仿录音，并在字母 g 发 /g/ 或 /dʒ/ 音的单词旁分别写上相应的音标，如 guide (/g/)。**

| manage ( ) | college ( ) | negative ( ) | grab ( ) |
|---|---|---|---|
| flag ( ) | fog ( ) | margin ( ) | intelligence ( ) |
| oblige ( ) | energy ( ) | gravity ( ) | telegraph ( ) |

**（八）模仿录音，并在字母 n 发 /n/ 或 /ŋ/ 音的单词旁分别写上相应的音标，如 nice (/n/)。**

| demand ( ) | mango ( ) | money ( ) | thank ( ) |
|---|---|---|---|
| hungry ( ) | tense ( ) | once ( ) | nest ( ) |
| nephew ( ) | hank ( ) | sing ( ) | slang ( ) |

## 五、专项训练

**（一）模仿录音，注意画线辅音字母的读音。**

| object | jot | jacket | box | text |
|---|---|---|---|---|
| excel | exit | exist | exact | yard |
| yellow | yell | zoom | zoo | zero |

**（二）模仿录音，注意画线辅音字母组合的读音。**

| chick | rich | school | headache | chemistry |
|---|---|---|---|---|
| machine | Chicago | brochure | knife | know |
| elephant | photo | quality | quite | quiet |

## （三）英音视听说练习。

以下是电影《傲慢与偏见》（*Pride and Prejudice*）的节选片段，请欣赏，并给画线字母或字母组合选择正确读音。

Jane: Yes. A thousand times yes.

Mrs. Bennet: Thank the Lord for that. I <u>th</u>ought (1. A. /s/ B. /θ/) it would never happen.

Mr. Bennet: I am confident they will do well together. Their tempers are much alike. They will be <u>ch</u>eated (2. A. /ʃ/ B. /tʃ/ ) assiduously by their servants. And be so <u>g</u>enerous (3. A. /ʒ/ B. /dʒ/) with the rest, they will always exceed their income.

Mrs. Bennet: Ex<u>c</u>eed (4. A. /s/ B. /z/) their income? He has 5,000 a year. I knew she did not be so beautiful for nothing.

Miss Bennet: ...must be free from all insincerity. She only can address herself effec<u>t</u>ually (5. A. /t/ B. /tʃ/) to the heart or the feelings of other<u>s</u> (6. A. /s/ B. /z/) whose mind glows with the warmth of sen<u>s</u>ibility (7. A. /s/ B. /z/) and whose argumen<u>ts</u> (8. A. /ts/ B. /dz/) result from conviction. She must feel the influence of those passions and emotions which she wishes to inspire...

1. _____   2. _____   3. _____   4. _____
5. _____   6. _____   7. _____   8. _____

# 第 14 课 辅音连缀

● **考一考**

● 请你和你的同伴分角色朗读下列对话：

● A: Hey, John, you look strong. It seems you are a good sportsman, aren't you?

● B: Well, I'm fond of sports, but I'm not a good player.

● A: What sports do you like to play?

● B: I like to play table tennis and go swimming.

● A: Have you been on any sports teams?

● B: I was a member of a basketball team in high school, but I didn't think team sports were fun, so I quit.

● 对话中画线的部分都是辅音连缀。认真听录音，注意画线部分的读音，并对比你的读音和录音里的读音有什么不同。你是否在辅音之间加上元音 /ɪ/、/ə/ 或 /ʊ/？本课将具体介绍辅音连缀，并做大量相关练习。

● **导入**

　　在第 6—10 课里，我们学习了如何正确发单个辅音。但在英语中常出现两个、三个或更多辅音连在一起的现象，这种语音现象被称为辅音连缀。根据其在单词中的位置，辅音连缀可分为两大类：词内辅音连缀和词间辅音连缀。词内辅音连缀是指单词里辅音与辅音的连缀，例如：great /greɪt/、request /rɪˈkwest/。词间辅音连缀是指单词与单词之间的连缀，例如：a dark sky /ə dɑːk skaɪ/。根据辅音连缀中辅音的数量，辅音连缀又可分为：二辅音连缀、三辅音连缀和四辅音连缀，例如：break /breɪk/、display /dɪˈspleɪ/、sixths /sɪksθ/。

　　辅音连缀的第一个音要读得轻而短，很快过渡到第二个音，即第一和第二个音之间不可以有停顿，不可以在任何两个辅音间加上元音 /ɪ/、/ə/ 或 /ʊ/；而第二个辅音则要读得长而响亮。声音是由弱到强，由轻到响，由短到长。

　　因为汉语中没有辅音连缀现象，所以辅音连缀是中国学生容易犯错且不容易掌握的发音规则。本课将具体介绍并提供大量练习，帮助学习者轻松、自然地掌握辅音连缀。

## 一、学习目标

——了解辅音连缀的基本概念及类型
——掌握辅音连缀的发音技巧
——纠正辅音连缀的常见发音错误

## 二、学习内容

### （一）词内辅音连缀

常见的词内辅音连缀有：词首辅音连缀、词中辅音连缀和词尾辅音连缀。

1. 词首辅音连缀

词首辅音连缀是指处在一个英语单词的第一个元音前的两个或两个以上的辅音组合。常见的词首辅音连缀有词首二辅音连缀和词首三辅音连缀。

（1）词首二辅音连缀

① /s+ 辅音 /

| /sf/ | sphere /sfɪə/ | spherical /ˈsferɪkl/ | sphinx /sfɪŋks/ |
| --- | --- | --- | --- |
| /sk/ | scan /skæn/ | scope /skəʊp/ | score /skɔː/ |
| /sl/ | slip /slɪp/ | sleeve /sliːv/ | slope /sləʊp/ |
| /sn/ | snack /snæk/ | sneeze /sniːz/ | sniff /snɪf/ |
| /sm/ | smash /smæʃ/ | smooth /smuːð/ | smile /smaɪl/ |
| /sp/ | space /speɪs/ | spoon /spuːn/ | spirit /ˈspɪrɪt/ |
| /st/ | stain /steɪn/ | style /staɪl/ | storm /stɔːm/ |
| /sw/ | switch /swɪtʃ/ | swag /swæg/ | swim /swɪm/ |
| /sj/ | suit /sjuːt/ | sue /sjuː/ | suicide /ˈsjuːɪsaɪd/ |

② / 辅音 +l/

| /bl/ | block /blɒk/ | blow /bləʊ/ | blame /bleɪm/ |
| --- | --- | --- | --- |
| /pl/ | plough /plaʊ/ | plead /pliːd/ | plain /pleɪn/ |
| /fl/ | flake /fleɪk/ | flute /fluːt/ | flame /fleɪm/ |
| /gl/ | glue /gluː/ | glance /glɑːns/ | glide /glaɪd/ |
| /kl/ | clue /kluː/ | cling /klɪŋ/ | clone /kləʊn/ |

③ / 辅音 +r/

| /br/ | bright /braɪt/ | brink /brɪŋk/ | break /breɪk/ |
|---|---|---|---|
| /kr/ | crown /kraʊn/ | cradle /ˈkreɪdl/ | crane /kreɪn/ |
| /fr/ | frog /frɒg/ | fringe /frɪndʒ/ | fridge /frɪdʒ/ |
| /gr/ | grief /griːf/ | grin /grɪn/ | grain /greɪn/ |
| /pr/ | praise /preɪz/ | pray /preɪ/ | pride /praɪd/ |
| /θr/ | thread /θred/ | thrill /θrɪl/ | throw /θrəʊ/ |
| /ʃr/ | shriek /ʃriːk/ | shred /ʃred/ | shrewd /ʃruːd/ |

④ / 辅音 +w/

| /dw/ | dwell /dwel/ | dwarf /dwɔːf/ | dwindle /ˈdwɪndl/ |
|---|---|---|---|
| /gw/ | linguist /ˈlɪŋgwɪst/ | language /ˈlæŋgwɪdʒ/ | |
| /kw/ | quarter /ˈkwɔːtə/ | quartz /kwɔːts/ | quiet /ˈkwaɪət/ |
| /sw/ | sweat /swet/ | swear /sweə/ | swig /swɪg/ |
| /tw/ | twist /twɪst/ | twig /twɪg/ | twin /twɪn/ |

（2）词首三辅音连缀

| /spr/ | sprawl /sprɔːl/ | sprout /spraʊt/ | spring /sprɪŋ/ |
|---|---|---|---|
| /spl/ | splash /splæʃ/ | spleen /spliːn/ | split /splɪt/ |
| /skr/ | scrub /skrʌb/ | scratch /skrætʃ/ | screen /skriːn/ |
| /skw/ | square /skweə/ | squeeze /skwiːz/ | squat /skwɒt/ |
| /stj/ | student /ˈstjuːdnt/ | studio /ˈstjuːdiəʊ/ | studious /ˈstjuːdiəs/ |

注：在摩擦音 /s/ 加爆破音 /p/、/t/、/k/ 所构成的词首二辅音连缀或三辅音连缀，即 /sp/、/st/、/sk/、/spr/、/spl/、/stj/、/skr/ 中的 /p/、/t/、/k/ 不送气，分别变为 /sb/、/sd/、/sg/、/sbr/、/sbl/、/sdj/、/sgr/，例如：splash /splæʃ/、skirt /skɜːt/、spray /spreɪ/ 分别读为 /sblæʃ/、/sgɜːt/、/sbreɪ/。

2. 词中辅音连缀

词中辅音连缀是指处在英语单词中两个元音间的两个或两个以上的辅音组合。词中辅音连缀很多样化，有词中二辅音、词中三辅音和词中四辅音连缀。在爆破音变、省音等单元还会对此做详细讲解，故本单元只做简单介绍。

词中二辅音连缀　　dislike /dɪsˈlaɪk/　　　　　chapter /ˈtʃæptə/
词中三辅音连缀　　pumpkin /ˈpʌmpkɪn/　　　symptom /ˈsɪmptəm/

词中四辅音连缀　expression /ɪkˈspreʃn/　　　exclude /ɪkˈsklu:d/

3. 词尾辅音连缀

词尾辅音连缀是指处在英语单词最后一个元音后的两个或两个以上的辅音组合。常见词尾辅音连缀可分为词尾二辅音连缀和词尾三辅音连缀。

（1）词尾二辅音连缀

① /l + 辅音 /

常见的 /l + 辅音 / 连缀有：/lb/、/ld/、/lf/、/lk/、/lt/、/lm/、/ln/、/ldʒ/、/ltʃ/、/lp/、/lv/、/lθ/、/ls/ 和 /lʃ/，例如：

bulb /bʌlb/　　　　　wild /waɪld/　　　　　shelf /ʃelf/
milk /mɪlk/　　　　　belt /belt/　　　　　　film /fɪlm/

② / 辅音 + l/

常见的 / 辅音 + l/ 连缀有：/bl/、/pl/、/fl/、/vl/、/tl/、/dl/、/ml/、/nl/、/sl/、/zl/、/kl/ 和 /gl/，例如：

feeble /ˈfi:bl/　　　　purple /ˈpɜ:pl/　　　　rifle /ˈraɪfl/
rattle /ˈrætl/　　　　 ankle /ˈæŋkl/　　　　 devil /ˈdevl/

③ / 辅音 + θ/

常见的 / 辅音 + θ / 连缀有：/fθ/、/tθ/、/dθ/、/nθ/、/lθ/ 和 /ŋθ/，例如：

twelfth /twelfθ/　　　eighth /eɪtθ/　　　　breadth /bredθ/
month /mʌnθ/　　　　health /helθ/　　　　strength /streŋθ/

④ / 辅音 + s/

常见的 / 辅音 + s/ 连缀有：/ns/、/ks/ 和 /ps/，例如：

defence /dɪˈfens/　　　fix /fɪks/　　　　　　collapse /kəˈlæps/

⑤ / 辅音 + t/

常见的 / 辅音 + t/ 连缀有：/nt/、/pt/、/kt/、/ft/ 和 /st/，例如：

faint /feɪnt/　　　　　adopt /əˈdɒpt/　　　 conduct /kənˈdʌkt/
shift /ʃɪft/　　　　　 nest /nest/　　　　　 list /lɪst/

⑥ / 辅音 + n/

常见的 / 辅音 + n/ 连缀有：/tn/、/dn/、/sn/ 和 /zn/，例如：

button /ˈbʌtn/　　　　sudden /ˈsʌdn/　　　 listen /ˈlɪsn/

此外，常见的辅音连缀还有：/ŋk/、/mp/、/ntʃ/、/nd/ 和 /nz/，例如：

thank /θæŋk/　　　　 jump /dʒʌmp/　　　　branch /brɑ:ntʃ/
end /end/　　　　　　 bronze /brɒnz/　　　 lens /lenz/

（2）词尾三辅音连缀

常见的辅音连缀还有：/spt/、/sps/、/skt/、/sks/、/pst/、/kst/、/ksθ/、/mpt/、/mps/、/mfs/、/nθs/、/lps/、/lmz/、/ŋkl/、/dnt/ 和 /nzd/，例如：

| | | |
|---|---|---|
| lisped /lɪspt/ | lisps /lɪsps/ | asked /ɑːskt/ |
| disks /dɪsks/ | lapsed /læpst/ | taxed /tækst/ |
| thanks /θæŋks/ | prompt /prɒmpt/ | glimpse /glɪmps/ |

## （二）词间辅音连缀

词间辅音连缀指词与词之间辅音的连缀，例如：

| | | |
|---|---|---|
| 二辅音连缀 | a long channel | /ə lɒŋ ˈtʃænl/ |
| 三辅音连缀 | She loves surprise. | /ʃiː lʌvz səˈpraɪz/ |
| 四辅音连缀 | to settle problems | /tə ˈsetl ˈprɒbləmz/ |
| 五辅音连缀 | next Friday | /nekst ˈfraɪdeɪ/ |
| 六辅音连缀 | next spring | /nekst sprɪŋ/ |
| 七辅音连缀 | the text's script | /ðə tekst skrɪpt/ |

> **注意**
>
> 英语中的辅音连缀最多为七辅音连缀，但在实际语言应用中，没有必要把每个辅音都清楚地读出来。关于这一点，涉及英语朗读技巧中的音变和音的连续，我们将在第 4 单元中介绍。

# 三、常见错误

## （一）连缀加音

汉语语音系统中最重要的组合关系是声韵配合关系，该组合有以下特点：第一，辅音一般只能出现在音节前面；第二，每个音节都有元音和声调；第三，汉语音节没有辅音连缀。受此影响，许多学生认为英语的音节也是辅音后面必须接元音，所以在英语的辅音连缀中会出现"加音"现象，即在两辅音间加上元音 /ɪ/、/ə/ 或 /ʊ/。例如：

1. 在 /s/ + 辅音的词首或词中辅音连缀中、在 /s/ 与辅音间加元音 /ɪ/，例如：

   | | | | | |
   |---|---|---|---|---|
   | scare | /ˈsɪkeə/ | × | /ˈskeə/ | √ |
   | dislike | /dɪsɪˈlaɪk/ | × | /dɪsˈlaɪk/ | √ |

2. 在辅音 /k/ 或 /g/ + /l/ 或 /r/ 的词首辅音连缀中，在 /k/ 或 /g/ 与 /l/ 或 /r/ 间加元音 /ə/，例如：

| clue | /kəluː/ | × | /kluː/ | √ |
| crane | /kəreɪn/ | × | /kreɪn/ | √ |
| glide | /gəlaɪd/ | × | /glaɪd/ | √ |
| gram | /gəræm/ | × | /græm/ | √ |

3. 在辅音 /b/、/p/ 或 /f/ + /l/ 或 /r/ 的词首辅音连缀中，在两者之间加元音 /ə/，例如：

| bless | /bəles/ | × | /bles/ | √ |
| please | /pəliːz/ | × | /pliːz/ | √ |
| pride | /pəraɪd/ | × | /praɪd/ | √ |

## （二）连缀停顿

辅音连缀的两大特点是：不加音；不停顿。很多学生会在两辅音之间停顿，即把第一个辅音读音拉长或是把两个辅音分开读，造成读音不够自然和连贯。例如：

1. 在辅音 /ʃ/ 或 /θ/+/r/ 的词首辅音连缀中，有些学生会把第一个辅音 /ʃ/ 或 /θ/ 的读音拉长或是把其与 /r/ 分开读，例如：

| shred | /ʃ…red/ | × | /ʃ-red/ | × | /ʃred/ | √ |
| three | /θ…riː/ | × | /θ-riː/ | × | /θriː/ | √ |

2. 在辅音 /k/ 或 /d/+/w/ 的词首连缀中，把 /k/ 或 /d/ 和 /w/ 分开读，例如：

| quest | /k-west/ | × | /kwest/ | √ |
| dwell | /d-wel/ | × | /dwel/ | √ |

3. 在辅音 /t/+/w/ 的词首连缀中，将二者分开读，例如：

| twin | /t-wɪn/ | × | /twɪn/ | √ |
| twilight | /ˈt-waɪlaɪt/ | × | /ˈtwaɪlaɪt/ | √ |

## （三）连缀省音

辅音连缀是指两个或两个以上的辅音相连在一起，但辅音连缀并非字母组合，辅音连缀中的辅音都有自己的发音。个别学生会把辅音连缀与字母组合混淆，省去连缀中一个辅音。这种现象在 /l/+ 辅音的词尾连缀或辅音 +/l/ 的词中连缀中更为常见。有些学生往往会把 /l/+ 辅音的词尾连缀或辅音 +/l/ 的词中连缀中的 /l/ 音省略，例如：

| hold | /həʊd/ | × | /həʊld/ | √ |
| culture | /ˈkʌtʃə/ | × | /ˈkʌltʃə/ | √ |

## 四、纠错训练

**（一）模仿录音，注意下列 /s/ + 辅音的词首和词中二辅音连缀单词。**

| smash | smuggle | sponsor | spoon |
| stall | stagnant | straw | streak |
| swag | swamp | stuffy | stunt |

**（二）模仿录音，注意下列辅音 /k/ 或 /g/ + /l/ 或 /r/ 的词首辅音连缀单词。**

| closet | club | cluster | clue |
| cross | crowd | crown | cruel |
| glare | glitter | gloss | glue |

**（三）模仿录音，注意下列辅音 /b/、/p/ 或 /f/ + /l/ 或 /r/ 的词首辅音连缀单词。**

| bloom | blind | blink | block |
| bride | broad | break | broom |
| plow | plot | plenty | pledge |

**（四）模仿录音，注意下列辅音 /ʃ/ 或 /θ/ + /r/ 的词首辅音连缀单词。**

| shrine | shrug | shrink | shrub |
| shrill | shrimp | shrew | shriek |
| throne | throw | through | threat |

**（五）模仿录音，注意下列辅音 /k/ 或 /d/ + /w/ 的词首辅音连缀单词。**

| quack | quad | quake | quality |
| qualify | quantity | quarter | queen |
| quake | dwell | dwarf | dwindle |

**（六）模仿录音，注意下列辅音 /t/ + /w/ 的词首辅音连缀单词。**

| twig | twice | twelve | twin |
| twinkle | twist | twit | twitter |
| two | twenty | twitch | tweet |

## 五、专项训练

**（一）模仿录音，注意下列带有词首辅音连缀的单词。**

| skull | skirl | skin | stage | still |
|---|---|---|---|---|
| stamp | spray | sprint | spike | scrap |
| scratch | script | squeal | squirrel | squeak |

**（二）模仿录音，注意下列带有词中辅音连缀的单词。**

| library | member | mischief | object |
|---|---|---|---|
| obstruct | obstacle | sanction | synchronize |
| obscure | excrete | explosion | explore |

**（三）模仿录音，注意下列带有词尾辅音连缀的单词。**

| sold | fold | wild | settle | crystal |
|---|---|---|---|---|
| rattle | wiggle | angle | eagle | lefts |
| gifts | shifts | inks | sinks | links |

**（四）英音视听说练习。**

欣赏电影《超级无敌掌门狗》（*Wallace & Gromit*）的片段，按照要求写出含有各种辅音连缀的单词。

Campanula: Thank goodness you've...

　　Victor: What ho! For you, my love.

Campanula: Victor. How lovely and... unexpected.

　　Victor: Heard you had a spot of rabbit bother and toodle straight on over, to sort the blighters out.

Campanula: Gosh, that is awfully sweet of you, but you really needn't bother.

　　Victor: It is no bother, little boo-boo, it is the least a chap can do for his filly. Don't want pests spoiling our beautiful manor house, do we?

Campanula: "Our" manor house? No one's mentioned marriage, Victor.

　　Victor: All in good time, my dear. Vermin first, though, what what. Come on, Phillip.

Campanula: Victor, we can deal with this humanely.

　Wallace: Very classy. Just the sort of client we should be dealing with, eh, lad?

Wallace: Burrowing bounders! They must be breeding like... well, rabbits. Only one thing for it, lad.

Campanula: Victor, hadn't we agreed? No more thoughtless killing.

Victor: Quite right, my dear. So I have thought this one through very carefully. It's off to bunny heaven for you, big ears.

Campanula: Victor! No.

Victor: What the...?

词首二辅音连缀单词：_____  _____  _____

三辅音连缀单词：_____  _____  _____

词中辅音连缀单词：_____  _____  _____

# 第4单元 语流音变

在前3个单元中，我们学习了英语中的20个元音音素、28个辅音音素以及音节、读音规则及辅音连缀等音素组合，这些都是学习语音的基础和关键。掌握正确的发音方法对掌握音素、音节或单词固然重要，但在实际语言运用过程中，朗读或说话双方的表情达意却是通过自然、连贯的语流来实现的。语流指一连串有连贯意义的语音过程。要想实现连贯自然的语流，必须学会音素在语流中的发音变化。本单元将从爆破音变、音素同化、音素连读、省音和缩读等五个方面进行讲解和训练。

# 第15课 爆破音变

### ● 考一考

下面的谜语中,哪两个英语字母意思是"无"?
What two letters in English mean nothing?

### ● 导入

"考一考"环节的谜底为"MT",即"MT means nothing"。MT 读音为 /ˈemtɪ/,恰好与单词 empty /ˈem(p)tɪ/ 发音相近,于是,仅从发音来看,谜面便成了:"Empty (MT) means nothing"(空即是无)。这个简单有趣的谜语背后所涉及的语音现象,就是本课即将讲解的知识:失去爆破。

失去爆破是实现英语连贯语流不可缺少的一种语流音变。除了失去爆破,本课还将介绍另外三种音变现象:不完全爆破、鼻腔爆破和舌侧爆破。掌握好以上各种爆破音变技巧,对提高英语发音质量、理解英语人士的自然语流很有帮助。

## 一、学习目标

——了解爆破音变的概念及类型
——掌握爆破音变的读音方法
——纠正爆破音变的常见发音错误

## 二、学习内容

### (一)爆破音变的概念

发音就是一系列由发音器官所产生的发音姿势,即音姿。发音是一种音姿运动,而不是发音器官的静态位置。*在语流环境中,相邻音素之间的音姿往往相互影响,形成音姿交叠,从而产生不同的发音变化,也就是音变。

爆破音变是由一个爆破音与另一个辅音构成的语音环境中所产生的音变。爆破音变可以出现在英语单词中(词中)、单词尾(词尾)以及单词与单词间(词间)。出

---

\* Peter Ladefoged. 2011. 语音学教程. 5 版. 北京:北京大学出版社,p. 66.

现失去爆破、不完全爆破的爆破音及其音标在本课中均用下划线"＿"表示，如：affect /əˈfekt/；因鼻腔爆破可省略的元音 /ə/ 用上移的"ᵊ"表示，如：shouldn't /ˈʃʊdᵊnt/。

## （二）爆破音变的类型及方法

爆破音变共有四种类型，即：失去爆破、不完全爆破、鼻腔爆破和舌侧爆破。以下逐一介绍各种爆破音变及其发音技巧。

1. 爆破音 + 爆破音

英语爆破音（/p/、/b/、/t/、/d/、/k/、/g/）在发音时大致要经过"成阻""持阻"和"除阻"三个步骤。所谓"除阻"，就是让气流冲破阻碍，爆破成音。但是，当两个爆破音相邻时，前一个爆破音只需完成成阻和持阻两个步骤，无须除阻爆破，这种现象在语音学上称为"失去爆破"，简称"失爆"。失爆现象的产生，究其原因，是因为两个辅音相邻太近，音姿交叠，发音器官尚未完成前一音姿目标便已需准备下一音姿目标。

失去爆破的发音技巧是：第一个爆破音只按其发音部位做好发音口形，形成阻碍但不爆破出来，稍作停顿后即发出后面的爆破音，后面的爆破音需完全爆破。以课前"考一考"中所涉及的单词 empty /ˈemptɪ/ 为例，单词中第一个爆破音 /p/ 发音时不爆破，气流只需在双唇处完成成阻和持阻两个步骤，省去除阻步骤，稍作停顿立即发出后面的爆破音 /t/，整个词的发音即为 /ˈemtɪ/。又如：

词中相邻，失去爆破：

apt /æpt/                              respective /rɪˈspektɪv/

词尾相邻，失去爆破：

robbed /rɒbd/                          infect /ɪnˈfekt/

词间相邻，失去爆破：

keep quiet /kiːp kwaɪət/               hard times /hɑːd taɪmz/

2. 爆破音 + 摩擦音 / 破擦音

当爆破音与摩擦音（/f/、/v/、/s/、/z/、/ʃ/、/ʒ/、/θ/、/ð/、/r/ 和 /h/）或破擦音（/tʃ/、/dʒ/、/tr/ 和 /dr/）相连时，爆破音只需部分爆破，这种现象在语音学上称为"不完全爆破"。具体发音技巧是：爆破音在发音时只完成除阻爆破的一半，即只让气流从狭小的缝隙中通过，形成不完全爆破，再立即过渡到后面的摩擦音或破擦音。例如，在发单词 picture /ˈpɪktʃə/ 中的两个相邻辅音时，先做好软腭音 /k/ 的发音姿势，在气流稍冲出时立即过渡到后面的破擦音 /tʃ/，形成不完全爆破，这种情况下的爆破音 /k/ 听起来非常轻微。又如：

词中相邻，不完全爆破：

absent /ˈæbsənt/                       advance /ədˈvɑːns/

词尾相邻，不完全爆破：

fix /fɪks/	eggs /egz/

词间相邻，不完全爆破：

take charge /teɪk tʃɑːdʒ/	get there /get ðeə/

3. 爆破音 + 鼻音

当爆破音和鼻音（/m/、/n/）在单词中或单词间相邻时，爆破音形成不完全爆破。例如，单词 midnight /ˈmɪdnaɪt/ 中的爆破音 /d/ 位于鼻音 /n/ 前只需轻微爆破。

需要注意的是，当爆破音 /t/ 和 /d/ 与鼻音在词尾相邻时产生的音姿交叠，即爆破音受鼻音发音部位的影响，爆破部位由口腔爆破改为鼻腔爆破。具体发音技巧是：保持舌尖紧贴上齿龈不变（爆破音 /t/ 和 /d/ 的发音部位），让气流改由鼻腔爆破而出，形成鼻腔爆破。例如：

词中相邻，不完全爆破：

utmost /ˈʌtməʊst/	kidney /ˈkɪdnɪ/

词尾相邻，鼻腔爆破：

hidden /ˈhɪdᵊn/	written /ˈrɪtᵊn/

词间相邻，不完全爆破：

broad-minded /ˈbrɔːd ˈmaɪndɪd/	odd number /ɒd ˈnʌmbə/

4. 爆破音 + 舌侧音

当爆破音和舌侧音 /l/ 在单词中或单词间相邻时，爆破音形成不完全爆破。例如，单词 lately /ˈleɪtlɪ/ 中的爆破音 /t/ 在舌侧音 /l/ 前只需轻微爆破。

需要注意的是，当爆破音和舌侧音 /l/ 在词尾相邻时产生的音姿交叠，即爆破音受舌侧音发音部位的影响，爆破部位由口腔爆破改为舌侧爆破。舌侧爆破的关键在于把握好各辅音的发音部位及方式，即双唇音 /p/ 和 /b/、齿龈音 /t/ 和 /d/、软腭音 /k/ 和 /g/，尤其要注意含糊 /l/ 音在齿龈部位的发音方式。以 apple /æpl/ 中的 /pl/ 为例。先将双唇紧闭，屏住气息，在做好此发音姿势的同时旋即将舌尖抵住上齿龈，舌身略微下垂，使气流由舌两侧泻出后爆破，发音时感觉到腮部因舌两侧的强烈送气而略微鼓起。更多例子如下：

词中相邻，不完全爆破：

loudly /ˈlaʊdlɪ/	outline /ˈaʊtlaɪn/

词尾相邻，舌侧爆破：

battle /ˈbætl/	uncle /ˈʌŋkl/

词间相邻，不完全爆破：

look like /lʊk laɪk/	white lie /waɪt laɪ/

## 三、常见错误

### （一）不知变通

当爆破音与其他辅音相邻时，不少英语初学者由于缺乏相关语音学知识，误以为每个音素在任何情况下都应读得标准、响亮，因而会认真地把第一个爆破音也完全爆破，使得前后两个辅音听起来一样响亮，结果却适得其反，造成读音生硬、不自然。例如：

| | | | | |
|---|---|---|---|---|
| 爆破音 + 爆破音： | adopt /əˈdɒpt/ | × | adopt /əˈdo̱pt/ | √ |
| 爆破音 + 摩擦音： | advice /ədˈvaɪs/ | × | a̱dvice /ədˈvaɪs/ | √ |
| 爆破音 + 破擦音： | assumption /əˈsʌmpʃᵊn/ | × | | |
| | assumption /əˈsʌmp̱ʃᵊn/ | | | √ |
| 爆破音 + 鼻辅音： | sadness /ˈsædnəs/ | × | sa̱dness /ˈsædnəs/ | √ |
| 爆破音 + 舌侧音： | outline /ˈaʊtlaɪn/ | × | ou̱tline /ˈaʊtlaɪn/ | √ |

**纠正办法**

要想轻松自然发出此类音，首先必须清楚各种爆破音变现象，再经过大量练习，掌握好不同辅音的发音部位和相应的失爆、不完全爆破等技巧。例如，在发 adopt /əˈdɒpt/ 中的 /pt/ 时，先将双唇紧闭，屏住气息，做出发双唇音 /p/ 的动作，但无须真正发出音来，而仅停顿留出半拍，与此同时舌尖抵住上齿龈，顺势发出齿龈音 /t/。其他单词的爆破音变也可同样采用这种方法加以练习。

### （二）他音介入

当爆破音 /t/、/d/ 和鼻音在词尾相邻时，部分学习者因要领掌握不到位，舌尖有瞬间离开齿龈的动作，导致气流停留在口腔中间部位的时间过长，如同汉语拼音 e 的发音，因而无法形成足够的鼻腔爆破。而当一个爆破音和舌侧音 /l/ 在词尾相邻时，许多学习者可能由于舌身在发音活动中移动过慢（如：/p/、/b/、/k/ 和 /g/），过渡时舌尖没有及时到达上齿龈 /l/ 的位置，或是由于舌尖移位（如：/t/ 和 /d/），也可能导致无法形成舌侧爆破，而以近似音 /əʊ/ 代替 /l/。例如：

| | | | | | |
|---|---|---|---|---|---|
| /t/+/n/: | Britain | /ˈbrɪtən/ | × | /ˈbrɪtᵊn/ | √ |
| /d/+/n/: | pardon | /ˈpɑːdən/ | × | /ˈpɑːdᵊn/ | √ |
| /t/+/l/: | beetle | /ˈbiːtəʊ/ | × | /ˈbiːtl/ | √ |
| /d/+/l/: | kindle | /ˈkɪndəʊ/ | × | /ˈkɪndl/ | √ |
| /p/+/l/: | ample | /ˈæmpəʊ/ | × | /ˈæmpl/ | √ |

| | | | | | |
|---|---|---|---|---|---|
| /b/+/l/: | amble | /ˈæmbəʊ/ | × | /ˈæmbl/ | √ |
| /k/+/l/: | tickle | /ˈtɪkəʊ/ | × | /ˈtɪkl/ | √ |
| /g/+/l/: | smuggle | /ˈsmʌgəʊ/ | × | /ˈsmʌgl/ | √ |

### 纠正办法

掌握正确的发音技巧。在发鼻腔爆破 /tⁿn/ 或 /dⁿn/ 时，确保舌尖紧贴上齿龈的动作不变，这是发音的关键。舌身先将气流阻挡在口腔内，再让气流冲破舌端与上齿龈的阻碍后由鼻腔爆破而出，形成自然的鼻腔爆破。发鼻腔爆破时的口腔张开程度较单独发爆破音 /t/ 和 /d/ 时小，两嘴角边微微上扬即可。

发舌侧爆破时，注意保持齿龈音 /t/ 和 /d/ 与其后的舌侧音 /l/ 发音位置不变，若是发双唇音 /p/ 和 /b/ 或软腭音 /k/ 和 /g/，则在做该发音姿势的同时迅速将舌尖紧贴上齿龈，舌身略微下垂，使劲用气流冲破舌端的阻碍后由舌两侧泻出爆破。初学者刚练习时会有"大舌头"的感觉，不容易控制好气流，但经过大量模仿练习后可逐渐掌握发音要领。

## （三）拼音影响

当爆破音与其他辅音相邻时，受汉语拼音"声母 + 韵母"结构的影响，有些学生会习惯性地在辅音之后加入一个补偿性的元音 /ə/ 或 /ʊ/。例如：

| | | | | |
|---|---|---|---|---|
| 爆破音 + 爆破音：adopt /əˈdɒpʊtə/ | × | adopt /əˈdɒpt/ | √ |
| 爆破音 + 摩擦音：advice /ədəˈvaɪs/ | × | advice /ədˈvaɪs/ | √ |
| 爆破音 + 破擦音：assumption /əˈsʌmpʊʃⁿn/ | × | assumption /əˈsʌmpʃⁿn/ | √ |
| 爆破音 + 鼻辅音：sadness /ˈsædənəs/ | × | sadness /ˈsædnəs/ | √ |
| 爆破音 + 舌侧音：outline /ˈaʊtəlaɪn/ | × | outline /ˈaʊtlaɪn/ | √ |

### 纠正办法

采用英汉对比发音练习的方法，逐渐区分两种不同的语音系统，摆脱汉语拼音的负面影响，在正确掌握单个英语辅音音素的发音技巧后，再尝试两个辅音相连的发音练习方法，反复练习直至熟能生巧。

## 四、纠错训练

**（一）模仿录音，注意下划线爆破音的失去爆破或不完全爆破。**

### 爆破音 + 爆破音（失去爆破）

| 词中 | 词尾 | 词间 |
|---|---|---|
| ado<u>p</u>tive /əˈdɒptɪv/ | stoppe<u>d</u> /stɒpt/ | sho<u>p</u>keeper /ˈʃɒpkiːpə/ |
| su<u>b</u>due /səbˈdjuː/ | rubbe<u>d</u> /rʌbd/ | bloo<u>d</u> bank /ˈblʌd bæŋk/ |
| vic<u>t</u>ory /ˈvɪktəri/ | looke<u>d</u> /lʊkt/ | ba<u>ck</u>pack /ˈbækpæk/ |
| selec<u>t</u>ive /sɪˈlektɪv/ | selec<u>t</u> /sɪˈlekt/ | ba<u>ck</u> pain /ˈbæk peɪn/ |
| tem<u>p</u>tation /tempˈteɪʃən/ | tugge<u>d</u> /tʌgd/ | pi<u>g</u>tail /ˈpɪgteɪl/ |

### 爆破音 + 摩擦音 / 破擦音（不完全爆破）

| 词中 | 词尾 | 词间 |
|---|---|---|
| a<u>d</u>vance /ədˈvɑːns/ | ta<u>p</u>s /tæps/ | nigh<u>t</u> show /naɪt ʃəʊ/ |
| a<u>b</u>sorb /əbˈsɔːb/ | ro<u>b</u>s /rɒbz/ | kee<u>p</u> silent /kiːp ˈsaɪlənt/ |
| a<u>d</u>venture /ədˈventʃə/ | ki<u>ck</u>s /kɪks/ | boo<u>k</u> shelf /bʊk ʃelf/ |
| su<u>cc</u>ess /səkˈses/ | bu<u>g</u>s /bʌgz/ | tha<u>t</u> child /ðæt tʃaɪld/ |

### 爆破音 + 鼻音（不完全爆破）

| 词中 | 词间 |
|---|---|
| Sy<u>d</u>ney /ˈsɪdni/ | goo<u>d</u> night /gʊd naɪt/ |
| par<u>t</u>ner /ˈpɑːtnə/ | star<u>t</u> now /stɑːt naʊ/ |
| wi<u>t</u>ness /ˈwɪtnəs/ | ca<u>t</u> nap /kæt næp/ |
| a<u>d</u>mire /ədˈmaɪə/ | goo<u>d</u> neighbors /gʊd ˈneɪbəz/ |
| nigh<u>t</u>mare /ˈnaɪtmeə/ | ta<u>k</u>e note /teɪk nəʊt/ |

### 爆破音 + 舌侧音（不完全爆破）

| 词中 | 词间 |
|---|---|
| la<u>t</u>ely /ˈleɪtli/ | I'<u>d</u> like to /aɪd laɪk tʊ/ |
| boo<u>k</u>let /ˈbʊklɪt/ | straigh<u>t</u> line /streɪt laɪn/ |
| regar<u>d</u>less /rɪˈgɑːdlɪs/ | goo<u>d</u> luck /gʊd lʌk/ |

## （二）模仿录音，注意画线部分的鼻腔爆破或舌侧爆破。

**鼻腔爆破**

didn't /ˈdɪdᵊnt/     needn't /ˈniːdᵊnt/     shouldn't /ˈʃʊdᵊnt/
harden /ˈhɑːdᵊn/     ridden /ˈrɪdᵊn/     burden /ˈbɜːdᵊn/
certain /ˈsɜːtᵊn/     button /ˈbʌtᵊn/     rotten /ˈrɒtᵊn/

**舌侧爆破**

title /ˈtaɪtl/     little /ˈlɪtl/     middle /ˈmɪdl/
riddle /ˈrɪdl/     article /ˈɑːtɪkl/     chuckle /ˈtʃʌkl/
google /ˈɡʊɡl/     giggle /ˈɡɪɡl/     couple /ˈkʌpl/

## 五、专项训练

### （一）模仿录音，给下列产生音变的爆破音画线。

**爆破音 + 爆破音（失去爆破）**

| | | | |
|---|---|---|---|
| let go | credit card | bad cold | third part |
| keep quiet | shop keeper | rob Kim | describe precisely |
| book ticket | take time | big pond | lag behind |

**爆破音 + 摩擦音 / 破擦音（不完全爆破）**

| | | | |
|---|---|---|---|
| sweet voice | pet shop | a good view | loud cheers |
| help them | stop shouting | big jug | big size |
| take risks | take charge of | job training | rub shoulders |

**爆破音 + 鼻音（不完全爆破）**

| | | | |
|---|---|---|---|
| at most | not much | odd numbers | good morning |
| take note | dark night | help me | stop now |
| stop mourning | take mine | quite near | loud noise |

## 第 4 单元 语流音变

**爆破音 + 舌侧音（不完全爆破）**

| | | | |
|---|---|---|---|
| at large | sound like | at last | at leisure |
| red lantern | good luck | black list | sick leave |
| at lunch | red light | good luck | at length |

**爆破音 + 鼻音（鼻腔爆破）**

| | | | |
|---|---|---|---|
| mitten | frighten | written | important |
| Britain | Briton | Boston | Washington |
| pardon | hidden | widen | gardening |

**爆破音 + 舌侧音（舌侧爆破）**

| | | | |
|---|---|---|---|
| fumble | rumble | table | gentle |
| handle | idle | ankle | nickel |
| cradle | obstacle | muddle | mumble |

（二）配对练习。下面有十组被拆散的复合词，表格中 A 栏为每个单词的前半部分，请根据提供的词义，将选项一栏中的单词填在 B 栏里，即将复合词还原。然后再大声朗读，注意失去爆破和不完全爆破。

| 选　　项 | A | B | 词　　义 |
|---|---|---|---|
| run | up | | 升起 |
| date | out | | 超过 |
| top | foot | | 立足点 |
| point | lap | | 笔记本电脑 |
| come | up | | 更新 |
| seeing | check | | 检查站 |
| case | out | | 成果 |
| rising | back | | 双肩包 |
| hold | suit | | 手提箱 |
| pack | sight | | 观光游览 |

121

### （三）英音视听说练习。

欣赏电影《哈利波特与魔法石》(*Harry Potter and the Philosopher's Stone*) 片段，用下划线划出对白中的爆破音变，然后模仿跟读。

Professor: Ronald Wesley.

Hat: Ha, another Wesley! I know just what to do with you. Gryffindor!

Professor: Harry Potter.

Hat: Em, difficult, very difficult. Plenty of courage, I see. Not a bad mind, either. There is talent, oh, yes. And a thirst to prove yourself. But where to put you?

Harry: Not Slytherin. Not Slytherin.

Hat: Not Slytherin, eh? Are you sure? You could be great, you know. It's all here, in your head. And Slytherin will help you on the way to greatness, no doubt about that. No? Well, if you're sure. Better be Gryffindor!

# 第16课 同化

● **考一考**

请给下面 3 个专有名词标注音标，注意画线部分的读音：

Asia　　　　Indonesia　　　　Russia
/　　　/　　/　　　　/　　　/　　　　/

● **导入**

若用前面我们学过的语音音素知识来判断，以上"考一考"中 3 个专有名词的音标应为：/ˈeɪzjə/、/ˌɪndəʊˈniːzjə/ 和 /ˈrʌsjə/，而事实上其真正发音为：/ˈeɪʒə/、/ˌɪndəʊˈniːʒə/ 和 /ˈrʌʃə/。黑体部分显示出的前后变化，即 /z/+/j/ 变为 /ʒ/，/s/+/j/ 变为 /ʃ/，就是本课即将介绍的音同化中的一种：融合同化。

音的同化有历史原因，也有语境方面的原因。早期英语中的一些发音正是由于同化发展而来，如以上介绍的 3 个例词；再如 cupboard /ˈkʌbəd/，其中的 /p/ 被后邻音 /b/ 所同化，也是属于语言的历史发展所导致的音同化现象。除此之外，还有一些词的发音是依据语境而变化的，如：let go 中的 /t/ 可以被 /g/ 同化成软腭音 /k/，don't you 中的 /t/ 和 /j/ 合并同化成 /tʃ/ 等。

音素同化与省音、连读一样，都属于连贯语流中的音变现象，在英语口语中非常普遍。对部分同化现象的了解和掌握有助于英语听力理解及发音。但对于快速语流环境下产生的同化，英语学习者只需了解，不必刻意追求和模仿。本课只介绍和训练对于中国英语学习者的发音具有实际指导意义的同化的内容。

## 一、学习目标

——了解同化的基本概念及类型
——掌握同化的发音方法
——纠正音的同化时的常见发音错误

## 二、学习内容

### （一）同化概念

音同化指一个音受其相邻音的影响变得与其相同或相近，或者两个相邻音互相影响，变为第三个音。同化可以发生在单词或复合词中，也可以发生在相邻的两个单词之间。同化的实质是为了发音方便，省力省时，是一种为了"偷懒"而采取的音变；换言之，就是说话时只需采用一种而非两种清浊方式或是发音部位、发音方式来发音。

在本课内容讲解及习题训练中，出现同化的音素部分用斜体表示，如：A*si*a。

### （二）同化的类型及方法

同化时相邻音的影响有三种情况：受前邻音的影响、受后邻音的影响以及前后两个相邻音相互影响。根据三种影响前后顺序的不同可以把同化分为三种类型：顺同化、逆同化和融合同化。但是，无论哪种同化，其产生均与以下三种原因有关联：受清浊变化的影响、受发音部位的影响以及受发音方式的影响。

1. 顺同化

两个相邻的音，后邻音受前邻音的影响变得与其相同或相近，这种同化叫作顺同化。顺同化主要出现在以 -s 或 -es 结尾的名词复数、名词所有格、一般现在时动词第三人称单数以及以 -ed 结尾的动词过去式、过去分词里。若前邻音发音为清音，则后邻音随之同化成清音；若前邻音发音为浊音，则后邻音也同化成相应的浊音。例如：

|  | 清音 | | 浊音 | |
| --- | --- | --- | --- | --- |
| 名词复数 | cap*s*<br>roof*s*<br>take*s* | /-s/<br>/-s/<br>/-s/ | citie*s*<br>cab*s*<br>knive*s* | /-z/<br>/-z/<br>/-z/ |
| 名词所有格 | Kate'*s* son<br>Mr. Smith'*s* pet | /-s/<br>/-s/ | teacher*s*'<br>girl*s*' | /-z/<br>/-z/ |
| 动词第三人称单数 | beat*s*<br>tap*s* | /-s/<br>/-s/ | need*s*<br>climb*s* | /-z/<br>/-z/ |
| 动词过去式/<br>动词过去分词 | look*ed*<br>watch*ed* | /-t/<br>/-t/ | claim*ed*<br>oblig*ed* | /-d/<br>/-d/ |

此外，以 -t 或 -d 结尾的一般动词过去式、过去分词，以 -ed 结尾的部分形容词以及以 -edly 结尾的部分副词，-ed 读音为 /ɪd/；以 /s/、/z/、/ʃ/、/ʒ/、/tʃ/、/dʒ/ 读音结尾的名词复数或动词单数形式须在词尾加 -es 或 -s，读音为 /ɪz/；以 -th 结尾的单词后接 -s 或 's 的读音视具体前邻音素而定。以上情况均视为语境中的顺同化。详见下表：

| 动词 /ɪd/ | 形容词 /ɪd/ | 副词 /ɪd/ | /ɪz/ |
|---|---|---|---|
| wanted<br>elected<br>adapted<br>donated<br>educated<br>added<br>needed<br>sounded<br>wounded<br>concluded<br>succeeded | learned<br>wicked<br>aged<br>naked<br>wretched<br>legged<br>dogged | fixedly<br>markedly<br>resignedly<br>deservedly | 名词复数<br>classes<br>noses<br>dishes<br>beaches<br>fridges<br>动词单数<br>fixes<br>buzzes<br>vanishes<br>matches<br>obliges |

| -th+-s 或 's 的读音 ||||
|---|---|---|---|
| /θs/ || /ðz/ | /θs/ 或 /ðz/ |
| 在短元音或 -rth 之后：<br>months<br>births || 在长元音、双元音之后：<br>paths<br>mouths | 两者兼可：<br>youths<br>truths |

2. 逆同化

两个相邻音中，前邻音受后邻音的影响变得与其相同或相近，这种同化叫作逆同化。逆同化的产生与清浊变化、发音部位或发音方式有关。本课仅列举较实用的前两类，详见下表：

| | | 同清 | 同浊（仅限个别单词） |
|---|---|---|---|
| 同清同浊 | | of course (/v/ → /f/)<br>newspaper (/z/ → /s/)<br>with pleasure (/ð/ → /θ/) | gooseberry (/s/ → /z/)<br>cupboard (/p/ → /b/)<br>raspberry (/s/ → /z/), (/p/ → /b/) |

| 发音部位 | 变为双唇音 | | 变为齿龈音 | |
|---|---|---|---|---|
| | /n/+/m/、/b/ 或 /p/ → /m/<br>te*n* minutes<br>o*n*e boy<br>seve*n* parcels<br>/t/+/m/、/b/ 或 /p/ → /p/<br>tha*t* man<br>shor*t* break<br>whi*t*e paper<br>/d/+/m/、/b/ 或 /p/ → /b/<br>ol*d* man<br>goo*d* boy<br>an educa*t*ed person | | /n/+/t/、/d/ 或 /n/ → /n/<br>i*n*tolerable<br>i*n*direct<br>i*n*numerable<br>/θ/+/s/ → /s/<br>the four*th* season | |
| | 变为腭龈音 | | 变为软腭音 | |
| | /s/+/ʃ/ → /ʃ/<br>thi*s* shirt<br>look*s* sharp<br>/z/+/ʃ/ → /ʒ/<br>hi*s* shoes<br>doe*s* she | | /t/+/g/ 或 /k/ → /k/<br>le*t* go<br>I couldn'*t* cook.<br>/d/+/g/ 或 /k/ → /g/<br>a goo*d* game<br>a ba*d* concert<br>/n/+/g/ 或 /k/ → /ŋ/<br>ha*n*dkerchief<br>o*n*e class<br>We ca*n* go out. | |

3. 融合同化

在英语的快速语流中，两个相邻音互相影响，变为第三个音，这种同化叫作融合同化。融合同化主要体现在 /t/、/d/、/s/ 或 /z/+/j/ 的情况之下。详见下表：

| /t/+/j/ → /tʃ/ | ac*tu*al | na*tu*ral | las*t y*ear | aren'*t y*ou | |
| --- | --- | --- | --- | --- | --- |
| /d/+/j/ → /dʒ/ | gra*du*al | gra*du*ate | di*d y*ou | woul*d y*ou | |
| /s/+/j/ → /ʃ/ | Ru*ss*ia | in*su*rance | mis*s y*ou | bles*s y*ou | |
| /z/+/j/ → /ʒ/ | A*si*a | Indone*si*a | u*su*al | ca*su*al | vi*su*al |
| /ts/+/j/ =/tʃ/ | She le*t's y*ou in. | | | | |
| /dz/+/j/=/dʒ/ | He sen*ds y*our sister a card each year. | | | | |

**你知道吗?**

音同化现象并非英语独有。在我们所熟悉的汉语口语中也有很多音同化现象。例如,年轻人开玩笑时说的"表""酱紫",其实就是通过对"不要""这样子"等词融合同化而成的。

## 三、常见错误

### (一)清浊不分

清浊不分是许多英语学习者的通病,即分不清英语中的清辅音和浊辅音。其结果是在遇到名词复数、名词所有格、一般现在时动词第三人称单数的屈折后缀 -s 或 -es 时一律读成 /s/;在遇到以 -ed 结尾的动词过去式、过去分词时又一律读成 /d/。

**纠正办法**

1. 分清清浊辅音。屈折后缀的顺同化规则就是:清随清,浊跟浊。英语的辅音中有很多是清浊对应的,剩余的除去 /h/ 外都是浊音。以下是本教材介绍的 28 个清浊辅音在一般情况下与屈折词缀相遇时的读音(不含灰色部分):

| 清 | -s → /s/ | p | t | k | f | θ | s | ʃ | ts | tʃ | tr | h | | | | | |
|---|---|---|---|---|---|---|---|---|---|---|---|---|---|---|---|---|---|
| 浊 | -s → /z/ | b | d | g | v | ð | z | ʒ | dz | dʒ | dr | | m | n | ŋ | l | w | r | j |
| 清 | -ed → /t/ | p | **t** | k | f | θ | s | ʃ | ts | tʃ | tr | h | | | | | |
| 浊 | -ed → /d/ | b | **d** | g | v | ð | z | ʒ | dz | dʒ | dr | | m | n | ŋ | l | w | r | j |

   从表中可以看出,除去灰色部分的一些特例及无法搭配发音的音素,需要记忆的内容并不多,只需平时多加注意观察和练习读音即可。例如:

   traps /træps/    briefs /briːfs/    established /ɪˈstæblɪʃt/

2. 强记特例规则。除去以上介绍的一般情况,灰色方框内黑体部分的音素在特殊情况下发音不同,这点必须牢记。具体详见本课知识内容介绍。

3. 加强听力输入。听力最难的部分往往与英语连贯语流中的各种音变现象有关。有些学生对英语的同化现象听辨不清,很大部分是由于听力输入不足造成的,进而影响到发音。在掌握了相关知识后,以足够的听力输入为前提保证和输出驱动,才能对英语中的同化现象有清楚的认识。

## （二）清音浊化

有些英语学习者受汉语发音习惯的影响，在快速语流中会将清辅音读成浊辅音，例如：

I li*k*e *t*ha*t* bla*c*k dog.

连读时斜体部分的清辅音 /k/、/t/、/k/ 听起来像被同化成了对应的浊辅音 /g/、/d/、/g/。这是错误的。清辅音 /k/、/t/、/k/ 虽与之后的 3 个浊辅音 /ð/、/b/、/d/ 相邻，但在正确的英语语流中应避免将其同化成对应的浊辅音。

**纠正办法**

> 英语快速语流中前浊后清时出现逆同化，即前面的浊音同化成清音的情况比较多见。但与其相反的一类，即前清后浊时出现逆同化则不存在。若采取这种发音处理方式，会有一种很重的外国腔。

## 四、纠错训练

### （一）模仿录音，注意区分屈折后缀的清浊辅音的同化。

**清辅音 + -s/-es → /s/**

| | | |
|---|---|---|
| chips | chops | loops |
| pants | beats | compacts |
| breaks | cracks | overlooks |
| cliffs | laughs | gulfs |
| months | lengths | breaths |

**浊辅音 + -s/-es → /z/**

| | | |
|---|---|---|
| cabs | bulbs | suburbs |
| awards | brands | decades |
| nags | rugs | handbags |
| knives | reserves | perceives |
| bathes (v.) | breathes (v.) | wreathes (v.) |
| combs | tombs | claims |
| stains | unions | mountains |

| polls | angles | symbols |
| rings | wings | strings |

**清辅音 + -ed → /t/**

| helped | wrapped | snapped |
| lacked | risked | shocked |
| puffed | engulfed | triumphed |
| assessed | collapsed | impressed |
| wished | polished | established |
| watched | twitched | approached |

**浊辅音 + -ed → /d/**

| mobbed | rubbed | climbed |
| hugged | dragged | plagued |
| dived | contrived | preserved |
| bathed (v.) | breathed (v.) | wreathed (v.) |
| eased | infused | confused |
| engaged | enlarged | exchanged |
| claimed | bombed | condemned |
| assigned | resigned | inclined |
| banged | hanged | twanged |
| cuddled | huddled | concealed |

**/s, z, ʃ, ʒ, tʃ, dʒ/ + -s 或 -es → /ɪz/**

| glasses | confesses | devises |
| buzzes | teases | criticizes |
| wishes | vanishes | polishes |
| garages | mirages | |
| matches | patches | bunches |
| ages | bridges | marriages |

### /t, d/ + -ed → /ɪd/

| wanted | toasted | roasted |
| elected | adapted | educated |
| boarded | blended | awarded |
| wounded | concluded | succeeded |

（二）模仿录音，注意不要将画线部分的清辅音读成相应的浊辅音 /d/ 或 /g/。

| si<u>t</u> back | no<u>t</u> bad | ge<u>t</u> behind | firs<u>t</u> glance |
| no<u>t</u> good | hear<u>t</u> break | chea<u>t</u> daddy | a<u>t</u> best |
| kic<u>k</u> brick | loo<u>k</u> like | blac<u>k</u> dog | ta<u>ke</u> them |

## 五、专项训练

（一）找错误。下面是一台装有自动语音识别系统的电脑在语音识别时记录下的句子。每个句子中都有一处由于音的同化而产生的音似错误。请在错误的单词下画线，并在所提供的单词栏里选出正确的写在后面的空格里。

| tried | bad | heart | coat | turn |
| cheat | beat | you | your | what's |

例：Mr. Smith <u>talk</u> classes this morning.  ( taught )

1. Wash the coke clean!  (_____)
2. Her harp broke when he left her.  (_____)
3. The government cheap people out of their pensions.  (_____)
4. Have you ever tribe Beijing beer?  (_____)
5. Tom always asks bag questions in class.  (_____)
6. You may have a left term before you arrive at the corner.  (_____)
7. I can beach you in the run.  (_____)
8. Watch your name?  (_____)
9. Don't chew like it?  (_____)
10. They need jaw help.  (_____)

**（二）双人练习。**两人一组，轮流扮演 Sloppy Michael 和 Neat Tony，根据所提供的情景及信息进行对话。

情景：Michael 和 Tony 是大学同窗室友，在过去的两年中，Michael 懒散邋遢，Tony 勤快整洁。用所提供的词汇描述两人的不同生活习惯，注意动词过去时态后缀 -ed 的正确发音。

例：Sloppy Michael never changed his bed sheets.

Neat Tony changed his bed sheets every other week.

| 动词 | 名词 | Sloppy Michael | Neat Tony |
|---|---|---|---|
| ★ wash<br>★ dust<br>★ dump<br>★ fold<br>★ rinse<br>★ polish<br>★ mop<br>★ scour<br>★ wipe<br>★ clean<br>★ change | ★ dishes<br>★ bookshelves<br>★ garbage<br>★ clothes<br>★ the laundry<br>★ shoes<br>★ the hallway<br>★ the toilet<br>★ windows<br>★ computer<br>★ bed sheets | ★ the next day<br>★ once a week<br>★ occasionally<br>★ almost never<br>★ on weekends<br>★ seldom<br>★ once a month<br>★ never<br>★ rarely<br>★ every other month<br>★ only when his girlfriend visited | ★ after every meal<br>★ whenever it was dirty<br>★ everyday<br>★ every night<br>★ often<br>★ every week<br>★ usually<br>★ once a week<br>★ frequently<br>★ routinely |

**（三）英音视听说练习。**

欣赏电影《英国病人》(*English Patient*)片段，画出对白中的融合同化，然后模仿。

Hanna: How are you?

Solider 1: Okay.

Hanna: Your leg will be fine. And a lot of shrapnel came out. And I saved you pieces.

Solider 1: You are the prettiest girl I've ever seen.

Hanna: I don't think so. Here.

Solider 1: Would you kiss me?

Hanna: No, I'll get you some tea.

Solider 1: It would mean such a lot to me.

Hanna: Would it?

Solider 1: Thank you.

Solider 2: Nurse, I can't sleep. Would you kiss me?

Solider 3: You are so pretty. Will you tuck me in, please?

Hanna: Very funny. Go to sleep now.

Woman 1: Where is the doctor?

Woman 2: Don't ask.

第 4 单元　语流音变

# 第17课　连读

### 考一考

请读出下面的单词、词组和句子：

time

the time

the timer

the timer fool

He said **the timer** fool.

请把最后一个句子默念几遍，注意感觉句子各部分的强弱，并根据语音猜猜这句话的逻辑意义。

### 导入

　　英语与汉语在语音学方面有很大的区别：汉语的音节结构封闭、独立，音节之间具有明显的离散性和排他性；而英语的音节结构具有开放性，音节与音节间具有明显的凝聚性和聚合性，音节间界限模糊。英语音节结构的这种特质为连读提供了可能。因此，与汉语字字铿锵有力的语言特色相比，英语则是行云流水、一气呵成。要形成这样一种连贯语流，势必会产生类似"考一考"中所听到的语流音变，即部分单词和词组在连读过程中产生的各种声音变化，致使原来为我们所熟知的词句突然间变得陌生起来。事实上，"耳尖"的人在听到这句话后是能够判断出其真正语义的，即：He said **that I am a** fool.

　　连读是英语自然语流中的一个重要现象，是英语学习者能听会说的一个重要前提。要想突破英语听力学习的瓶颈，提高英语话语的流利程度，摆脱一字一顿的"中国腔"，除了基础的音素学习外，还必须了解英语的各种自然语流现象，掌握好诸如连读、同化、省音、缩读、节奏等连贯语流技巧。

## 一、学习目标

——了解连读的基本概念及类型

——掌握连读的读音方法

——纠正连读中的常见发音错误

## 二、学习内容

### （一）连读的概念

连读是快速语流的自然结果，在自然流畅的英语口语中比比皆是。连读是同一意群中，两个相邻单词的词尾和词首音素自然流畅地连接在一起的发音技巧。连读时首尾相邻的音素只需顺其自然地一带而过，不宜读得太重，也不能省音。

本课的连读符号用一个下沉的弯弧线"‿"表示。

### （二）连读的类型及方法

根据连读时邻接词词尾及词首音素的不同性质，本书将连读划分成四大类型，即：元音+元音型、辅音+元音型、辅音+半元音型、辅音+辅音型。

1. "元音+元音型"连读

在英语的自然语流中，当前一单词以元音音素结尾，后一邻接词以元音音素开头时，两词之间通常通过添加一个轻读的 /w/、/j/ 或 /r/ 进行连读。听音时感觉好像第二个单词产生了音变。/w/、/j/、/r/ 在语音学中又称为无擦通音，介乎元音和辅音之间。在英语连读中添加这几个音无形中起到了很好的连接作用。

"元音+元音型"连读包含四种子类型。

（1）/ɪ/、/i:/、/eɪ/、/aɪ/、/ɔɪ/ + 元音

在自然语流中，若前一单词以扁口型元音 /ɪ/、/i:/、/eɪ/、/aɪ/ 和 /ɔɪ/ 等结尾，后一单词起首也是元音，两个单词往往通过连读自然衔接在一起，正如我们在课前"考一考"中所听到的 the timer 中的 that I ‿ am a 之间的连读现象。

此种连读的技巧是：在两个元音之间加上一个轻读的外加音 /j/。具体学习时可尝试在延长前一个元音的同时将口型放扁，中间不断气滑到 /j/ 音，再顺势连上后续元音。例如：

    /j/      /j/
   I ‿ am    try ‿ it

（2）/əʊ/、/aʊ/、/u:/ 和 /ʊ/ + 元音

说话或朗读时，若前一单词以圆唇型元音 /əʊ/、/aʊ/、/u:/、/ʊ/ 等结尾，后一单词起首也是元音时，两个单词往往通过连读自然衔接在一起。

此种连读的技巧是：在两个元音之间加上一个轻读的外加音 /w/。具体学习时可尝试先将前一个元音的唇形收拢，中间不断气滑到 /w/ 音，再顺势连上后续元音。例如：

    /w/      /w/
   who ‿ is    how ‿ often

（3）–r 或 -re+ 元音

在自然语流中，如果单词后邻接词以元音开头，并且两个词在意义上密切相关、中间无停顿隔开时，两词之间通常会添加一个连读音 /r/，此时的 /r/ 音较之在其他单词起首时的发音要弱而含糊得多。例如：

　　　　　　　/r/　　　　　　　　　　/r/
　　　　for ⌣ a while　　　　after ⌣ all

需要注意的是，当出现以下两种情形时，即使后面的邻接词以元音开头，也不宜连读：

① 同一个音节中前后都有字母 -r 或 -re，例如：

　　a roar of laughter　　　a rare animal　　　nearer and nearer

② 两词之间有意群停顿（即使该停顿并没有真正产生），例如：

　　She peeped from the door | and slipped in.

（4）/ə/、/ɜː/、/ɪə/ 和 /eə/ + 元音

英语连读还包括一种特殊现象，即：单词拼读里虽没有字母 r 或 re 结尾，但单词以带有中性元音 /ə/ 的音素结尾，而后邻接词的词首也是元音，此时为了避免让这两个意义相关的邻接词的末首元音分立而读，两单词之间会添加一个轻微的外加音 /r/ 进行连读。此种类型的连读对许多英语学习者来说比较陌生。例如：

　　　　　　/r/　　　　　　　　　　　　/r/
　　　the idea ⌣ of　　　　　　　media ⌣ event

2. "辅音 + 元音型" 连读

在英语的自然语流中，当同一意群中的前一单词以辅音音素结尾，后一邻接词以元音音素开头时，两个单词通常会自然地连读在一起。听音时感觉好像前一个辅音"脱离"了原单词，与后一个元音重新组合变成新的音节，如：turn ⌣ off 听起来就像 tur noff。

"辅音 + 元音型" 连读包含五种子类型。

（1）爆破音 + 元音

以爆破音 /p/、/b/、/t/、/d/、/k/、/g/ 结尾的单词，其后的邻接词若以元音音素开头，可以连读。例如：

　　stop ⌣ it　　　　　　　　good ⌣ idea

　　disturb ⌣ it　　　　　　　speak ⌣ English

　　first ⌣ of all　　　　　　　dig ⌣ out

（2）摩擦音 + 元音

以摩擦音 /f/、/v/、/θ/、/ð/、/s/、/z/、/ʃ/ 结尾的单词，其后的邻接词若以元音

音素开头，可以连读。例如：

two of ‿ us          leave ‿ alone
a wealth ‿ of        with ‿ a start
a box ‿ of           is ‿ out
fresh ‿ oranges

（3）破擦音 + 元音

以破擦音 /tʃ/、/dʒ/、/ts/、/dz/ 结尾的单词，其后的邻接词若以元音音素开头，可以连读。例如：

much ‿ of            manage ‿ it
parts ‿ of           kinds ‿ of

（4）鼻辅音 + 元音

以鼻辅音 /m/、/n/、/ŋ/ 结尾的单词，其后的邻接词若以元音音素开头，可以连读。例如：

come ‿ in            come ‿ along
one ‿ evening        in ‿ an hour
the meaning ‿ of     being ‿ a step-mother

（5）舌侧音 + 元音

以舌侧音 /l/ 结尾的单词，其后的邻接词若以元音音素开头，可以连读。需要注意的是，舌侧音 /l/ 处于词尾时，音系学中称为含糊 /l/ 音，与处于词首的清晰 /l/ 音有区别。因此在与邻接词的元音连读时，较之在正常词首发音时要弱而含糊。例如：

all ‿ of us          a bottle ‿ of

3. "辅音 + 半元音 /j/ 型" 连读

此类连读主要包括 /t/、/d/、/s/ 和 /z/+/j/。在快速语流中，以辅音 /t/、/d/、/s/、/z/ 结尾的单词之后若紧接一个以半元音 /j/ 起首的单词，将产生融合同化，即前后两种音素共同融合，向第三种发音转化，具体为：/t/+/j/ → /tʃ/、/d/+/j/ → /dʒ/、/s/+/j/ → /ʃ/、/z/+/j/ → /ʒ/。例如：

/tʃ/                 /dʒ/
won't ‿ you          did ‿ you

/ʃ/                  /ʒ/
this ‿ year          has ‿ she

（此类连读技巧涉及音的同化，因此在"音的同化"一课中有具体介绍和习题操练。在此只做总结归纳，以便学习者对连读现象有系统的认识和了解。）

4. "辅音 + 辅音型"连读

在流畅的英语口语中，当同一意群中的前后单词都以辅音音素结尾和起首时，两个单词往往出现连读。"辅音 + 辅音型"连读大致可分成两种。

（1）辅音 + 其他辅音：轻微音变

在快速语流中，当前后邻接词的首尾音素均为辅音时，往往出现连读。连读时两词之间不做停顿，前一词尾辅音产生轻微音变，以便轻松过渡。例如：

   with ⌣ them  a warm ⌣ breeze  one ⌣ class  （音的同化）

此类连读需要注意以下两种情况：

第一，若前一单词的词尾音素为爆破音，后一单词为爆破音或爆破音之外的其他辅音，则连读时产生相应的失去爆破或不完全爆破。例如：

heart ⌣ break  make ⌣ bread  look ⌣ good  （失去爆破）
stop ⌣ now  take ⌣ long  great ⌣ changes（不完全爆破）

第二，当第二个邻接词以 /h/ 音素起首时，/h/ 往往不发音，此时的第一个单词的词末辅音与 /h/ 后的元音自然连读在一起。例如：

ask ⌣ (h)im  tell ⌣ (h)er  come ⌣ (h)ere  （省音）

（详见"同化""失去爆破和不完全爆破"及"省音"中的相关讲解及习题训练。但当 /t/ 或 /d/ 出现在 /h/ 之前时，通常不省音。例如：left ⌣ handed, seemed ⌣ happy。）

（2）前后同辅：延长发音

在快速语流中，当前后邻接词的首尾音素为同一英语辅音时，可以通过延长该辅音的方法进行连读，也就是将两个辅音发音处理成一个辅音延长音。例如：

half ⌣ finished    give ⌣ Vicky
miss ⌣ Sam     Mrs ⌣ Zebra
worth ⌣ thanks    with ⌣ them
Danish ⌣ ship     some ⌣ milk

需要注意的是，当 /tʃ/ 和 /tʃ/、/tʃ/ 和 /dʒ/、/dʒ/ 和 /tʃ/ 或 /dʒ/ 和 /dʒ/ 首尾相邻时，前后两个音往往都要发出来，以免造成歧义。例如：

much cheaper  orange juice  village jail  large cherries

**你知道吗？**

> 不同的语言之间虽有差异，但也具有共性。汉语的自然语流中也存在许多像英语一样的连读现象。以叹词"啊"为例：
>
> "快看啊！" "谁啊！" "快走啊！"

以上 3 个感叹句在快速语流中，因分别受到前邻音 n，i(y)，u(w) 的影响而产生音变，听起来就成了：

"快看哪 (na) ！" "谁呀 (ya) ！" "快走哇 (wa) ！"

这与英语中辅元音连读、添加外加音 /j/ 及外加音 /w/ 何其相似！认识这一点，可以帮助我们消除学习英语连读时的顾虑，加深对语言连读现象的认识，树立语音学习的信心。

## 三、常见错误

### （一）"越界"连读

在学习连读时，有些学生看到单词能连读就连读，不分情况随意连读，结果往往导致"越界"连读。这里说的"界"，指的是英语中的意群。以下句子为不正确连读的示例：

I had ⌣ a party for him ⌣ | in my home ⌣ in New York.

**纠正办法**

了解英语连读的基本概念。同一意群中的邻接词间可以产生连读，而超越意群概念的邻接词间即使可以连读也是不合适的。

在上述例句中，in my home 及 in New York 均为介词结构，后者作为 my home 的后置定语，与介词短语 in my home 构成了一个具有相对独立的语义及语法意义的意群单元，充当整个句子的地点状语。而句子 I had a party for him 是一个完整的主谓宾补结构的句子，构成另一个独立的意群单元。处于这两个意群之间的 him 和 in 虽看似可以连读，但已经超越意群概念，所以不宜连读。以下句子的连读处理也存在同样的问题：

She ⌣ asked | ⌣ if ⌣ I could call her ⌣ again.

### （二）过度概括

有些学生对"词尾 -r 或 -re + 词首元音"具有连读的可能性比较了解，遇见这类情况也都一概连读，结果往往无视一个音节中前后都有 -r 或 -re 的情况，如以下句子中的不恰当连读：

The Spring Festival is coming nearer ⌣ and nearer.

The barrier ⌣ at the gate prevented us from getting in.

**纠正办法**

领会英语连读的目的和意义。英语连读的目的是在语句达意的基础上寻求语流更为顺畅。当一个音节的前后都含有字母 -r 或 -re 时不宜连读，这是为了避免带来过多近似 /rə/ 音的混淆，造成词不达意。因此，语音学习不仅仅是机械模仿和记忆，还需理智判断和思考。

## （三）含糊其辞

部分学生在学习了英语连读后把英语连读规则视为说一口地道英语的"金科玉律"，为达到行云流水的效果会十分刻意地把前后相邻词都连读在一起，造成虚声矫音，给人含糊其辞的感觉。

**纠正办法**

英语连读是一种自然的语流现象，是在快速的说话或朗读中自然形成的，换言之，连读只是说话的某种方式，不是必须连读，不能为了连读而刻意连读；连读必须以实现语言表达为最终目的。因此，学习英语连读必须循序渐进，要在确保表达信息准确、顺畅的基础上进行连读。

## （四）"言"之过重

与上述第三种现象相反，部分学生连读时往往"言"之过重，一字一顿，听起来总是一口别扭的"中式英语腔"，达不到英语行云流水般的韵律效果。例如，"Not ⌣ at ⌣ all!"这句话，部分学生口中蹦出的连读是生硬的 /'nɒ 'tæ 'tɔːl/，共三个明显的重音模式，而非弱化成两个重音模式的 /'nɒt(ə) 'tɒl/。

**纠正办法**

1. 掌握好英语单词的弱读式。英语的连读常常涉及弱读式，强弱读交错构成的重读音节与非重读音节才使得英语的连贯语流成为可能。因此，掌握好弱读式是保证英语连读的一个前提。
2. 英语连读中，外加音 /w/、/j/、/r/ 往往读得比其在正常单词起首时更弱、更含糊，以确保语流的连贯和顺畅。学习者在学习时应认识到这一点，连读时注意滑读而非拼读技巧，多听多练，以使口腔肌肉和舌头更加灵活。

## 四、纠错训练

**（一）下列句子中的连读，有些是不恰当的"越界连读"，请在相应的连读符号下划"×"。**
　　**注意：不在同一意群中的两个单词不宜连读。**

1. She ‿ is ‿ out, ‿ of course.
2. She ‿ asked ‿ if ‿ I had ‿ ever been ‿ to Hainan.
3. They ‿ ate ‿ breakfast ‿ together ‿ and ‿ on ‿ weekdays drove ‿ together.
4. I came ‿ upon ‿ him ‿ in ‿ a clearing ‿ at ‿ the ‿ end ‿ of ‿ the month.
5. Linking occurs when ‿ a word ends ‿ in ‿ a consonant ‿ and ‿ the following ‿ word starts ‿ with ‿ a vowel.

**（二）下列句子中均含有"-r 或 -re+ 元音型"连读，请在连读不恰当的句子后划"×"。**

1. She made an error ‿ of judgment.
2. WeChat is more ‿ interesting than QQ.
3. Mother is going to buy some more ‿ eggs.
4. She is a girl of superior ‿ intelligence.
5. Would you like to share ‿ it?
6. Panda is a rare ‿ animal.

**（三）模仿录音，注意不要将连读时的前辅音读得过重。**

| /j/ | /j/ | /j/ |
|---|---|---|
| I ‿ am | say ‿ it | stay ‿ up |
| /j/ | /j/ | /j/ |
| see ‿ off | we ‿ agree | study ‿ English |
| /w/ | /w/ | /w/ |
| so ‿ I | do ‿ I | so ‿ honest |
| /w/ | /w/ | /w/ |
| how ‿ often | who ‿ is | two ‿ others |
| /r/ | /r/ | /r/ |
| there ‿ is | there ‿ are | here ‿ are |
| /r/ | /r/ | /r/ |
| for ‿ instance | air ‿ attack | a matter ‿ of fact |

# 第 4 单元  语流音变

## 五、专项训练

**（一）找错误。** 下面是一台装有自动语音识别系统的电脑在语音识别时记录下的句子。每个句子中都有一处由于音的连读而产生的音似错误。请在错误的单词或词组下画线，并在所提供的单词或词组里选出正确的写在后面的空格里（注：个别单词可选两遍）。

| eight | I | ears | stage joked | up |
| age | time and | addiction | joined us | |

1. Timer time again I ask myself who I am.　　　　　　（　　　　）
2. His long hair is over the years.　　　　　　　　　　　（　　　　）
3. I was penniless when I was about your rage.　　　　　（　　　　）
4. Do why need to come?　　　　　　　　　　　　　　　（　　　　）
5. When did you pick cup your English?　　　　　　　　（　　　　）
6. Don't go out after rate.　　　　　　　　　　　　　　（　　　　）
7. It's now a quarter to wait.　　　　　　　　　　　　　（　　　　）
8. The Smiths join does for dinner.　　　　　　　　　　（　　　　）
9. Computer in diction has many negative consequences.　（　　　　）
10. The actor on stay joked with the audience.　　　　　（　　　　）

**（二）模仿录音，并在相应的连读处画上连读符号。**

**元音 + 元音 ( 外加音 /j/、/w/、连音 /r/)**

| I agree | may I | stay on the track |
| try it | my arm | stay in shape |
| do I | go away | too often |
| too easy | who else | how old |
| our own | more over | a pair of |
| far and wide | for example | over and over |

**爆破音 /t/、/d/、/k/、/g/、/p/、/b/ + 元音**

| out of date | out of temper | heart and soul |
| ahead of time | second edition | head on crash |
| plug in | bug off | plug and play |

| keep up with | up and down | a cup of tea |
| rob a bank | grab a bag | job interview |
| speak English | work it out | thick and thin |

### 摩擦音 /f/、/v/、/θ/、/ð/、/s/、/z/ 和 /ʃ/+ 元音

| half an hour | on behalf of | puff away |
| above all | leave it alone | starve a fever |
| month after month | breathe out | a place of interest |
| ups and downs | lose out | rush in |

### 破擦音 /tʃ/、/dʒ/、/ts/、/dz/+ 元音

| which apple | large orange | a page of |
| lots of | hands up | ants in one's pants |

### 鼻辅音 /n/、/m/、/ŋ/+ 元音

| an hour | one evening | on and off |
| come here | come at eight | time and tide |
| bring up | anything else | tongue in cheek |

### 舌侧音 /l/+ 元音

| fell off | a bowl of rice | a bottle of ink |
| full of anger | fill up the cup | all of a sudden |

### 辅音 + 辅音（前后同辅）

| hot tea | next topic | part-time job |
| relate to | resort to | at times |
| blind date | good dream | shoot to fame |
| big gap | case study | false start |
| home made | a life friend | flat tire |

## （三）英音视听说练习。

欣赏电影《哈利波特与密室》（*Harry Potter and the Chamber of Secrets*）片段，注意以下对话中的各种音变，用所学过的连读、同化、失去爆破和不完全爆破符号表示出来。

Snape: You were seen by no less than 7 Muggles. Do you have any idea how serious this is? You have risked the exposure of our world. Not to mention the damage you inflicted on a Whomping Willow that's been on these grounds since before you were born.

Ron: Honestly, Professor Snape, I think it did more damage to us.

Snape: Silence! I assure you that were you in Slytherin, and your fate rested with me, the both of you would be on the train home tonight. As it is...

Dumbledore: They are not.

Harry: Professor Dumbledore.

## 第18课 省音

### 考一考

下面句子中，黑体单词的两种读音是否正确？

The nurse will **probably** take your son's **temperature** shortly.

- probably      A: /ˈprɒ-bə-blɪ/      B: /ˈprɒ-blɪ/
- temperature      A: /ˈtem-pə-rə-tʃə/      B: /ˈtem-prə-tʃə/

### 导入

在快速语流中，英语本族语者有时不会把某些音节弱化成中性元音 /ə/，而是将某个音素或音节直接省略掉，这种现象称为省音。省音在快速、随意的语流中很常见，目的是为了提高语速，使发音简单省力，同时也使说话更为自然、流利。但是，在正式场合和语速较慢的情况下，省音不是必须的。以上"考一考"中，尽管两个单词的 A、B 选项音节数目不同，两种发音却都是正确的：A 选项是我们所熟知的正式发音；B 选项则是随意口语中的省略式发音。省音是连贯语流的自然音变现象，了解省音的特点对英语听力训练大有裨益，而适当掌握常见的省音技巧对提高口语表达的流利性和自然性也很有帮助。

## 一、学习目标

——了解省音的基本概念及类型
——掌握省音的读音方法
——纠正省音中常见的发音错误

## 二、学习内容

### （一）省音的概念

在快速、非正式场合的言语中，省略某个元音、辅音或音节的发音叫省音。省音可以发生在单词内部，也可以发生在相邻的单词之间。

在"爆破音变"一课中，我们曾使用"ᵊ"表示因鼻腔爆破可以省略的元音 /ə/，如：mustn't /ˈmʌsᵊnt/。在本课及下一课的内容讲解及习题训练中，为便于标注和统一，出现省音的音素或音节在单词及音标中均用"( )"表示，如：pro(ba)bly /ˈprɒ(bə)blɪ/。

## （二）省音的类型及方法

省音大致可分为元音或音节的省略和辅音的省略两类。元音或音节的省略主要体现在单词中及相邻单词之间。辅音的省略主要涉及辅音 /t/、/d/、/h/、/l/、/v/ 的省略。

1. 元音的省略

（1）单词中非重读元音 /ə/ 的省略

此类省音通常出现在音素 /r/、/l/、/n/ 之前。例如：

出现在 /r/ 之前

ordin(a)ry /ˈɔːdɪn(ə)rɪ/         diction(a)ry /ˈdɪkʃ(ə)n(ə)rɪ/

int(e)rest /ˈɪnt(ə)rəst/          Janu(a)ry /ˈdʒænjʊ(ə)rɪ/

出现在 /l/ 之前

caref(u)lly /ˈkeəf(ə)lɪ/          thankf(u)lly /ˈθæŋkf(ə)lɪ/

fam(i)ly /ˈfæm(ə)lɪ/             espec(ia)lly /ɪˈspeʃ(ə)lɪ/

出现在 /n/ 之前

fright(e)ning /ˈfraɪt(ə)nɪŋ/      gard(e)ning /ˈgɑːd(ə)nɪŋ/

length(e)ning /ˈleŋθ(ə)nɪŋ/      educati(o)nal /ˌedjʊˈkeɪʃ(ə)nəl/

（2）单词中非重读元音 /ɪ/ 的省略

veg(e)table /ˈvedʒ(ɪ)təbl/       eas(i)ly /ˈiːz(ɪ)lɪ/

med(i)cine /ˈmed(ɪ)sən/         bus(i)ness /ˈbɪz(ɪ)nɪs/

（3）单词间元音或音节的省略

此类省音有三种情况：第一种是重音在第二个音节的双音节词，当说话语速快时，第一个非重读元音经常省略；第二种是单词的第一个非重读音节完全省略；第三种形式在口语中很常见，即把部分单词的音节省略后合并读音。例如：

① 重音在第二个音节的双音节词，第一个元音省略

p(er)haps /p(ə)ˈhæps/           t(o)day /t(ə)ˈdeɪ/

② 单词的第一个非重读音节完全省略

try (a)gain                      not (a)lone

go (a)way                       walk (a)way

(Re)member when we first met last year?

(A)nother drink, Mr. Simpson?

③ 单词部分音节省略或合并

    G(ood) morning!

    How('re) you doing?

    I am (going to) go. (gonna)

    I (want to) take a day off. (wanna)

2. 辅音的省略

（1）/d/ 或 /t/ 的省略

当 /t/ 或 /d/ 出现在两个辅音之间时往往会完全失音。例如：

    res(t)less                    exac(t)ly

    frien(d)ship               han(d)bag

此外，功能词 and 中的 /d/ 常常省略，读成 /ən(d)/ 甚至 /(ə)n(d)/（详见第22课"强读式和弱读式"）。例如：

    here an(d) there            now an(d) then

以下几点需要注意：

① 词尾三辅音连缀 /skt/ 在元音或 /h/ 前时，常常省略 /k/，读成双辅音连缀 /st/；在辅音前时省略 /kt/，读成 /s/，与后面的辅音形成另一个双辅音连缀。例如：

    She as(k)ed Anne. /ɑːs(k)t æn/    He ris(k)ed (h)is life. /rɪs(k)t (h)ɪz/

② 当 /d/ 出现在 /l/、/w/、/r/ 和 /s/ 前，通常不省音。例如：

    Do you min<u>d</u> <u>l</u>ending me a book?

    Do you min<u>d</u> <u>w</u>alking?

    Oliver lik<u>ed</u> <u>w</u>riting when he was young.

    Remember to sen<u>d</u> <u>S</u>am a postcard.

（2）/h/ 省略

人称代词 he、her、his、him，助动词 have、has、had，疑问词 who 或代词 here 中的 /h/ 在快速语流中常常省音。例如：

    tell ‿ (h)im                  Come ‿ (h)ere!

    Mr. Simpson ‿ (h)as arrived.

以下几点需要注意：

① 当 /h/ 出现在词首时不能省音。例如：

    <u>H</u>ave you heard about him?

② 当 /h/ 需要重读强调时。例如：

    This is my suitcase, not <u>h</u>is!

③ 当 /t/ 或 /d/ 出现在 /h/ 之前时，通常不省音 ( 详见第 17 课 "连读" )。例如：

left handed　　　　　　　looked happy

（3）/l/ 省略

元音 /ɔː/ 后的 /l/ 也常常会省音。例如：

a(l)so　　　　　　　a(l)ways　　　　　　　a(l)right

（4）/v/ 省略

若音素 /v/ 后紧跟一个辅音，/v/ 有时会省音。此外，在辅音音素之前的 of /ɒv/ 通常省去 /v/，读成中性元音 /ə/（另见第 22 课 "弱读式和强读式" 的介绍）。例如：

gi(ve) me　　　　　　　as a matter o(f) fact
a waste o(f) time　　　　a bottle o(f) wine

**你知道吗？**

省音在英语口语中很常见，在书面文本中则一般采用正规写法。但是，某些文学作品中的英语单词也会采用省音的写法来表现人物的口音特点，使作品人物表现更具张力。例如，以下节选的美国作家约翰·斯坦贝克（John Steinbeck）的作品《人鼠之间》（*Of Mice and Men*，1937）中就使用了很多省音：

"Well, we ain't got any," George exploded. "Whatever we ain't got, that's what you want. God **a'mighty**, if I was alone I could live so easy. I could go get a job **an' work**, **an'no** trouble... **An'** I could do all that every damn month. Get a gallon of **whisky**, or set in a pool room and play cards or shoot pool." ... "**An' whatta** I got," George went on furiously. "I got you! You can't keep a job and you lose me **ever' job** I get. **Jus' keep** me **shovin' all** over the country all the time." (1.89)*

# 三、常见错误

## （一）口语生硬无省音

有些英语学习者的口语常显生硬，无省音、同化、连读等语流音变，缺乏口语自然表现力。例如，friendship /ˈfren(d)ʃɪp/ 和 blind man /blaɪn(d) mæn/ 中的 /d/ 和 /t/ 无省音，over and over /ˈəʊvə (ə)nd ˈəʊvə/ 中的虚词发音过重等。

---

\* John, Steinbeck. *Of Mice and Men*. Retrieved from http://en.wikipedia.org/wiki/Elision.

导致英语发音生硬的原因是因为英语教学长期重读写、轻听说，学生对鲜活的英语省音现象缺乏了解和体验。在实际生活中，英语的省音现象十分普遍。

**纠正办法**

加大听力输入，以真实的听力输入为前提，提高对语言的敏感度，同时驱动"说"的输出环节，多模仿，以提高英语口语的流利度及自然度。

## （二）回避式吞音

吞音是中国英语学习者说英语时常见的坏习惯，尤其是遇到辅音连缀时此现象尤其严重。究其原因，主要是出于回避策略，避免难发的音素而有意吞音或含糊带过。这样做的结果有时的确会"歪打正着"，将一些可省音的部分省去，但更多的则是胡乱省音，尤其是遇到三辅连缀时，常常把三辅连缀省略成一辅或错误的二辅连缀。例如：

| | | |
|---|---|---|
| She as(ked) Anne. | /ɑːs(kt) æn/ | × |
| She as(k)ed Anne. | /ɑːs(k)t æn/ | √ |
| He ris(ked) his life. | /rɪs(kt) hɪz/ | × |
| He ris(k)ed (h)is life. | /rɪs(k)t (h)ɪz/ | √ |

**纠正办法**

省音不是吞音。英语本族语者的省音有规律可循，省音不影响听力理解与交流，而错误的吞音则是毫无根据的省音乱象。因此，必须端正学习态度，排除畏难心理，了解正确的省音规则，多听多练，以实现英语表达的可理解性。

## 四、纠错训练

### （一）模仿录音，注意快速语流中的省音。

1. 元音的省略（A组读音语速较慢，发音清晰；B组是省音后的读音）

**-r 前非重读元音 /ə/ 的省音**

| A | B | A | B |
|---|---|---|---|
| factory | fact(o)ry | history | hist(o)ry |
| robbery | robb(e)ry | suffering | suff(e)ring |
| general | gen(e)ral | sovereign | sov(e)reign |

## 第 4 单元　语流音变

### -l 前非重读元音 /ə/ 的省音

| A | B | A | B |
|---|---|---|---|
| porcelain | porc(e)lain | bachelor | bach(e)lor |
| carefully | caref(u)lly | thankfully | thankf(u)lly |
| family | fam(i)ly | especially | espec(ia)lly |

### -n 前非重读元音 /ə/ 的省音

| A | B | A | B |
|---|---|---|---|
| evening | ev(e)ning | student | stud(e)nt |
| national | nat(io)nal | educational | educat(io)nal |
| traditional | tradit(io)nal | deafening | deaf(e)ning |

### 非重读元音 /ɪ/ 的省音

| A | B | A | B |
|---|---|---|---|
| easily | eas(i)ly | believe | b(e)lieve |
| family | fam(i)ly | university | univers(i)ty |
| business | bus(i)ness | medicine | medic(i)ne |

### 重音在第二个音节的双音节词，第一个元音的省音

| A | B | A | B |
|---|---|---|---|
| tomato | t(o)mato | perhaps | p(er)haps |
| today | t(o)day | correct | c(o)rrect |
| believe | b(e)lieve | suppose | s(u)ppose |

2. 辅音的省略

### 辅音 /t/、/d/ 的省音

| A | B | A | B |
|---|---|---|---|
| restless | res(t)less | mostly | mos(t)ly |
| firstly | firs(t)ly | friendly | frien(d)ly |
| mindless | min(d)less | landlord | lan(d)lord |

### 辅音 /d/ 的不省音

Do you min<u>d l</u>ending me a book?
Remember to sen<u>d S</u>am a postcard.
Do you min<u>d w</u>alking?
Oliver like<u>d w</u>riting when he was young.

### 辅音 /h/ 的省音

can ‿ (h)e          will ‿ (h)e          come ‿ (h)ere
tell ‿ (h)im         does ‿ (h)e         was ‿ (h)e
is ‿ (h)e            love ‿ (h)er         leave ‿ (h)im
for ‿ (h)im          with ‿ (h)im         stop ‿ (h)er

Is ‿ (h)e there?
Can ‿ (h)e do it?
Tell ‿ (h)er I miss her.
Leave ‿ (h)im alone.
Ask ‿ (h)er to send me a message.

### 辅音 /l/ 的省略音

| A | B | A | B |
| --- | --- | --- | --- |
| also | a(l)so | always | a(l)ways |
| alright | a(l)right | almost | a(l)most |
| already | a(l)ready | although | a(l)though |

（二）下列黑体单词中的辅音音素有的可以省音，有的不可以省音。用"( )"标出可以省音的音节，再试着朗读句子，体会省音后发音是否更自然、流利。

例：He basically **as(ked) the** same questions.

1. The man outside **asked for** you.
2. This is our **first lesson** in the new semester.
3. His parents chose to **send him** to a boarding school.
4. I **changed trains** when I went home.

5. I went **next door** to the bathroom.
6. We **sailed a** small boat out to the sea.
7. He is a **world champion**.
8. She **looked good**.
9. Let's **just leave** then.
10. Now we come to the **second part** of the scene.

## 五、专项训练

**（一）听录音，用"( )"标出下文中有可能出现元音及辅音省略现象的音素。然后想象自己正在接受节目访谈，尝试用自然流利的语调朗读省音后的短文。**

I experienced great stress in my study last year. I just couldn't do things correct and I lost interest in everything. I've tried every means to adjust and relieve my stress. Finally I found a way out in my leisure. Leisure time is very important and necessary for me. Without it I am sure I would go insane definitely. I spend most of my extra time reading, listening to music, talking to my family, my real life friends, or talking on the Internet with people I meet. I especially enjoy going out into a quiet place and reading my favorite poetry or books. It's a marvelous experience. If I do not make time for all of this I will not be able to handle everything else in life and I will feel like a prisoner. Along with reading to relax, listening to music is very important to me. If I feel sad, I listen to slow songs, while I am happy I like listening to fast songs. Music is the universal language and it can express different feelings. It can relate to the soul, or as a matter of fact I think it is the soul of feelings.

**（二）双人练习。听录音，注意下列对话中黑体单词的各种音变，用所学过的连读、省音、同化、失去爆破和不完全爆破符号表示出来，再模仿录音。**

M: **Good morning. Can I come in**?

W: Yes. **Come on in**!

M: I'd **like** to enroll **for an English** course **at this** college. Can you tell me when the **next course starts**?

W: Right. Well the next **Intermediate English** course **begins on** Monday 10th **September**. You could **probably** join that one—otherwise **you'd have** to **wait until January** or **February**.

M: I **think I'd like to** do the **next** course. I'm **gonna take more** other courses **next year**.

W: OK. **Could you take a** seat and I'll get **one of** the teachers to **have a word with** you.

（三）英音视听说练习。

欣赏电影《哈利波特与密室》（*Harry Potter and the Chamber of Secrets*）片段，注意对话中的各种音变，用所学过的连读、省音、失去爆破和不完全爆破符号表示出来。

Boy1: Ron, is that your owl?

Ron: Bloody bird's menace. Oh, no!

Samus: Look everyone, Wesley's got himself a Howler.

Neville: Go on, Ron. I ignored one from my gran once. It was horrible.

Ron's Mother: Ronald Wesley! How dare you steal that car! I am absolutely disgusted. Your father's now facing an inquiry at work and it's entirely your fault! If you put another toe out of line, we'll bring you straight home! Oh and Ginny dear, congratulations on making Gryffindor! Your father and I are so proud.

## 第19课 缩读

● 考一考

下面是一段幽默短对话。听录音，补全空格：

(In a car in the middle of Colorado)

Wife: "Oh dear George, 1._____ the house's gonna burn down, 2._____ I left the iron on."

George: "The house 3._____ burn down dear, 4._____."

Wife: "How can you make a statement like that?"

George: "'Cause I r'member I 5._____ turned off the water in the bathtub!"

● 导入

在前一课中，我们学习了省音。此外，英语口语中还存在一种相当普遍的缩读现象。以上"考一考"中 1–5 空格处分别对应的答案为：I'm (afraid)、I'm (sure)、won't、don't (worry) 以及 haven't。以上带有撇号的单词发音即为"缩读"，与正常情况下原单词发音有所不同，如：I'm /aɪm/ 与 I am /aɪ əm/、won't /wəʊnt/ 与 will not /wɪl nɒt/、don't /dəʊnt/ 与 do not /duː nɒt/、haven't /'hævnt/ 与 have not /hæv nɒt/，在书写形式上也有所差异。

## 一、学习目标

——了解缩略的基本概念及类型

——掌握缩读的读音方法

——纠正缩读中的常见发音错误

## 二、学习内容

### （一）缩读的概念

英语本族语者在快速流畅地讲话时，常将某些词组中的音素省略掉，将词组合二为一，这种省音现象称作"缩读"。缩读的书面形式叫"缩略式"，往往用一个撇号"'"将两个英语单词缩略在一起。从宽松的定义上讲缩读也是省音，如"考一考"中的 5 个例子缩读后的单音节就是由原来的两个音节省音而成。但是，省音和缩读之间并非完全一一对等，例如：gonna 与 going to，其本身是省音，但并非缩读；cannot 与 can not，其本身是缩读，但并没有省音。

英语中的缩读十分自然，是流畅口语表达的一种常见形式。缩读和省音一样，既不会影响理解，也不会引起误解。了解和掌握英语中常见的缩读对英语听力理解十分有利。一般来说，构成缩略的词语前一部分通常是人称代词、指示代词、WH 疑问词等，后一部分通常是系动词、助动词和情态动词等功能词，因此缩读是有规律的，是"有迹可循"的。

## （二）常见缩读及其缩略式

下表是常见的英语缩略式及缩读方法的几个例子：

| 1. 人称代词 + 系动词 / 助动词 / 情态动词 ||||||
|---|---|---|---|---|---|
| 完全形式 | 完全读音 | 缩 读 | 缩略式 | 例 句 ||
| I am | /aɪ əm/ | /aɪm/ | I'm | I'm more than happy to help. ||
| I will | /aɪ wɪl/ | /aɪl/ | I'll | I'll be there by 7:00. ||

| 2. 系动词 / 助动词 / 情态动词 +no/not ||||||
|---|---|---|---|---|---|
| 完全形式 | 完全读音 | 缩 读 | 缩略式 | 例 句 ||
| is not | /ɪz nɒt/ | /'ɪz(ə)nt/ | isn't | Larry isn't coming until tomorrow. ||
| are not | /ɑː nɒt/ | /ɑːnt/ | aren't | I'm late again, aren't I? ||

| 3. 情态动词 + 助动词 ||||||
|---|---|---|---|---|---|
| 完全形式 | 完全读音 | 缩 读 | 缩略式 | 例 句 ||
| should have | /ʃʊd hæv/ | /'ʃʊd(ə)v/ | should've | You should've come to the party last night, Mary. ||
| could have | /kʊd hæv/ | /'kʊd(ə)v/ | could've | It could've been much worse. ||

| 4. 疑问代词 + 系动词 / 助动词 / 情态动词 ||||||
|---|---|---|---|---|---|
| 完全形式 | 完全读音 | 缩 读 | 缩略式 | 例 句 ||
| what is | /wɒt ɪz/ | /wɒts/ | what's | What's the matter with you? ||
| what has | /wɒt hæz/ | /wɒts/ | what's | What's happened to my pie? ||

## 你知道吗?

在第 16 课音的同化中，我们曾经介绍过汉语的同化现象，如"这样子"变为"酱紫"。除此之外，汉语在日常口语中同样也存在缩读现象。例如，"你造吗"这个新潮句子，其实就是对"你知道吗"中的"知道（zhi dao）"进行缩读，去掉中间部分后形成了"造（zao）"句。

## 三、常见错误

### （一）"懒虫式"误读

部分英语学习者在遇到不认识或不熟悉的缩略式时懒于查询正确读音，而是想当然地按照自己错误的认知发音。例如：

| it will /ɪt wɪl/ | it'll /ˈɪtəl/ | √ | it'll /ɪl/ | × |
| shall not /ʃəl nɒt/ | shan't /ʃɑːnt/ | √ | shan't /ʃənt/ | × |
| were not /wə(r) nɒt/ | weren't /wɜːnt/ | √ | weren't /wəʊnt/ | × |

这种懒惰的学习方法不仅导致发音错误，同时也导致听听力时的"不知所云"。

**纠正办法**

勤查字典，同时多做"影子练习"，即听音跟音模仿训练。

### （二）回避式吞音

在前一课的省音部分我们提到过英语学习者的回避式吞音，这是中国英语学习者说英语时常见的坏习惯。当遇到英语缩读时许多学习者同样采取回避策略，把缩略式中的辅音吞掉不发音。例如，在遇到与 would 连接的缩略式，即：I'd、you'd、he'd、she'd、we'd、they'd、there'd 等情况时，常常将尾音 /d/ 直接吞掉；在遇到与 have 连接的缩略式，即：I've、you've、they've、we've 等情况时，则将尾音 /v/ 吞掉。

出现这种回避式吞音的现象是因为英语学习者在词尾辅音发音方面比较困难。汉语拼音发音特点绝大多数为辅元式，而英语则多为辅元辅式。英语缩略式是将两个词语的音素合二为一，往往弱化掉一个响亮的元音部分，用中性元音 /ə/ 替代，或只剩余词尾辅音，这就给中国的英语学习者带来了发音上的困难。

**纠正办法**

加强"影子练习"，注意听辨缩读与完全发音之间的细微差别。

## （三）缩略无缩读

在发音策略上，除了回避式吞音，部分英语学习者会选择将缩略式读成完全形式的发音。例如，与 are 连接的缩略式，常常被拆分读成原单词的发音，即：

| | | | | |
|---|---|---|---|---|
| we're | /wɪə/ | √ | /wi: ɑ:/ | × |
| you're | /jɔ:r/ | √ | /ju: ɑ:/ | × |
| they're | /ðeɪə/ | √ | /ðeɪ ɑ:/ | × |
| why're | /ˈwaɪə/ | √ | /waɪ ɑ:/ | × |
| who're | /hu:ə/ | √ | /hu: ɑ:/ | × |

**纠正办法**

加强"影子练习"，注意听辨缩读与完全发音之间的细微差别。

## 四、纠错训练

### （一）模仿录音，注意下列常见缩读的正确读法。

| 完全形式 | 完全读音 | 缩略式 | 缩读 | 例　句 |
|---|---|---|---|---|
| I will | /aɪ wɪl/ | I'll | /aɪl/ | I'll be there by 7:00. |
| you will | /ju: wɪl/ | you'll | /ju:l/; /jʊl/; /jəl/ | You'll have to do it yourself. |
| we will | /wi: wɪl/ | we'll | /wi:l/; /wɪl/ | We'll do better next time. |
| they will | /ðeɪ wɪl/ | they'll | /ðeɪl/ | They'll be here any minute. |
| she will | /ʃi: wɪl/ | she'll | /ʃi:l/; /ʃɪl/ | She'll recover soon. |
| he will | /hi: wɪl/ | he'll | /hi:(ə)l/; /hi(ə)l/; /ɪ(ə)l/ | He'll never agree. |
| it will | /ɪt wɪl/ | it'll | /ˈɪtəl/ | It'll be hard to find a helper. |
| who will | /hu: wɪl/ | who'll | /hu:l/; /hʊl/; /ʊl/ | Who'll you be seeing tonight? |
| that will | /ðæt wɪl/ | that'll | /ðæt(ə)l/; /æət(ə)l/ | That'll do. |
| there will | /ðeə wɪl/ | there'll | /ðeəl/; /ðəl/ | There'll be a live show tonight. |
| Why will | /waɪ wɪl/ | why'll | /waɪəl/ | Why'll it be tomorrow? |
| will not | /wɪl nɒt/ | won't | /wəʊnt/ | He won't get married with you. |

| 完全形式 | 完全读音 | 缩略式 | 缩读 | 例　句 |
|---|---|---|---|---|
| are not | /ɑː nɒt/ | aren't | /ɑːnt/ | I'm late again, aren't I? |
| were not | /wə nɒt/ | weren't | /wɜːnt/ | Weren't we lucky with the weather? |
| might not | /maɪt nɒt/ | mightn't | /ˈmaɪt(ə)nt/ | Young people mightn't like the idea. |
| ought not | /ɔːt nɒt/ | oughtn't | /ˈɔːt(ə)nt/ | Larry oughtn't to do that. |
| shall not | /ʃəl nɒt/ | shan't | /ʃɑːnt/ | I shan't be able to come to your party. |

**（二）模仿录音，注意缩读不是吞音。**

| 完全形式 | 完全读音 | 缩略式 | 缩读 | 例　句 |
|---|---|---|---|---|
| who have | /huː hæv/ | who've | /huːv/; /hʊv/; /ʊv/ | Who've you invited to the party? |
| who would | /huː wʊd/ | who'd | /huːd/; /hʊd/; /ʊd/ | Who'd have thought Joey was going to become so successful? |
| who had | /huː hæd/ | who'd | /huːd/; /hʊd/; /ʊd/ | Who'd sent her the mysterious email? |
| why have | /waɪ hæv/ | why've | /waɪv/ | Why've you come so early? |
| why did | /waɪ dɪd/ | why'd | /waɪd/ | Why'd you do that? |
| there would | /ðeə wʊd/ | there'd | /ðeəd/; /ðəd/ | She assured me there'd be a practice this morning. |
| there have | /ðeə hæv/ | there've | /ðeəv/; /ðəv/ | There've been enough quarrels. |
| there has | /ðeə hæz/ | there's | /ðeəz/; /ðəz/ | There's been entirely too much said on this subject. |
| there had | /ðeə hæd/ | there'd | /ðeəd/; /ðəd/ | They put up the sign because there'd been an accident recently. |
| that would | /ðæt wʊd/ | that'd | /ðætəd/ | That'd be nice, don't you think? |
| that had | /ðæt hæd/ | that'd | /ðætəd/ | When it happened, I didn't realize that'd been the reason. |
| they have | /ðeɪ hæv/ | they've | /ðeɪv/ | They've really made a mess of things now. |

| 完全形式 | 完全读音 | 缩略式 | 缩读 | 例　　句 |
|---|---|---|---|---|
| they had | /ðeɪ hæd/ | they'd | /ðeɪd/ | They'd had three bottles of wine and were very drunk. |
| they would | /ðeɪ wʊd/ | they'd | /ðeɪd/ | They'd love to see the film. |
| we have | /wi: hæv/ | we've | /wi:v/; /wɪv/ | We've been married eight years. |
| we had | /wi: hæd/ | we'd | /wi:d/; /wɪd/ | We'd better be more careful in the future. |
| we would | /wi: wʊd/ | we'd | /wi:d/; /wɪd/ | We'd be grateful for an answer. |
| she had | /ʃi: hæd/ | she'd | /ʃi:d/; /ʃɪd/ | She'd gone before I got there. |
| she would | /ʃi: wʊd/ | she'd | /ʃi:d/; /ʃɪd/ | She'd be a great managing director. |
| he had | /hi: hæd/ | he'd | /hi:d/; /hɪd/; /ɪd/ | He'd already spent all his money by the second day of the trip. |
| he would | /hi: wʊd/ | he'd | /hi:d/; /hɪd/; /ɪd/ | He'd be able to do it, if anyone could. |
| you have | /ju: hæv/ | you've | /ju:v/; /jəv/ | If you've finished your pasta, then you can have some cake. |
| you had | /ju: hæd/ | you'd | /ju:d/; /jʊd/; /jəd/ | You'd better be off now. |
| you would | /ju: wʊd/ | you'd | /ju:d/; /jʊd/; /jəd/ | You'd get many surprises. |
| I have | /aɪ hæv/ | I've | /aɪv/ | I've been waiting an hour already. |
| I had | /aɪ hæd/ | I'd | /aɪd/ | I'd just got in the bath when the phone rang. |
| I would | /aɪ wʊd/ | I'd | /aɪd/ | Of course I'd love to see you. |

**（三）模仿录音，注意缩读与完全读音的区别。**

| 完全形式 | 完全读音 | 缩略式 | 缩读 | 例　　句 |
|---|---|---|---|---|
| we are | /wi: ɑ:/ | we're | /wɪə/ | We're very encouraged by your support. |
| you are | /ju: ɑ:/ | you're | /jɔ:/; /jʊə/ | You're the boss of yourself. |

| 完全形式 | 完全读音 | 缩略式 | 缩读 | 例 句 |
|---|---|---|---|---|
| they are | /ðeɪ ɑː/ | they're | /ðeɪə/ | They're so in love. |
| why are | /waɪ ɑː/ | why're | /waɪə/ | Why're you late? |
| who are | /huː ɑː/ | who're | /huːə/ | The film begins with a young couple, who're just about to get married. |
| there are | /ðeə ɑː/ | There're | /ðeə/; /ðər/ | There're tons of mistakes in his speech. |
| should have | /ʃʊd hæv/ | should've | /ˈʃʊd(ə)v/ | You should've come to the party last night, Mary. |
| could have | /kʊd hæv/ | could've | /ˈkʊd(ə)v/ | It could've been much worse. |
| would have | /wʊd hæv/ | would've | /ˈwʊd(ə)v/ | I would've believed you until you started laughing. |
| must have | /mʌst hæv/ | must've | /ˈmʌst(ə)v/ | Someone must've entered his room. |

## 五、专项训练

**（一）找错误。下面是一台装有自动语音识别系统的电脑在语音识别时记录下的句子。每个句子中画线部分的缩略式都被电脑理解成其后括号中的词语。请在理解错误的词语旁画"×"，并把正确的词语写在后面。**

1. He's paid for the dinner. (He is)  _____
2. She's done his homework. (She is)  _____
3. She's the Prime Minister at the moment. (She is)  _____
4. "This is ridiculous, who's got the remote control now?" moaned dad. (who is)  _____
5. It's been a wonderful day. (It is)  _____
6. He'd already spent all his money by the second day of the trip. (He had)  _____
7. He'd be able to do it, if anyone could. (He had)  _____
8. That'd be nice, don't you think? (That had)  _____
9. Why's she doing that? (Why is)  _____
10. Why's the TV been turned off? (Why is)  _____

### （二）听录音，在横线上填写相应的缩略式。

Today I met my friends. In fact _____ my best friends. I _____ seen them for a while and we had lots to catch up on. _____ been friends for years. _____ never forget the day we all got stuck in a lift. _____ never been so scared. Paul, the oldest of us all, got us out. Gill, _____ the youngest, said _____ never go in a lift again. I _____ blame her because we _____ think we were going to get out.

### （三）英音视听说练习。

欣赏英剧《唐顿庄园》（*Downton Abbey*）片段，将以下对白中的缩略式补充完整，填在相应的横线上，再模仿跟读。

Thomas: And 1._____ off.
Mrs. Hughes: No rest for the wicked.
Mrs. Patmore: Lady Mary. Are the tea trays ready?
Anna: All ready, Mrs. Patmore, if the 2._____ boiled. Could you give us a hand to take the other two up?
Miss O'Brien: 3._____ got her ladyship's to carry.
Anna: 4._____ help.
Mrs. Hughes: Back door.
Mr. Carson: The papers, at last. William.
William: 5._____ late!
Mailman: Yeah, I know, but ....
William: But what!
Mailman: You'll see.

1._____    2._____    3._____    4._____
5._____

# 第5单元 音律节奏

　　英语是节奏感极强的语言，富于韵律美。中国的英语学习者因受母语影响，缺乏弱读意识，习惯于将每个音节读得同样强、同样的长或同样的高。更缺乏意群意识，随意停顿，节奏模式趋于一字一顿，语流不连贯、生硬牵强。想要说出一口自然流畅、富有节奏感和韵律美的英语，学习者必须在发音的长短（音长）、发音的强弱（音强）和发音的高低（音高），以及意群、停顿等方面多下功夫。本单元将针对这些方面的问题，从单词重音、句子重音，强读式和弱读式、节奏以及停顿等五个方面重点进行讲解和训练。

# 第20课 单词重音

● 考一考

下面是一则小故事，请仔细阅读，并完成文后问题：

　　I was once talking with a university freshman and he was telling about himself, his hobbies, his personality and so on. At one point, he was trying to tell me that he was quite "unique"/juːˈniːk/, but unfortunately he had poor pronunciation and put the stress on the first syllable, so that it sounded like another word /ˈjuːnək/. Thus, his sentence, "I must tell you, I'm unique" sounded like "I must tell you, I'm a _____".

你知道这个被误发重音的单词是什么吗？

● 导入

　　重音在英语语音中无处不在，重音是我们在发某个音素或音节时，相对于其他音素或音节的音长更长、音强更强、音高更高，从而形成重读音节和非重读音节的对立现象。对于以英语为母语的人来说，重音位置和轻重音之间的对照是他们通过听觉识辨单词的关键，一旦说话人对重音把握出现错误，就会造成交流障碍，甚至闹出笑话，如"考一考"中把"unique"（/juːˈniːk/，"独一无二的"）说成"eunuch"（/ˈjuːnək/，"太监"）。可见，英语重音的学习对于有效的听说交流极为关键。英语重音分为单词重音和句子重音。

## 一、学习目标

——了解单词重音的基本概念及类型
——掌握单词重音的一般规则
——纠正单词重音中的常见发音错误

## 二、学习内容

### （一）单词重音的概念

　　在一个包含有两个音节以上的英语单词中，至少有一个音节发音比其他音节响亮，这个音节称为"重读音节",其他发音较轻的称为"非重读音节";词的这种轻重音节对立现象就叫"单词重音"。

重读音节要强读,音高响亮,音质完整饱满,发音时长较长;非重读音节要弱读,声音相对低弱而含糊,发音时长较短。例如:better /ˈbetə/ 中的 /ˈbe/ 为重读音节,/tə/ 为非重读音节。

重读音节在词典中有明确的标注,用重音符号 "ˈ" 表示,加在重读音节的左上方,如:feature /ˈfiːtʃə/。

英语单词根据所含音节的多少可分为单音节词、双音节词、三音节词以及多音节词。单音节词单独念时一律要重读,但在单独注音时不必加重音符号,例如:bay /beɪ/、wife /waɪf/。包含两个音节以上的单词需使用重音符号,例如:双音节词 buyer /ˈbaɪə/,三音节词 family /ˈfæm(ə)lɪ/,多音节词 democracy /dɪˈmɒkrəsɪ/。

## (二)单词重音的类型

英语单词重音根据其强弱程度可分为三种,即:主重音(又称第一重音)、次重音(又称第二重音)和零重音。标在音节左上方的重音符号 "ˈ" 用来表示主重音,如 announce /əˈnaʊns/。次重音强度仅次于主重音,介于主重音和零重音之间,以次重音符号 "ˌ" 表示,加在次重读音节的左下方,如:independent /ˌɪndɪˈpendənt/、preparation /ˌprepəˈreɪʃ(ə)n/。零重音即没有重音的音节,又称非重读音节,如上例 independent /ˌɪndɪˈpendənt/ 以及 preparation /ˌprepəˈreɪʃ(ə)n/ 中除去主重音和次重音以外的其他音节,即 /dɪ/、/dənt/、/pə/ 以及 /ʃ(ə)n/。

## (三)单词重音的一般规则

1. 双音节词中,名词或形容词重音一般落在第一个音节上,动词重音一般落在第二个音节上。例如:

   名词 / 形容词:　ˈincrease　　　　　ˈobject　　　　　ˈpresent
   动词:　　　　　inˈcrease　　　　　obˈject　　　　　preˈsent

2. 含有长元音、双元音、响亮单元音(除 /ə/ 和 /ɪ/ 外)的双音节词,或元音后含有双辅音字母的单词,重音往往落在相应音节上,此时非重读音节一般都被弱化成中性元音 /ə/ 或 /ɪ/。例如:

   长元音:regard /rɪˈgɑːd/　　appeal /əˈpiːl/　　　fortune /ˈfɔːtʃ(ə)n/
   双元音:assign /əˈsaɪn/　　　obtain /əbˈteɪn/　　mountain /ˈmaʊntɪn/
   响亮单元音:happen /ˈhæpən/　comer /ˈkʌmə/　　Oxford /ˈɒksfəd/
   双辅音字母:distinct /dɪˈstɪŋkt/　acclaim /əˈkleɪm/　detect /dɪˈtekt/

3. 三音节词重音一般落在第一个音节上,即"重—轻—轻"。例如:

   ˈfamily　　　　　　　　ˈbarbecue　　　　　　　ˈcommunist

4. 多音节词（四个音节以上）重音一般落在倒数第三个音节上，如四音节词的"轻—重—轻—轻"，也可以为"次重—轻—主重—轻（一轻）"。例如：

    de'mocracy　　　　　　a'cademy　　　　　　ˌinde'pendence

5. 复合名词（N+N；Adj+N；V-ing+N）重音落在第一个单词重音。例如：

    'desktop　　　　　　'greenhouse　　　　　　'driving license

6. 复合动词（Prep+ V）重音落在动词。例如：

    down'load　　　　　　over'look　　　　　　outper'form

    down'play　　　　　　under'state　　　　　　out'do

7. 复合形容词（Adj/Adv + Adj /PP/ N; N + Adj; N + PP）多为均重音（又称双重音），即有两个音节重读；有时为非均重音，即一个主重音和一个次重音。例如：

    'fast-'developing　　　'well-'meant　　　　　'world-'famous

8. 短语动词（V + Adv; V + Prep）多为双重音（均重音）。例如：

    'turn 'off　　　　　　'buckle 'up　　　　　　'hand 'out

9. 英语复合专有名词主重音通常落在第二个单词重音上；但含有 street 和 day 的复合专有名词主重音落在第一个单词重音上，次重音落在 street 和 day 上。例如：

    Great 'Britain　　　　Beach 'Hotel　　　　　Harvard 'University

    Third 'Avenue　　　　'Forest Street　　　　'Valentine's Day

10. 英语词缀（包括前缀和后缀）一般不重读；部分来自法语或拉丁语的外来词后缀本身需重读。例如：

    in'tact　　　　　pre'dict　　　　　con'tend

    eco'nomic　　　　es'sential　　　　de'mocracy

    ob'scure　　　　　lemo'nade　　　　refu'gee

> **你知道吗？**
>
> 一般说来，英语双音节名词的重音通常落在第一个音节。但有些英语中的外来词，如法语双音节词 ma'chine、ho'tel、po'lice 等，至今仍保留了重读在第二个音节的特点。

## 三、常见错误

### 重音概念缺乏

由于缺乏重音概念，英语学习者在读单词时常常无视重音落点，想当然地"望文

生音", 对单词重音定位随意性大, 既不讲规则, 也不遵循惯例。主要表现在以下三点:

1. 在遇到某些同形异义词时, 采用"一刀切"的处理方式, 无论名词、动词或形容词, 一律读成同一种重音模式, 例如:

   There is a remarkable *contrast* between the two brothers. ( 'contrast 名词, 意为"差别")

   His actions and his promises *contrast* sharply. (con'trast 动词, 意为"相反")

   英语单词重音具有区分词性及意义的作用。在同形异义的英语双音节词中, 名词或形容词重音通常在第一个音节, 动词重音在第二个音节, 单词意义也各不相同。

### 纠正办法

勤查字典, 培养良好的学习习惯, 树立严谨的求学态度。尤其需要指出的是, 某些电子词典和网络词典并没有严格区分开一些同形异义词, 对不同词性和意义的单词只提供一种发音标注, 这对学习者是一种误导。鉴于此, 建议学习者在学习过程中多查询权威字典。

2. 无视英语复合词与修饰性短语之间区别性的重音落点, 例如:

   复合名词: a 'blackboard     一块黑板(不一定是黑色, 也可能是其他颜色)
   
   修饰性短语: a ˌblack 'board    一块黑色的板

   英语复合词中, 除复合动词外, 绝大多数复合名词重音落在第一个音节, 其表示的含义已经约定俗成, 往往不是构成该复合词的两个单词原始意义的简单叠加。随意选择重音模式将带来词义的完全改变乃至理解上的误会。

### 纠正办法

加强英语重音意识, 勤查字典, 在此基础上加大听力输入, 正确掌握复合名词不同于修饰性短语的发音特点及特殊意义。

3. 一律以词根作为重读音节, 例如:

   'science         'scientific    ×      scien'tific    √
   
   'accident        'accidental    ×      acci'dental    √

   部分英语派生词(即词根相同的词)的重音和词根重音一致, 例如词根 'act 及其派生词: 'actor、'active、'action、re'act、'actually。但有些派生词的重音却会发生变化, 与词根重音模式不同。部分学习者对此不求甚解, 一旦认识了某些词根的重音模式, 便过度概括, 套用到所有派生词。

> **纠正办法**
>
> 熟悉掌握基本的词缀重音模式，同时勤查字典，多听多读，培养正确的英语语感。

## 四、纠错训练

**（一）模仿录音，朗读下列句子，用重音符号标出下列各组画线部分单词的重音，并写出其词性及词义。**

例：They're studying an interesting 'subject.（名词，科目）

1. China usually <u>imports</u> wool from Australia.

   What's the <u>import</u> of his statement?

2. <u>Increase</u> in population made emigration necessary.

   The driver <u>increased</u> speed when he realized it was getting dark soon.

3. You've <u>progressed</u> well this semester.

   I'd like to see even more <u>progress</u>.

4. His actions <u>contrast</u> sharply with his promises.

   His white hair was in sharp <u>contrast</u> with his dark skin.

5. He's reading a <u>digest</u> of the week's news.

   She couldn't <u>digest</u> food properly.

6. The guards <u>permitted</u> me to bring my camera.

   He has to apply for a <u>permit</u> to work in the foreign country.

7. His <u>perfect</u> performance killed the audience.

   The real goal of a person's life is to keep <u>perfecting</u> himself.

8. The drug is known to <u>produce</u> side-effects in women.

   We manage to get most of our <u>produce</u> in farmers' markets.

9. Mrs. Roding's husband <u>deserted</u> her years ago.

   His father died in the Sahara <u>Desert</u>.

10. They're studying an interesting <u>subject</u>.

    Ancient Rome <u>subjected</u> most of Europe to her rule.

    The plan is <u>subject</u> to confirmation.

**（二）听录音，根据录音对画线词语进行重音标注，并勾出正确选项，注意复合名词与修饰性短语重音模式的不同。**

1. Be careful with that yellow jacket.
   A. 黄蜂　　　　　　　　B. 黄色的夹克
2. My friend brought me a red coat toy from England.
   A. 英国兵　　　　　　　B. 红色外套
3. My grandma's dream is to have a greenhouse.
   A. 温室　　　　　　　　B. 绿色的房子
4. Cold cream is favored by many ladies.
   A. 冷霜　　　　　　　　B. 冰冻的奶油
5. He lives in the White House.
   A. 白宫　　　　　　　　B. 白色的房子
6. She is describing the blue print to them.
   A. 蓝图　　　　　　　　B. 蓝色的图案
7. Mr. Kitting is a famous head doctor.
   A. 精神病医生　　　　　B. 主治大夫
8. Look at that hot dog.
   A. 面包夹熏红肠热狗　　B. 发怒的狗
9. He's now in his dark room.
   A. 冲洗胶卷的暗房　　　B. 阴暗的房间
10. Have you ever heard of the Whitehall?
    A. 白厅　　　　　　　　B. 白色的大厅
11. The floor was stacked high with bales of dry goods.
    A. 布匹　　　　　　　　B. 干货
12. The blue book the government released concealed many facts.
    A. 蓝皮书　　　　　　　B. 蓝色的书

**（三）听录音，给下列单词进行重音标注，并将各单词的音节数目填在相应括号内。**

例如：'occupy　　　（3）　　　occu'pation　　　（4）

1. operate　　　（　）　　　operation　　　（　）
2. harmony　　　（　）　　　harmonious　　　（　）
3. curious　　　（　）　　　curiosity　　　（　）

| | | | |
|---|---|---|---|
| 4. subject ( ) | | subjective | ( ) |
| 5. object ( ) | | objective | ( ) |
| 6. industry ( ) | | industrial | ( ) |
| 7. agriculture ( ) | | agricultural | ( ) |
| 8. economy ( ) | | economic | ( ) |
| 9. major ( ) | | majority | ( ) |
| 10. accident ( ) | | accidental | ( ) |
| 11. product ( ) | | production | ( ) |
| 12. continent ( ) | | continental | ( ) |
| 13. beautify ( ) | | beautification | ( ) |
| 14. qualify ( ) | | qualification | ( ) |
| 15. photograph ( ) | | photographic | ( ) |
| 16. educate ( ) | | education | ( ) |
| 17. confidence ( ) | | confidential | ( ) |
| 18. nominate ( ) | | nomination | ( ) |
| 19. converse ( ) | | conversation | ( ) |
| 20. person ( ) | | personality | ( ) |

## 五、专项训练

**(一) 模仿录音，朗读下列单词，注意单词重音落点。**

**法语词缀重读**

| | | |
|---|---|---|
| lemo'nade | enter'tain | employ'ee |
| refu'gee | trai'nee | domi'neer |
| engi'neer | auctio'neer | pre'pare |

**后缀前一音节重读**

| | | |
|---|---|---|
| mini'sterial | bene'ficial | edi'torial |
| mu'sician | his'torian | mathema'tician |
| geo'metric | e'lectric | scien'tific |

### 倒数第三音节重读

| | | |
|---|---|---|
| pho'tography | au'tography | psy'chology |
| cal'ligraphy | de'mocracy | bu'reaucracy |
| i'dentify | ge'ometry | imma'turity |

### 复合动词：重音位于动词重音之上

| | | |
|---|---|---|
| down'load | in'put | outper'form |
| up'date | over'work | under'estimate |
| ill-'treat | over'do | under'pay |

### 复合形容词：重音为均重音（双重音）或非均重音

| | | |
|---|---|---|
| 'deaf-'mute | 'old-'fashioned | 'fast-'developing |
| 'well-'meant | 'world-'famous | 'heart-'broken |
| 'kind 'hearted | 'three-'legged | 'second-'hand |

### 短语动词：重音为双重音（均重音）

| | | |
|---|---|---|
| 'turn 'off | 'buckle 'up | 'hand 'out |
| 'take 'away | 'drive 'in | 'sit 'on |

### 复合专有名词：主重音位于第二个单词的重音上（除 street 和 day 外）

| | | |
|---|---|---|
| United 'States | United 'Nations | Pacific 'Ocean |
| Third 'Avenue | Easter 'Sunday | Harvard 'University |
| New 'York | Long 'Island | Beach 'Hotel |

### 多音节词

| | | |
|---|---|---|
| ˌuni'versity | a'cademy | po'litical |
| ˌinde'pendence | ˌprepa'ration | ˌmathe'matics |
| exˌcita'bility | acˌcounta'bility | faˌmili'arity |

### （二）模仿录音，朗读下列句子，注意画线部分复合名词的重音的位置。

1. Mr. Thompson went out during the <u>lunch hour</u> and bought a <u>newspaper</u>.
2. When I have tea with my <u>girlfriend</u>, she always gives me jam <u>sandwiches</u>.
3. I am meeting my <u>grandparents</u> at the <u>bus stop</u>, not at the <u>airport</u>.
4. I forget to bring with me my <u>sun glasses</u> and <u>flashlight</u>.
5. Mum never does any <u>housework</u> on <u>weekdays</u>.
6. It gets so hot in the <u>sitting room</u> that we've had to fit an <u>air-conditioner</u>.
7. She works as a <u>shop assistant</u> in the <u>drugstore</u>.
8. My <u>housemate</u> is terrified of <u>fireworks</u>.
9. Don't forget to take <u>a toothpaste</u> to the <u>bathroom</u>.
10. Michael didn't like <u>baseball</u> when he was in <u>middle school</u>. He liked <u>basketball</u>.

### （三）英音视听说练习。

欣赏英剧《唐顿庄园》（*Downton Abbey*）片段，给以下对白画线部分的单词或词组标注重音，并按不同重音模式规则分类后填写表格。

Robert: Is her <u>ladyship</u> awake?

Miss O'Brien: Yes, my lord. I'm just going to <u>take in</u> her breakfast.

Robert: Thank you.

Cora: Hello?

Robert: May I <u>come in</u>?

Cora: Isn't this terrible? When you think how excited Lucy <u>Rothes</u> was at the <u>prospect</u>, it's too awful for any words. Did J. J. Astor <u>get off</u>? Of course that <u>new wife</u> of his is bound to be <u>rescued</u>.

Robert: I've had a telegram from George <u>Murray</u>. One of his partners is in <u>New York</u>.

Cora: Yes?

Robert: It seems James and Patrick were on board.

Cora: What? They can't have been. They weren't <u>going over</u> until May.

Robert: Then they changed their plans. They're definitely on the <u>passenger list</u>.

Cora: Thank you, O'Brien. That'll be all for the moment. But surely they were <u>picked up</u>?

Robert: Doesn't look like.

Cora: What? Neither of them? You must tell Mary. She can't hear about it from anyone else.

| 类别 | 词语 | 重音模式规则 |
|---|---|---|
| 双音节名词 |  |  |
| 三音节词 |  |  |
| 复合名词 |  |  |
| 修饰性词组 |  |  |
| 复合动词 |  |  |
| 专有名词 |  |  |

# 第21课 句子重音

### ● 考一考

请和同伴分角色朗读下列对话，并录音：

A: It's great.

B: It's not great.

A: It is great.

B: No. It isn't.

A: Yes, it is. It's truly great.

B: As far as I'm concerned, it stinks!

请认真聆听原录音，并和自己的录音做比较，发现有什么不同吗？

### ● 导入

英语重音分为单词重音和句子重音。在20课，我们学习了单词重音。本课将着重学习句子重音。句子重音不仅能让对话双方更加清楚地表达和传递思想，而且还能体现句子的节奏感和韵律感，对说话者的感情表达也起着重要作用。例如"考一考"中，说话双方的感情色彩是通过句子重音表现出来的。这段对话正确的句子重音模式应为：

A: It's 'great.

B: It's 'not great.

A: It is great.

B: 'No. It 'isn't.

A: Yes, it 'is. It's 'truly great.

B: As far as I'm concerned, It 'stinks!

## 一、学习目标

——了解句子重音的基本概念

——掌握句子重音的一般规则

——纠正句子重音常见的发音错误

## 二、学习内容

### （一）句子重音的基本概念

每个单词在单独出现的时候都有重音，但在句子里，一些单词保留其重音，一些单词则失去原有的重音，这些保留下来的原有重音就是句子重音。句子中的重音读得相对较重、慢、清晰，而非重音部分则读得相对较轻、快、含糊。本课中，句子重音用 "'" 标注。

### （二）句子重音的一般规则

句子重音通常分为语法重音和语义重音。

1. 语法重音

语法重音的规则是：实词重读，虚词轻读。英语中实词含有重要的词汇意义，通常需要重读；而虚词（也称功能词）只起功能作用，没有特别的含义，在句子中通常不重读。实词包括：名词、形容词、副词和实义动词（即情态动词、助动词以外的动词）；虚词包括：介词、代词、冠词、连词、助动词和情态动词。数词和感叹词是介于实词和虚词之间的词类，通常也重读。在语法重音规则下，说话人说话时不受个人情感影响，也没有特意将句中的某一信息加以强调，只对句中的实词一视同仁地加以强调，因此，语法重音也称表意重音 (sense stress)。例如：

'How 'time 'flies!

'Conscience and 'hard 'work are 'valued.

'AIDS has 'killed about '204,000 'Americans.

A 'world with 'clones was 'suddenly 'argued.

但实词重读，虚词轻读并不是不变的语音现象。实词也有不重读的情况：

（1）名词在以下几种情况下一般不重读：

① 当名词在一个句子或较短的语境中重复出现时，例如：

'Business is business.

The 'little 'boy 'turned to the 'next boy.

② 当名词表示整体概念，如 person、fellow、thing、matter、affair、business、place 等，且前面有修饰语时，例如：

'Can you 'explain the matter?

'Who's the fellow on the 'playground?

③ 当名词用做对比时，例如：

'We can 'do it 'this way or 'that.

④ 当名词在句末作称呼语时，例如：

'Come 'on, boy!

⑤ 当名词 street 用作街名时，例如：

'Downing Street　　　　'Main Street　　　　'Oxford Street

⑥ 当名词被名词修饰时，例如：

'reference book　　　　'Christmas Day　　　a 'joke gift

（2）形容词用于问候语时不重读，例如：

Good 'morning, Madame.

Sweet 'dreams, boys.

（3）副词在以下几种情况下一般不重读：

① 当程度副词 about、a little、almost、much、too、very、hardly、pretty、rather、slightly 等后面接的是重读词时，程度副词不重读，例如：

The 'man almost 'lost his 'mind.

He 'feels too 'nervous to 'find an 'excuse.

② 副词 so 在 think、do 等词后时不重读，例如：

'Yes, I 'think so.

'Sorry, I 'didn't 'say so.

③ 副词 so、now、then 用在语气上连接上下文时不重读，例如：

So he 'went to 'sleep.

Now 'let's 'begin from the 'very 'beginning.

④ 关系副词 why、where、when 一般不重读，例如：

He 'wasn't quite 'sure of the 'time when he 'murdered the 'woman.

（4）倒装句中的实义动词一般不重读，例如：

"'Oh," said the 'man.

'After a 'storm came a 'windy 'day.

虚词在以下几种情况下需要重读：

（1）介词位于句首或句尾时需重读，例如：

'What on 'earth are you 'talking 'about?

'Of the '100 'students, about '30% of the 'parents 'attend 'special 'meetings.

（2）指示代词、强调代词、物主代词、疑问代词一般需重读，例如：

'That's what I 'mean.

He's a 'friend of 'mine.

（3）人称代词用作并列主语或宾语时需重读，例如：

'He and 'I are 'twins.

She 'looked at 'him and 'me with 'puzzles.

（4）人称代词用作对比意义或位于句末作主语时一般需重读，例如：

'Who are 'you?

'You 'like it but 'I 'don't.

（5）从属连词位于句首并且后接不重读的词时需重读，例如：

'When I 'came to 'concern about his 'health, it was too 'late.

'After I 'met 'Mark, I 'found him a 'charming and 'intelligent guy.

（6）双音节或多音节连词 therefore、before、because、although、however、otherwise、nevertheless 等一般需重读，例如：

'Do what've been 'told, 'otherwise you'll be 'punished.

We, 'therefore, 'save most 'personal 'visiting for 'after-work 'hours.

（7）助动词在以下几种情况下重读：在句首时；在对一般疑问句作简略回答时；与否定词 not 构成缩略式时；do、does、did 出现在肯定句中表强调时，例如：

'Have you 'finished your 'book?

'Yes, I 'am.

We 'haven't been 'through so 'much 'together.

We 'did 'come to the 'spot 'yesterday.

（8）情态动词在以下几种情况下重读：在句首时；在对一般疑问句作简略回答时；与否定词 not 构成缩略式时；当情态动词表示可能性、惊讶和强烈的肯定时，例如：

'May I 'ask you for a 'favor?

'Sure, you 'can.

I 'mustn't 'believe his 'words.

They 'may 'go 'shopping this 'afternoon.

2. 语义重音

英语中除了语法重音还有语义重音（也称逻辑重音或强调重音）。语义重音指的是，句子中的重音取决于说话者的意思，即一句话中，任何一个词都可以按照说话者的意图用重读加以突出。这样，通常重读的实词有可能不重读，而通常轻读的虚词也有可能重读。例如：

I 'say I 'love you.（正常句子重音）

'I say I love you.（强调是我说而不是其他人说爱你）

I 'say I love you.（强调我是说而不是写爱你）

I say 'I love you.（强调是我爱你而不是别人）

I say I 'love you.（强调我是爱你而不是恨你）

I say I love 'you.（强调我爱的人是你而不是别人）

3. 节奏重音

除了语法重音和语义重音外，句子重音也可以为句子的节奏感和韵律感服务。为了使句子的节奏感和韵律感更强，我们也会在句子重音上灵活地做出相应变化，形成重音转移，即同一个单词在一个句子中的读法和其被单独读时的读法不一样，重音位置有所变化，例如：

sixteen

a) How many? 'Six'teen.

b) There're 'six'teen members in our team.

c) 'Sixteen thousands of people have been reported to suffer from AIDS.

d) I'm just six'teen years old.

sixteen 这个词单独读时为双重音 'six'teen，如句子 a。句子 b 强调具体数目，'six'teen 第一和第二音节都重读。句子 c 中的 sixteen 和 thousands 共同组成一个意群，为了使句子保持良好的节奏感和韵律感，第二个音节上的重音被省略，即 'sixteen。句子 d 强调 just 一词，为了使句子保持良好的节奏感和韵律感，第一个音节上的重音被省略，即 six'teen。类似的例子有：

Chinese

a) Chi'nese.

b) Da Shan can speak very good Chi'nese.

c) We all believe that 'Chinese people are very hard-working and brave.

unknown

a) Un'known.

b) To be or not to be is still un'known.

c) This is a large 'unknown land.

## 三、常见错误

### （一）母语迁移

受汉语的影响，学生会把每个英语单词都读得一样重，一样长，致使语句听起来生硬，既没节奏感又没韵律感，例如：

| | |
|---|---|
| 'A 'friend 'in 'need 'is 'a 'friend 'indeed. | × |
| A 'friend in 'need is a 'friend 'indeed. | √ |

## （二）规则不清

1. 名词：名词作为实词通常是需要重读的，但这并不是绝对规律，名词在几种情况下是不需重读的。许多同学并不了解这一规则，导致遇到名词都重读，例如：

   | | | | |
   |---|---|---|---|
   | 'Hurry 'guys! | × | 'Renmin 'Street | × |
   | 'Hurry guys! | √ | 'Renmin Street | √ |

2. 介词：介词是虚词，一般不重读，但介词位于句首或句尾时要重读。很多同学没有掌握这个规则，通常轻读所有介词，例如：

   | | |
   |---|---|
   | The 'hard 'work 'paid off. | × |
   | The 'hard 'work 'paid 'off. | √ |

3. 人称代词：人称代词一般不重读，但有时又需要重读。有些同学并不了解这点，所有的人称代词都按不重读处理，例如：

   | | |
   |---|---|
   | 'Who are you? | × |
   | 'Who are 'you? | √ |

4. 助动词：助动词一般不重读，但当 do、does、did 出现在肯定句中表强调时需要重读。有些同学并不了解这点，在这种情况下没有重读助动词，致使说话者的强调意愿没能表达出来，例如：

   | | |
   |---|---|
   | Do 'remember! | × |
   | 'Do 'remember! | √ |

5. 情态动词：情态动词一般是不重读的，这点大多数学生都知道，但当情态动词表示可能性、惊讶和强烈的肯定时是需要重读的。很多学生由于不了解这个规则，在这些情况下情态动词不重读，这样说话者的意思或某种情绪就不能清楚地表达出来，例如：

   | | |
   |---|---|
   | She must be in 'good 'condition 'now. | × |
   | She 'must be in 'good 'condition 'now. | √ |

6. 实词重读，虚词不重读，此为句子重音的语法重音。但句子重音除语法重音外，还有语义重音，即句子重音取决于说话人的意思。有些同学只是套用句子重音的一般规则，重读实词，轻读虚词，忽略说话者的意图，但该重读的没重读，以致错误传达或误读说话者的意思，例如：

   （他昨天承诺借 1000 美元给"她"）

   | | |
   |---|---|
   | He 'promised to 'lend her '$1,000 'yesterday. | × |
   | He 'promised to 'lend 'her '$1,000 'yesterday. | √ |

# 四、纠错训练

## （一）模仿录音，注意句子重音。

'Ever 'since 'early the 'last 'century, 'electricity has 'become an 'essential 'part of our 'modern 'life. Our 'industrial and 'agricultural 'production 'depends on it to 'run 'various 'kinds of 'machines. The 'modern 'wonder 'computers 'work on 'electricity too. It 'provides 'light, 'heat and 'power for us. If we 'want to 'watch 'TV or 'films or to 'listen to the 'radios we 'also need it. 'Nobody can 'deny that the 'development of our 'civilization 'depends on electricity.

## （二）模仿录音，在句子中不需要重读的名词下画线。

1. Could you show me the way to Da Tong Street?
2. When he does these things he never looks exactly like I do.
3. My success tells me that the key to successful creative emulation is to emulate the successful people.
4. At first they were just "just friends", and after their marriage I think they'll still be good friends.

## （三）模仿录音，注意介词在句首和句末需要重读。

1. You will do a lot more growing up.
2. Inside the card, she saw that he had written a note.
3. He will come five times that day, in case you should be out.
4. With loneliness and solitude, that tragedy has become her fate.
5. She brought the roses in and then just looked at them in astonishment.

## （四）模仿录音，注意画线人称代词的重读。

1. Which one is <u>you</u>?
2. Leo looked down upon <u>her</u> and <u>me</u>.
3. You appreciate that but <u>I</u> don't.
4. Who are <u>you</u>?

## （五）模仿录音，注意画线助动词的重读。

1. They <u>did</u> want to divorce.
2. <u>Do</u> stop talking!
3. Please <u>do</u> take care of yourself.
4. She <u>does</u> work hard enough.

## （六）模仿录音，注意情态动词表示可能性、惊讶和强烈的肯定时需要重读。

1. You ought to take care of your silly girlfriend.
2. They may go shopping this afternoon.
3. Can he graduate from college?
4. She must be the one he's been looking for.

## （七）根据所标出的重音朗读下列句子，并写出不同的重音所表达的不同含义。

1. ˈJim bought Susan a dog yesterday. _____
2. Jim ˈbought Susan a dog yesterday. _____
3. Jim bought ˈSusan a dog yesterday. _____
4. Jim bought Susan a ˈdog yesterday. _____
5. Jim bought Susan a dog ˈyesterday. _____

# 五、专项训练

## （一）模仿录音，注意语句的重音。

1. How are you?
2. Here we are.
3. Where do you like?
4. I beg your pardon?
5. Thank you very much.

## （二）听录音，在重读词上标注重音符号"ˈ"。

A: What sports appeal to you?
B: I like almost every kind of sport.
A: Is there anything you like especially?
B: Well, I like X-sports in particular.
A: X-sports? You don't look like the extreme sports type.
B: I have even tried bungee jumping and surfing.
A: Wow, you certainly surprised me!

## （三）视听说练习。

欣赏电影《傲慢与偏见》(*Pride and Prejudice*)片段，写出演员朗读为重音的虚词，并填在文后所示的横线上。

Bingley: ... since I was a child and then she died. I have a beautiful grey. Of course, Caroline's a much better rider than I, of course.

Mrs. Bennet: Oh, yes. We fully expect a most advantageous marriage. And my Jane, marrying so grand, must throw her sisters in the way.

Elizabeth: Clearly my family are having a competition to see who can expose themselves to the most ridicule.

Charlotte: At least Bingley has not noticed.

Elizabeth: No. I think he likes her very much.

Charlotte: But does she like him? There are few of us who are secure enough to be in love without proper encouragement. Bingley likes her enormously, but might not do more if she does not help him on.

Elizabeth: She is just shy and modest. If he cannot perceive her regard, he is a fool.

Charlotte: We are all fools in love. He does not know her character as we do. She should move fast and snap him up. There is plenty of time for us to get to know him afterwards.

Caroline: I can't help feeling that someone is going to produce a piglet and make us chase it.

Gentleman: Oh, dear!

Mrs. Bennet: I do apologize, sir. I'm awfully sorry. Do forgive me.

Lady: Emily, please!

Mr. Bennet: Mary, my dear Mary. Oh dear, oh dear, oh dear.

Mary: I've been practising all week.

Mr. Bennet: I know, my dear.

Mary: I hate balls.

Mrs. Bennet: Mr. Bennet, wake up. Oh, I've never had such a good time in my life!

Caroline: Charles, you cannot be serious.

Mrs. Bennet: We'll be having a wedding here in Netherfield in less than three months if you ask me, Mr. Bennet. Mr. Bennet!

Mrs. Bennet: Mary, please.

Mr. Bennet: Thank you, Mr. Hill.

Collins: Mrs. Bennet, I was hoping, if it would not trouble you, that I might solicit a private audience with Miss Elizabeth in the course of the morning.

Mrs. Bennet: Oh, certainly, Lizzie would be very happy indeed. Everyone, out. Mr. Collins would like a private audience with your sister.

Elizabeth: Wait, please. I bet Mr. Collins have nothing to say to me that anybody need not hear.

Mrs. Bennet: No, nonsense, Lizzie. I desire you will stay where you are. Everyone else to the drawing room.

Mrs. Bennet: Mr. Bennet.

Mr. Bennet: … But…

Mrs. Bennet: …now!

Mrs. Bennet: Jane, Jane, don't… Jane! Jane.

Elizabeth: Papa, stay.

1_____  2_____  3_____  4_____
5_____  6_____  7_____  8_____

# 第22课 强读式和弱读式

● **考一考**

● 听录音，写出你所听到的单词：
● A: Why is the Grand Canyon so beautiful?
● B: Because it's all _____.

● **导入**

　　"考一考"中的填空题，有人会写出"gorgeous"（/ˈɡɔːdʒəs/ 壮观的），答案没错，形容词 gorgeous 回答了问题的后半段；还有人可能会填上"gorges"（/ˈɡɔːdʒɪz/ 峡谷），答案也没错，巧妙地呼应了问题的前半段。这其中蕴含的语音现象，就是我们在本课即将学习的主要内容：强读式和弱读式。

　　许多英语常用词有两种或两种以上的读音，一种是强读式；一种是弱读式。在实际交际中，我们听到的英语有许多弱读现象，并非完全按词典标注的音去读。弱读式只出现在非重读中。不会弱读，就听不懂别人说话；不会弱读，就难以正确地传递意思。此外，把弱读形式读成强读形式也会影响说话的流利程度，导致说出的话缺乏节奏感。

　　弱读形式是中国人学习英语的一大难点。受母语发音影响，我们更习惯读单词的强读式，例如我们更习惯把 and 读成 /ænd/，而不是 /ənd/、/nd/、/ən/、/n/。又如，英语元音（/ɔɪ/ 和 /aʊ/ 除外）在非重读中通常可弱化为 /ə/ 或 /ɪ/，其中弱化为 /ə/ 最为常见。这就解释了为什么"考一考"环节中填 gorgeous 和 gorges 均可。此外，音的弱化不仅体现在元音，也会出现在辅音中，如 /ɪz/ 中的辅音 /z/ 通常会弱化成 /s/ 音，如 gorgeous /ˈɡɔːdʒəs/ 和 gorges /ˈɡɔːdʒɪz/ 中的两个辅音 /s/ 和 /z/。

　　本课将介绍强读式和弱读式的概念、使用情形及读法，并指出学习者的常见错误。

## 一、学习目标

　　——了解强读式和弱读式的基本概念
　　——掌握强读式和弱读式的使用情形及读法
　　——纠正强读式、弱读式中常见的错误发音

## 二、学习内容

### （一）强读式和弱读式的概念

一个英语单词在强读或弱读时具有不同发音，这些不同的发音形式就构成了词的强读式和弱读式。强读式是一个单词在重读时的读音形式。弱读式是一个单词非重读时的读音形式，包含元音或辅音音素的弱化或省略。

采用强读式的词多数是实词，即具有实际语义的词，如名词、动词、形容词、副词等。采用弱读式的词多数是虚词，即没有完整的词汇意义，但有语法意义或功能意义的词，包括助动词、介词、连接词、冠词以及代词等。在连贯语句中，用弱读式的时候多于用强读式的时候，这是一个重要的英语语音现象。

### （二）强读式和弱读式的使用情形及读法

1. 强读式的使用情形

强读式主要用于重读或孤立提及某个单词时，该单词通常为实词。一般说来，虚词在句子中不重读，而是采取弱读形式，但这并不是绝对的，虚词在以下情形必须用强读式。

(1) 在意群末或句末时：

Do you know who I **am**?

When I heard **that**, I almost hit the roof.

(2) 用重音表示强调时：

She **was** here just now.

You **must** come to see me right now.

(3) 孤立地提到或引用一个词时：

"**Can**" is a modal verb.

Are you sure that we should choose "**or**"?

(4) 助动词、情态动词和 be 与 not 连在一起时：

You **shouldn't** behave like that!

We **don't** really mean that!

(5) 对比时：

This toy is for **her**, not for **him**.

We're doing this for **you**, not for **us**.

(6) 并列使用介词时：

The letter is **from** me, not **to** me.

A work **of** and **about** youth

2. 弱读式的读法

　　弱读式在英语语音学习中不易掌握，且常被忽视。学习者说话不流利，节奏感不强，一个重要的因素是没有掌握好弱读式。弱读式究竟该怎么读？有三种方法：①弱化为元音 /ə/，如 as /æz/ 和 an /æn/ 通常被弱化为 /əz/ 和 /ən/；②缩短元音的长度，如 he、she、me、we、be、been 中的长元音 /i:/ 变为短元音 /ɪ/，who、you、to 中的长元音 /u:/ 变为短元音 /ʊ/；③省掉元音或辅音，如 from /frɔm/、some /sʌm/ 和 his /hɪz/ 通常会被分别省掉元音或辅音读为 /frm/、/sm/ 和 /ɪz/。

　　以下是常见的虚词弱读形式及例子。为便于学习者掌握，我们同时也提供了每个虚词的强读式。

（1）冠词的强弱读形式

| 冠词 | 弱读式 | 强读式 | 弱读例子 |
| --- | --- | --- | --- |
| a | /ə/ | /eɪ/ | a marriage; in a short time |
| an | /ən/ | /æn/ | an egg; an honest boy |
| the（元音前） | /ðɪ/ | /ði:/ | the hour; the other day |
| the（辅音前） | /ðə/ | /ði:/ | The more, the better. |

（2）代词的强弱读形式

| 代词 | 弱读式 | 强读式 | 弱读例子 |
| --- | --- | --- | --- |
| my | /mɪ/ | /maɪ/ | My joy of life mostly comes from my son. |
| his | /ɪz/ | /hɪz/ | I like his beautiful eyes. |
| your | /jʊə/ | /jɔ:/ | I put your coat in the box. |
| me | /mɪ/ | /mi:/ | Could you tell me the time? |
| us | /əs/ | /ʌs/ | He came to visit us every month. |
| him | /ɪm, əm/ | /hɪm/ | Send him my wishes. |
| her | /hə, ə/ | /hə:/ | Her words shocked all around. |
| them | /ð(ə)m/ | /ðem/ | Invite them to the party. |
| he | /i:, hɪ, ɪ/ | /hi:/ | He came back yesterday. |
| she | /ʃɪ/ | /ʃi:/ | She learned well. |
| we | /wɪ/ | /wi:/ | We must do it now. |
| you | /jʊ/ | /ju:/ | You're late again! |
| they | /ðe/ | /ðeɪ/ | They looked at us doubtfully. |
| some | /səm, sm/ | /sʌm/ | I need some cheese. |

（3）连词的强弱读形式

| 连词 | 弱读式 | 强读式 | 弱读例子 |
|---|---|---|---|
| as | /əz/ | /æz/ | as far as I know |
| or | /ə/ | /ɔː/ | Why or why not? |
| and | /ənd/、/nd/、/ən/ 或 /n/ | /ænd/ | It's raining cats and dogs. |
| but | /bət/ | /bʌt/ | We're slaves to nothing but the clock. |
| that | /ðət/ | /ðæt/ | He said that he would forgive me. |
| than | /ðən/ 或 /ðn/ | /ðæn/ | It's easier said than done. |

（4）助动词的强弱读形式

| 助动词 | 弱读式 | 强读式 | 弱读例子 |
|---|---|---|---|
| am | /əm/ 或 /m/ | /æm/ | I'm going to skate this afternoon. |
| is | /ɪs/ | /ɪz/ | It's so desperate. |
| are | /ə/ | /ɑː/ | Those are valuable data. |
| be | /bɪ/ | /biː/ | I'll be crazy if I were his wife. |
| was | /wəz/ | /wɒz/ | At that time I was a student. |
| were | /wə/ | /wəː/ | We were compelled to say that. |
| do | /dʊ/ | /duː/ | What do you say? |
| does | /dəz/ | /dʌz/ | Does anyone know the fact? |
| has | /həz/、/əz/ 或 /z/ | /hæz/ | He has finished the job beforehand. |
| had | /həd/ 或 /əd/ | /hæd/ | These seats had been reserved. |
| have | /həv/、/əv/ 或 /v/ | /hæv/ | I have tried to forget the past. |
| been | /bɪn/ | /biːn/ | He has been to many countries. |

（5）情态动词的强弱读形式

| 情态动词 | 弱读式 | 强读式 | 弱读例子 |
|---|---|---|---|
| can | /kən/ | /kæn/ | You can ask her for a favor. |
| may | /me/ | /meɪ/ | You may ask her for a dance. |
| must | /məst/ | /mʌst/ | I must hand it in before Friday. |
| will | /wəl/、/əl/ 或 /l/ | /wɪl/ | She will go as planned. |

| | | | | |
|---|---|---|---|---|
| would | /wəd/、/əd/ 或 /d/ | | /wʊd/ | Nothing would change my love. |
| shall | /ʃəl/ 或 /ʃl/ | | /ʃæl/ | I shall come ten minutes later. |
| should | /ʃəd/ 或 /ʃd/ | | /ʃʊd/ | You should take the medicine now. |

（6）介词的强弱读形式

| 介词 | 弱读式 | 强读式 | 弱读例子 |
|---|---|---|---|
| at | /ət/ | /æt/ | at work; all at once |
| of | /əv/ | /ɒv/ | of course; be made of |
| to | /tə/ 或 /tʊ/ | /tu:/ | to Shanghai; from bad to worse |
| for | /fə/ | /fɔ:/ | for example; for good |
| from | /frəm/ 或 /frm/ | /frɒm/ | from New York; from Class 1 |

# 三、常见错误

## （一）习惯使然

中国人学习英语时常受母语影响，每个单词习惯读得清晰到位，却忽略了英语中的弱读现象，导致说出的英语节奏感不强，也无法听懂地道的英语。例如：

Time seems to stand still. 此句中的 to /tu:/ 读成弱读式 /tʊ/ 才更自然。

She is too weak for conversation. 将 is /ɪs/ 和 for /fɔ:/ 分别读成弱读式 /ɪz/ 和 /fə/ 才显得地道自然。

## （二）规则不清

通常情况下，英语中实词一般是强读，虚词一般是弱读，但这并不是绝对的，大多数英语学习者会在下列情况下出错：

1. 虚词在意群或句末时没有被强读，例如：

    Which one is she (/ʃɪ/)?　　　×

    Which one is she (/ʃi:/)?　　　√

2. 虚词在表示强调时没有强读，例如：

    It does (/dəz/) have rhythm.　　×

    It does (/dʌz/) have rhythm.　　√

    They do (/dʊ/) look alike.　　×

    They do (/du:/) look alike.　　√

3. 虚词被孤立地提到或引用时没有强读，例如：

   "Must" (/məst/) is a modal verb.　　　　　　×

   "Must" (/mʌst/) is a modal verb.　　　　　　√

   Is it a "he" (/hɪ/) or a "she" (/ʃɪ/)?　　　　　　×

   Is it a "he" (/hiː/) or a "she" (/ʃiː/)?　　　　　　√

4. 虚词在对比时没有被强读，例如：

   I'm here for you (/jʊ/) not for your mother!　　　　　　×

   I'm here for you (/juː/) not for your mother!　　　　　　√

   I'm talking about this one, not that (/ðət/) one.　　　　　　×

   I'm talking about this one, not that (/ðæt/) one.　　　　　　√

5. 介词并列使用时没有被强读，例如：

   This is a work of (/əv/) and about youth.　　　　　　×

   This is a work of (/ɒv/) and about youth.　　　　　　√

   I regret greatly that I didn't transfer my father from (/frəm/) Hainan to (/tʊ/) Guangdong.　　　　　　×

   I regret greatly that I didn't transfer my father from (/frɔm/) Hainan to (/tuː/) Guangdong.　　　　　　√

## 四、纠错训练

### （一）模仿录音，注意实词和虚词的强弱读。

A: Do you like classical music?

B: No, I don't like it at all.

A: What type of music do you like?

B: I'm a real fan of pop songs.

A: Who's your favorite singer or group?

B: Jay Chou. What do you think about him?

A: I can hardly bear pop songs. They are all noise to me.

### （二）模仿录音，注意虚词在意群或句末时强读。

1. Sure does.
2. Yes, I think so.
3. You might not believe this.

4. I can't bear her laughing at me!
5. I hate to tell you this but it's a fake.

### （三）模仿录音，注意虚词在表示强调时强读。

1. Do stop that noise!
2. They did have broken up.
3. He does care about her.
4. Do make sure to come on time.
5. That's exactly what he did say.

### （四）模仿录音，注意虚词被孤立地提到或引用时强读。

1. "At" is a preposition.
2. Do you mean "will" or "would"?
3. It's not easy to grasp the usage of the word "may".
4. We were required to copy the word "shall".
5. "A" should be put here instead of "an".

### （五）模仿录音，注意虚词在对比时强读。

1. This is his dog, not hers.
2. This toy is for her, not for him.
3. We're doing this for you, not for us.
4. I'm here for you not for your mother!
5. I'm talking about this one, not that.

### （六）模仿录音，注意介词在并列使用时强读。

1. This is a work of and about youth.
2. The train is leaving from Hainan to Wuhan.
3. I regret greatly that I didn't transfer my father from Hainan Hospital to Guangdong Hospital.

## 五、专项训练

### （一）模仿录音，写出黑体词的弱读形式。

1. Better late **than** never. /        /
2. Time and tide wait **for** no man. /        /

3. An apple a day keeps **the** doctor away. /           /
4. The man with a new idea **is** a crank until the idea succeeds. /           /
5. If you don't learn **to** think when you are young, you may never learn. /           /

### (二) 模仿录音，注意需要弱读的单词。

1. — I thought you might be interested in this article.
   — Why, what's it about?
2. — How are you getting on these days?
   — Not too bad.
3. — How long do you need to keep that up?
   — It all depends.
4. — Professor Smith, do you spend a lot of time on teaching?
   — Yes. I have to prepare class notes, give lectures and hold office hours.

### (三) 听录音，写出空白处被弱读的虚词。

M: Darn! You've spilled red wine 1._____ me. My new dress 2._____ ruined.

J: I'm terribly sorry! What 3._____ I do to help? Here's some water to wash it off.

M: Stop splashing water on me! Oh, this 4._____ so embarrassing! I'm 5._____ mess.

J: Well, you do look upset. Please don't blow up. Don't lose your cool.

M: Hmm, you've got the nerve talking like that! Who wouldn't fly 6._____ the handle? This dress cost 7._____ fortune.

J: You look really cute when you're mad. I kid you not. Some people do look attractive when they are 8._____ a rage.

| 1._____ | 2._____ | 3._____ | 4._____ |
| 5._____ | 6._____ | 7._____ | 8._____ |

### (四) 模仿录音，并标出必须强读的虚词。

Hello, how are you? When most people do learn English as a second language, they learn formal English. Unfortunately, learning it like this tends to make you feel distant and bored. The truth is, most people in English-speaking countries don't speak to each other in such a formal way. They speak in a casual way to their friends and families. When speaking casually, people tend to use a lot of informal or colloquial words, and also shorten and connect their phrases. They say things like "Hey, what's up" or "Hey! Whatcha been doin'?" These expressions are both common and natural, and make you seem like a native speaker. Using them may make people more interested in talking to you. This type of English is more like what you will hear in movies and TV shows. Speaking this way makes native speakers feel more relaxed and you will sound like a friendly person who speaks English well.

### (五) 英音视听说练习。

欣赏电影《僵尸新娘》(*Corpse Bride*) 片段，在弱读单词下画线。

Victor: Victoria.

Victoria: Victor? I'm so happy to see you. Come by the fire. Where have you been? Are you all right?

Victor: I.. I... oh, dear.

Victoria: You're as cold as death. What's happened to you? Your coat.

Victor: Victoria, I confess. This morning I was terrified of marriage. But then, on meeting you, I felt I should be with you always... and that our wedding could not come soon enough.

Victoria: Victor, I feel the same.

Victor: Victoria, I se— I se— I seem to find myself married. And you should know it's unexpected.

Emily: My darling, I just wanted to meet— Darling? Who's this?

Victoria: Who is she?

Emily: I'm his wife.

Victoria: Victor?

Victor: Victoria, wait. You don't understand. She's dead. Look.

Emily: Hopscotch.

Victor: No! No! Victoria!

Emily: You lied to me! Just to get back to that other woman.

Victor: Don't you understand? You are the other woman.

Emily: No! You're married to me. She's the other woman.

Skeleton: She's got a point.

Emily: And I thought... I thought this was all going so well.

Victor: Look, I'm sorry, but... this just can't work.

Emily: Why not? It's my eye, isn't it?

Victor: No, your eye is… lovely. Listen, under different circumstances, well, who knows? But we're just too different. I mean, you are dead.

Emily: You should've thought about that before you asked me to marry you.

Victor: Why can't you understand? It was a mistake. I would never marry you.

# 第23课 节奏

## ● 考一考

以下是诗经开篇《关雎》中的一段名句及其英译文。请大声朗读，仔细体会这段中英文诗节在节奏韵律方面的区别：

| 关关雎鸠， | By riverside are cooing |
| 在河之洲， | A pair of turtledoves; |
| 窈窕淑女， | A good young man is wooing |
| 君子好逑。 | A fair maiden he loves. |

## ● 导入

　　和音乐一样，语言也有节奏。简单来说，语言的节奏是由语音的长短、高低、强弱（轻重）这三方面特质决定的。英语和汉语虽然都讲究节奏，但英语的节奏讲究轻重搭配，汉语普通话的节奏则讲究声调（平仄）搭配。

　　"考一考"中《关雎》的汉语诗节，共16字16个音节，每行4字，一字一顿，每字之间时距大抵相等。全诗音形兼备，朗朗上口，体现出汉语言独有的节奏特点。与之相比的英译文乍一看则"参差不齐"，似乎毫无规律可循，但只要稍作分析亦可见其"洞里乾坤"。从诗歌音步的角度看（诗歌音步是诗行中按一定规律出现的轻音节和重音节不同组合而成的韵律最小单位），全诗采用的是英语诗歌韵律中使用最为广泛的抑扬格（一轻一重），一、三行均为四音步，（By ri/verside/are coo/ing; A good/young man/is woo/ing），二、四行均为三音步（A pair/of tur/tledoves; A fair/maiden/he loves）。因此，尽管英译诗在音节数量方面看似与原文不相吻合，但在传神翻译的同时兼顾了英语的节奏特点，读起来抑扬顿挫，每个音步之间时距也大抵相等，充满音乐特质和动势变化。

　　由此可见，英语节奏与汉语节奏迥然不同。本书在"单词重音"一课中曾经介绍过，汉语属于"音节计时"（syllable-timed）语言，节奏以一个音节一节拍的形式出现，除轻读语气词以外，每个音节需要的时长大抵相等。原则上句子的字数多，用的时间就长，音节之间界限比较明显，讲究字正腔圆、一字一顿。英语节奏规律则表现为：话语句子所用时长以重音的数目决定，重读音节之间，不论音节多少，发音时长大抵相等，属于"重音计时"（stress-timed）的语言；连贯语篇中轻重音交替出现，实词重读，虚词弱读，从而形成同化、连读、省音、弱化等现象。

## 一、学习目标

——了解节奏及节奏群的基本概念
——掌握节奏的基本特点
——纠正英语节奏的常见错误

## 二、学习内容

### （一）节奏的概念

在英语的连贯语流中出现的一系列音节都有轻重、长短、高低、快慢等有规律的交替现象，该现象称为节奏。例如：

He 'jogs 'every 'morning. ( • ●● • ● • )

此句共含有 6 个音节，其中重读音节 3 个，非重读音节 3 个。在说话时，重读音节（包括名词、动词、形容词、副词、数词等）读得更重、更长、更慢、更清晰；非重读音节（包括冠词、介词、代词、助动词、连词等）读得更轻、更短、更快、更含糊。这种以重音为基础自然形成的轻重、长短、高低、快慢等有规律的语音交替就构成了英语的基本节奏。本课中，我们用实心大圆圈"●"表示重读音节，实心小圆圈"•"表示非重读音节，如上例。

### （二）节奏群的概念

节奏群是英语节奏的基本单位。一个节奏群由一个重读音节或一个重读音节及若干个非重读音节组成。重读音节是节奏群的核心，一个句子有多少个重读音节就有多少个节奏群。节奏群类似音乐里的"节拍"，一个节奏群即一拍。

关于节奏群的划分，通常规定第一个音节是重读音节，其后的音节为非重读音节。若句首音节为非重音，则第一个重音前形成一个"空拍"。两个重读音节之间的非重读音节，划归到前一节奏群。但如果中间的非重读音节在意义上与后面的重读音节联系更为紧密，则划归后一节奏群。本课中，节奏群用"|"来划分，放在句子的每一个重音之前；空拍用"?"表示，放在句首的非重音之前。例如，以下是 2014 年 8 月 30 日 CNN 报道中关于美国即将制裁俄罗斯的一则新闻句子：

The U.S. is warning Russia of new sanctions, economic penalties if it doesn't pull back.

该句单词重音标注如下：

The 'U.'S. is 'warning 'Russia of 'new 'sanctions, eco'nomic 'penalties if it 'doesn't 'pull 'back.

该句节奏群划分如下：

| ?The | 'U. | 'S. is | 'warning | 'Russia of | 'new | 'sanctions, eco | 'nomic | 'penalties | if it 'doesn't | 'pull | 'back.

以上例句可划分成12个节奏群，其中第一个为空拍，节奏群 | if it 'doesn't | 的划分因考虑语义上的前后联系而将非重读音节 if it 与 doesn't 划归同一个节奏群，每一个节奏群所占用时长大致相等。

### （三）节奏的基本特点

1. 重音计时。两个重读音节之间无论非重读音节数目多少，所需时长大致相等。例如：

   ① | one | two | three ( | ● | ● | ● )

   ② | one and | two and | three ( | ● •| ● •| ● )

   ③ | one and then | two and then | three ( | ● ••| ● ••| ● )

   ④ | Birds | eat | worms. ( | ● | ● | ● )

   ⑤ | Birds have | eaten | worms. ( | ● •| ● •| ● )

   ⑥ | Birds should have | eaten | worms. ( | ● ••| ● •| ● )

   英语的话语时间并非取决于该话语中含有的单词数目或音节数目，而是取决于有多少个重音。尽管以上例句中的单词数目及音节数目各不相同，重读音节数却都是三个，因此朗读每个句子时间大致相等，即三拍，每个节奏群为一拍，两拍之间应把非重读音节读完。

   英语节奏的这种重音计时特点自然会对语速造成影响。一般来说，重读音节之间的间隔越短，即每个节奏群中的非重读音节出现得越少，语速就会越慢，音节听起来会更清晰；反之，重读音节之间的间隔越长，非重读音节出现得越多，语速就会越快，音节听起来会更含糊。例如以上例句中，①和④句中的每个节奏群只有一个实词重读音节，非重读音节为零，因此朗读时显得从容、缓慢、清晰，就像声音被"拉长"的感觉；而②、③、⑤、⑥中的每一个节奏群都分别多加了一个或两个非重读音节，单位时间里拥挤的音节数量达到两个或三个，远比①句多，因此其中的非重读音节朗读时相对要急促、轻快、含糊些，就像被"挤紧"的感觉。

   由于重读音节决定时长，因此重读音节数量越多，连贯语流所需时长就越长。一般说来，以下各句朗读时所需时长随重读音节数量（或者说节奏群或音步数量）的增加而依次增加：

   ⑦ | ?The | bear | likes | eating | meat. (•●●● •●)

   ⑧ | ?The | big | bear | likes | eating | meat. (•●●●● •●)

   ⑨ | ?The | big | brown | bear | likes | eating | meat. (•●●●●● •●)

   ⑩ | ?The | big | brown | bear | likes | eating | fresher | meat. (•●●●●● •● •●)

2. 轻重音交替出现。英语的节奏是以重音为主干，轻音为陪衬，轻重音交替形成错落有致的韵律。在连贯语流中，重读音节之间往往由数个非重读音节隔开，如：

some bread and some milk. (•● ••●)

但有时也会出现连续几个重读音节的现象。在语言的实际运用中，可以通过交替弱化某些相邻的重读音节实现重音转移，从而形成节奏型重音，以达到韵律上轻重交替、起伏跌宕的效果。以句⑩为例：

| ?The | big | brown | bear | likes | eating | fresher | meat. (•●●●● •● •●)

其实，这个原本 8 个节奏群的句子也可以读成以下 6 个节奏群，听起来会更富有音乐节奏和律动美感：

| ?The | big brown | bear likes | eating | fresher | meat. (•● •● •● •● •●)

**你知道吗？**

节奏训练有很多辅助性手段：①运用视觉效应标出重读、连读、省音等特征；②运用听觉效应"唱"出单词和句子的音节；③运用知觉效应，通过肌肉运动，如拍掌、跺脚、摆手、打响指、踏步等身体语言来强调重读音节的响亮度特征。例如，可以采用拉橡皮筋的方法，即双手拇指绷起橡皮筋，以一伸一缩为一拍的方式，读重读音节时拉紧橡皮筋（可以适当夸张地拉长），读非重读音节时松开橡皮筋。这些手段可以让学习者清楚直观地感受到元音长度和响度的区别。

# 三、常见错误

## （一）节奏感淡薄

不少英语学习者，尤其是具备了一定基础的学习者常常错误地认为英语说得快就是说得好，因此在说英语时一味贪时求快，没有节奏感，给人以不知所云、废话连篇的感觉。

其实，一口优美动听的英语往往快慢得当、轻重并举，听起来流畅错落，语义清晰。具备一定基础的英语学习者在平时更需加强对英语节奏的认识和训练，纠正错误的说英语习惯，培养正确的英语节奏感。

## （二）汉腔节奏

中国的英语学习者在学习和运用英语节奏时常常会受"汉腔英语"影响。"汉腔英语"指节奏规律偏离英语规范、靠近汉语规则的一种英语变体。这种不正确的节奏模式主要表现为以下两点：

1. 重音多而不重，轻音少而不轻。

"重音多而不重"主要表现为句中音节无论重读与否常常被强化，而实际需要重读的音节却用力不够，时长不足。由此产生的"轻音少而不轻"自然就表现为句中非重读音节未被正确弱化，需要轻读的音节用力过大，时长过长，元音约简不够，听起来类似重读音节。两种现象综合后的结果是：句中每个音节所承载的轻重力度大致相同，重读音节不够突显，重读音节与非重读音节间的时长差异也不明显。例如，下面句子的正确重音应为黑体部分标注的三处，朗读时在两个意群（用"/"表示）之间形成自然停顿：

| ?I am a | stu**dent** / and I | **like** | **Chi**na.

但有些学习者会像朗读汉语一样将句子分解成以下汉腔英语节奏，致使每个音节都成了重读音节，且每个音节间都形成短暂的非自然停顿：

| I | am | a | stu | dent | and | I | like | Chi | na.

显然，中国英语学习者容易练成汉腔英语的主要原因其实是英语节奏习得环境的缺失以及母语的负迁移结果——学习者将母语的节奏模式应用于英语，忽视了汉语与英语节奏类型截然不同。

2. 句首多重读。

中国的英语学习者习惯重读句首英语单词，这主要是因为对英语句子重音特点了解不够。事实上，英语中一般疑问句和陈述句的句首单词往往是虚词，无须重读；特殊疑问句、祈使句、感叹句等句子的句首单词往往是实词，一般情况均需重读。句首多重读这一现象从另一个侧面也反映出了以上第一点所提到的"重音多而不重"的问题。

**纠正办法**

充分认识和了解英汉语节奏模式的不同特点，建立起一套新的节奏模式，提高节奏意识，了解相应规则，并在此基础上多听多练。

## 四、纠错训练

（一）模仿录音，注意感觉句子的节奏和速度，并用节奏群符号"/"划分以下句子或短语。

1. Dog eats meat.
2. The dog is eating the meat.

3. The dog there has eaten the meat.
4. The dog there must have eaten the meat.

● ● ●

1. Cats eat fish.
2. The cat is eating the fish.
3. The cats there have eaten the fish.
4. The cats there must have eaten the fish.

● ● ●

1. Birds eat worms.
2. The birds are eating the worms.
3. The birds there have eaten the worms.
4. The birds there must have eaten the worms.

● ● ● ●

1. one two three four
2. one and two and three and four
3. one and a two and a three and a four
4. one and then a two and then a three and then a four

● ● ● ●

1. Tom John Steve Sam
2. Thomson Johnson Steven Samson
3. Thomson and Johnson and Steven and Samson
4. Thomson and then Johnson and then Steven and then Samson

（二）模仿录音，注意重读音节与非重读音节的不同。

节奏类型1：• ●

1. destroy
2. pretend
3. at once
4. some more
5. my choice
6. Of course.

节奏类型2：● ●

1. Not me!
2. Where to?
3. So what?
4. Why not?
5. Good luck!
6. Come here.

节奏类型 3：• ● •

1. advantage
2. I hope so.
3. Of course not.
4. Excuse me.
5. With pleasure.
6. I'd like to.

节奏类型 4：● • ●

1. run away
2. long ago
3. Do it now.
4. Try again.
5. Write it down.
6. Put it there.

节奏类型 5：• • ● •

1. imitation
2. analytic
3. I've a pocket.
4. Mr. Donald
5. my to-do list
6. We are students.

节奏类型 6：● • • ●

1. wonderful play
2. terrible rain
3. go for a walk
4. Throw it away.
5. Candy is sweet.
6. Roses are red.

节奏类型 7：• ● • ●

1. a cup of tea
2. a pile of books
3. a ton of work
4. a herd of sheep
5. We have to go.
6. They did it well.

节奏类型 8：• ● • ● •

1. a lot of people
2. a gang of robbers
3. You'd better hurry.
4. It doesn't matter.
5. I like it better.
6. It's nice to see you.

节奏类型 9：• ● • ● • ●

1. I can't believe it's true.
2. It's all the same to me.
3. I'd like a piece of cake.
4. I'm sorry I'm late again.
5. I'd like to have a drink.
6. It's not the one I like.

节奏类型 10：• ● • ● • ● •

1. I used to play it every day.
2. He left the home without a word.
3. I've told you not to come again.
4. He ought to know the way by now.

## 五、专项训练

**（一）找错误。下面是一台装有节奏模式自动识别系统的电脑在语音识别时记录下的句子节奏。每个句子中都有一处节奏群划分错误。请找出错误划分的节奏群，画线标示，并改正。**

例：| Where do | you | want them to | start?

改：| Where do you | want them to | start?

1. | ?Will | Jack go | there to | gether with him?
2. | ?For | get what you have | heard from | that | guy.
3. | This isn't | quite the | moment for it.
4. | The | man | who is | now | speaking is the | boss.
5. | Whom are you | going to | meet?

**（二）双人练习。用 1—6 句替换 B 句，与 A 句组成对话。两人一组，轮流大声朗读对话，注意其●·●·●·●的节奏模式。**

例：A：Twinkle twinkle little star.

　　B：How I wonder what you are.

1. Let me help you find your keys.
2. Find a space and park your car.
3. Don't forget the bread and milk.
4. Thanks a lot for all your help.
5. Tell me why you don't agree.
6. Don't forget to leave a tip.

**（三）英音视听说练习。**

欣赏英剧《唐顿庄园》（*Downton Abbey*）片段，注意剧中对白的节奏模式。按示范要求填写表格，并模仿练习。

| 对白句子 | 重音模式 |
| --- | --- |
| So, the young Duke of Crowborough is asking himself to stay. | ●·●·●·●···●·●·● |
| And we know why. | |
| You hope you know why. | |
| That is not at all the same. | |
| You realize the Duke thinks Mary's prospects have altered. | |

| 对白句子 | 重音模式 |
|---|---|
| I suppose so. | |
| There is no "suppose" about it. | |
| Of course, this is exactly the sort of opportunity that will come to Mary if we can only get things settled in her favor. | |
| Is Robert coming around? | |
| Not yet. To him the risk is we succeed in saving my money but not the estate. | |
| He feels he'd be betraying his duty if Downton were lost because of him. | |
| Well, I'm going to write to Murray. | |
| He won't say anything different. | |
| Well, we have to start somewhere. | |
| Our duty is to Mary. | |
| Well, give him a date for when Mary's out of mourning. | |
| No one wants to kiss a girl in black. | |

## 第 24 课 停顿

● **考一考**

试着为下面的句子在不同的位置进行语调停顿划分，揣摩停顿对句义的影响。
Woman without her man is nothing.

● **导入**

  停顿是英语语流中经常被忽视、但又十分重要的一种语音现象。停顿不仅是为了让说话者在说话的间歇调整呼吸，更是保证信息准确传递的关键。"考一考"中的句子写成书面语会产生语义模糊，即读者不容易明白作者强调的重点；但若以口语形式，说话者可以利用语调停顿来表现不同的强调信息，例如：

  Woman / without her man / is nothing. /

  Woman / without her / man is nothing. /

  同样的单词，同样的语序，仅仅借助两处不同位置上的停顿和语调，前者的核心信息被锁定为"Woman is nothing"，后者的核心信息则变成了"Man is nothing"。

  停顿不仅广泛存在于日常口语交流中，在演讲中也扮演着重要角色。优秀的演讲者在演讲中都善于控制语速，注意句子的意群和停顿，使演讲或似湍急河水，奔腾起伏，或如涓涓小溪，轻流慢淌，以达到收放自如的效果。

## 一、学习目标

——了解停顿及意群的基本概念
——掌握停顿的基本方法
——纠正关于停顿的常见错误

## 二、学习内容

### （一）停顿和意群的概念

  停顿指话语的短暂停歇，是人们在说话或朗读中为了使意思表达得更清楚或出于换气的需要而采取的策略。

停顿是训练句子节奏的重点，其核心是意群的辨认。意群是小于句子的语音单位。一个句子根据其语义和语法结构可以划分出若干成分，每个成分称为一个意群。意群必须是有相对完整意义的一个词、词组或短语，或者一个分句、从句或主句。同一意群中词与词之间关系紧密相关，密不可分。本教材中意群用符号"/"表示。例如：

① Will you go out with me / or stay at home?

② That he will come here / is certain.

③ On this weekend, / my friends and I / are going to have a picnic.

意群在句子中具有语义、语法和语调三种特征。以上句子中，①和②都分别包含了两层语义、两个语法单位和两个语调单位（升降）；句子③则包含了三层语义、三个语法单位和三个语调单位（升升降）。显然，意群不仅确保了我们说话或朗读较长句子时得以停顿和喘息，而且进一步凸显了独具特色的英语节奏和韵律，增加了语流中语意的清晰度。

### （二）停顿的基本方法

停顿通常有三种方法：标点符号之间的停顿；连词之间的停顿；短语、从句或句子等语法单位之间的停顿。例如：

I saw ① / that you were perfect ② / and I loved you. ③ / Then I saw ④ / that you were not perfect ⑤ / and I loved you even more.

上述例句中，①和④均为宾语从句停顿，②和⑤均为连词停顿，③为标点符号停顿。

一般说来，段落与段落之间的停顿最长，句与句之间的停顿较短，意群之间的停顿则更短，或者可以不停顿。需要注意的是，同一意群各个单词之间不宜停顿，否则会出现破句，造成意思中断甚至歧义。

> **你知道吗？**
>
> 和英语一样，汉语其实也存在语气停顿对语义影响的现象。譬如，"拉长绳子"与"打死老虎"，究竟是"拉 / 长绳子""打 / 死老虎"呢，还是"拉长 / 绳子""打死 / 老虎"？这都需要靠语气的停顿来解决。

## 三、常见错误

### （一）缺少停顿

英语中存在一种同音异形异义现象，即相邻两个可连读单词所构成的语音组与另外一对不同单词构成的语音组发音相同，但意义不同。例如：

1a) Where're those stools? 　　 1b) Where're those tools?

2a) What're these sticks? 　　 2b) What're these ticks?

这类语音结构易引起歧义现象的产生，听者若不借助有效语境很有可能将 1a) 及 2a) 分别理解成 1b) 和 2b)。

**纠正办法**

> 在词与词之间稍做停顿，互不粘连，以避免歧义产生。

## （二）错误停顿

错误停顿往往表现在一些易造成歧义的句法结构，如下面的"修饰语＋名词＋名词"的短语结构：

young women and men

此句可以有两种理解：

a) young women / and men 年轻的女人们和所有男人

b) young / women and men 所有年轻的男女

这类结构在书面语中往往令人困惑，不知修饰语究竟修饰哪一个名词。在口语中若停顿不当则易导致歧义现象的产生。书面语中，句子的意义单位是通过句法结构或标点符号来确定的，而口语中则是借助语调单位来实现。语调单位可以区分出不同意义和语法单位的意群，这有助于排除句法结构本身的模糊性，使信息表达更为清晰。但错误的语调会产生错误的停顿，进而影响到语义表达。又如：

The conservatives who like the proposal are pleased.

本句可以有以下两种理解：

a) The conservatives who like the proposal / are pleased. 赞成该建议的部分保守党人高兴了。

b) The conservatives, / who like the proposal, / are pleased. 赞成该建议的所有保守党人都高兴了。

**纠正办法**

> 加强对英语句法结构的了解，培养正确的英语停顿意识，在口语交际中使用恰当的停顿、拖音和连续连音等手段，明确界定不同的意群，提高信息清晰度，避免歧义现象出现。

## （三）过多停顿

中国的英语学习者易受汉语节奏模式的影响，导致在说话或朗读时停顿过多。

停顿是语义、语法、语调及说话人调整呼吸的需要，意群和意群间视具体情况可以有一定的停顿，但在同一意群各个单词之间过多停顿势必造成意群逻辑意思的中断。

**纠正办法**

加强英语句法知识，正确把握英语语调，提高英语节奏意识，并在此基础上多听多练。

## 四、纠错训练

### （一）模仿录音，注意在单词之间给予适当的停顿。

1. a bee feeder — a beef eater
2. a trained deer — a train dear
3. grey day — grade A
4. a nice girl — an ice girl
5. a name — an aim
6. What're these sticks? — What're these ticks?

### （二）下列每组句子都含有两种不同的停顿，先大声朗读，再用英语在横线上写出相应的句意。

例：

a) I wasn't listening / all the time.
   <u>For the whole time I wasn't listening.</u>

b) I wasn't listening all the time.
   <u>I was listening sometimes.</u>

1a) Must I stick the stamp on / myself?
   _____

1b) Must I stick the stamp on myself?
   _____

2a) She did not become a teacher / because teaching was easy.
___

2b) She did not become a teacher because teaching was easy.
___

3a) They do not know how good / coffee tastes.
___

3b) They do not know / how good coffee tastes.
___

4a) Those who sold / quickly made a profit.
___

4b) Those who sold quickly / made a profit.
___

5a) Go and ask the Dean / who will teach us English.
___

5b) Go and ask the Dean who will teach us English.
___

**（三）模仿录音，注意在停顿处划上"/"符号。**

1. I came, I saw, I conquered.
2. A quick tour of the city would be nice.
3. If you see him give him my message.
4. Go down this road and turn left at the second crossing.
5. Presumably he thinks he can.
6. This is how he studies English.
7. He told me where I could find my way home.
8. Both my brother and I are fond of collecting stamps.
9. The house, it seemed to him, is smaller than before.
10. He read a great deal, and made full notes while he read.

## 五、专项训练

**（一）找错误。** 下面是一台装有语音自动识别系统的电脑在语音识别时记录下的句子及停顿。每个句子中都有一处停顿划分错误。请按正确的句法结构予以改正。

例：Usually he / comes on Sunday.

改：Usually / he comes on Sunday.

1. I have become most aware of my poor education whenever I have had the chance / to put it to the end.
2. One problem is that / I don't look any different from other people.
3. So / sometimes / some children in my primary school / would laugh / when I got out of breath after running a short way / or had to stop and rest halfway up the stairs.
4. Sometimes, too, / I was too weak to go to school / so my education suffered.
5. Every time I returned / after an absence, / I felt stupid / because I was behind the others.

**（二）双人练习。** 学生 A 念出以下五组句子，并向 B 提问句后问题，学生 B 仔细听辨并回答。

例：

a. "John", said the teacher, "is a fool".
b. John said the teacher is a fool.

Question: Who is a fool?

1a) The teacher said, "That student is lying."
1b) "The teacher", said that student, "is lying".

Question: Who was lying?

2a) He sold his house, boat, and shop.
2b) He sold his houseboat and shop.

Question: How many things did he sell?

3a) Do you want super salad?
3b) D you want soup or salad?

Question: How many things were you offered?

4a) Wooden matches are used to start fires.

4b) Wood and matches are used to start fires.

Question: How many kinds of things are used to start fires?

5a) "I'll ask her," said the manager.

5b) "Alaska", said the manager.

Question: What did the manager say?

### （三）英音视听说练习。

欣赏英剧《唐顿庄园》(*Downton Abbey*)片段，注意以下对白的停顿，并模仿练习。

Duke: I think I'd rather like to go exploring.

Mary: Certainly. Gardens or house?

Duke: Oh, house I think. Gardens are all the same to me.

Mary: Very well, we can begin in the hall, which is one of the oldest...

Duke: No, not all those drawing rooms and libraries.

Mary: Well, what then?

Duke: I don't know. The... The secret passages and the attics.

Mary: Well, it seems a bit odd, but why not? I'll just tell mama.

Duke: No, don't tell your mama.

Mary: But there's nothing wrong in it.

Duke: No, indeed. I'm... I'm only worried about the others who will want to join us.

# 第6单元 语调

　　语调是超音段音系学术语。总体来说，语言学家对语调的定义可分为狭义定义和广义定义。狭义上的语调指的是句子中的音高变化；广义上的语调指的是句子中的一切语音特征，包括重音、音调、节奏、停顿等，通常通过音高、音强、音长、停顿、响度、语速以及音色等声学指征来实现。

　　英语语调高低起伏、抑扬顿挫并充满旋律，其突出特点是各种句式除了一种默认语调类型与其形成基本的匹配关系外，还可任意搭配并形成不同的语调含义，说话人借此来表达态度、情绪或言外之意。例如，用降调说 Thank you. 这一句子可体现说话者的真诚，是非常正式的道谢；若使用升调就会显得随意，甚至漫不经心。使用错误的语调容易引起听者的误解，阻碍正常的交际。英语本族语者能够辨认出非英语国家英语学习者所犯的语法或语音错误，但却无法辨别说话人的语调错误，因此很容易产生误解。

　　本单元将介绍英语语调的相关内容，希望帮助学生了解并掌握这些语调知识，为学生讲出地道、流利的英语助一臂之力。

# 第25课 语调简介

● **考一考**

请你和你的同伴根据语调、音高提示，朗读下面的句子：

Hello, Helen dear. It's so nice to see you.

Hello, Helen dear. It's so nice to see you.

请讨论一下，用不同的语调来读这个句子，听者的感受会有什么样的变化呢？

● **导入**

  人们对英语语调的研究由来已久，其研究和描写方式主要分为三类：构型方式、调阶方式和 AM（auto-segmental-metrical）方式。第一类构型方式：将音高变化作为英语语调的基本单位，而音高变化的基本形式为升调、降调和平调。这三种基本语调组合在一起又可以形成降升调、升降调等不同语调，但最常用的语调模式还是降调、升调和降升调。构型方式中把英语语调成分分为调头、调核、前调头、调体及调尾。第二类调阶方式：也是将音高变化作为英语语调的基本单位，但音高分为四个层次，即极高调、高调、中调和低调。第三类 AM 方式：用 H（high）和 L（low）作为音高描述中的基础音调。本单元将采用最形象明了的构型方式来解释英语语调的相关知识。

## 一、学习目标

——了解语调的基本概念及基本模式
——掌握语调的基本功能、语调成分及其音高
——纠正常见的语调错误

## 二、学习内容

### （一）语调的定义和基本模式

  语调是超音段音系学术语，指英语口语中的音高模式。英语语调中除了降调、升调、

平调外，还有几种降调和升调合并形成的曲折调：降升调、升降调、降升降调、升降升调。这些语调中最常用、最基本的当属降调、升调和降升调。

1. 降调

（1）表示强调、肯定、终结、命令等。

（2）降调都用在有句子重音的词上，如果这个词是单音节词，就在此音节下降；如果这个词是多音节词，就在其重读音节下降，之后的非重读音节或其他单词则用低平调。

（3）常用在陈述句、特殊疑问句、祈使句和感叹句等句型中。

（4）本书中降调用符号"⌒"表示。

2. 升调

（1）表示不确定、疑问、请求、建议等。

（2）升调都从有句子重音的单词开始，如果这个词是单音节词，就在此音节上升；如果这个词是多音节词，就在其重读音节上升，之后的非重读音节或其他单词的音高依次递升；

（3）常用于一般疑问句、选择问句的前一个选择项、并列选项中除最后一项的所有项、表示疑问的陈述句、表示说话者对事情的把握较小时的反义疑问句中的附加问句、表示客气请求的祈使句、复合句中位于主句之前的状语从句和作状语的短语、带有宾语从句的主句的末尾。

（4）本书中升调用符号"⌒"表示。

3. 降升调

（1）表示有待继续、有所保留、夸张、急切的希望等。

（2）降升调都用在有句子重音的词上，如果这个词是单音节词，就在此音节完成降升，音高从高到低，再从低到高；如果这个词是多音节词，就在其重读音节下降，之后的非重读音节或其他词的音高逐步上升。

（3）常用在祈使句、感叹句、并列句中前面的分句、省略句等的句末。

（4）本书中降升调用符号"√"表示。

## （二）语调的基本功能

1. 语法功能：语调中所包含的信息能使听者更好地识别句法结构，听者通过语调的变化确定句子的具体含义，或者界定不同的语调群来明确句子的含义。例如：

    a) She is a teacher ⌒.

    b) She is a teacher ⌒?

    句子 a 以降调结尾，表明说话者陈述事实，语气肯定；句子 b 以升调结尾，表明说话者对此不确定，表示疑问。

2. 表态功能：通过语调的变化来确定说话者的情感、态度等。例如：

   a) Come with me ↘.

   b) Come with me ↗?

   c) Come with me ∨.

   句子 a 以降调结尾，表示说话者提出要求、建议或发布命令；句子 b 以升调结尾，表示说话者询问听者的意见；句子 c 以降升调结尾，表示说话者对听者的鼓励。

3. 强调功能：说话者常重读最重要的信息，以引起听者的注意。例如：

   a) Jane ↘ is a doctor.

   b) Jane is a doctor ↘.

   句子 a 强调在场的人中只有"简"是医生；句子 b 强调"简是位医生"，而不是其他职业。

## （三）语调成分及音高

1. 语调群

   一个语调群通常包括以下成分：

（1）调核（nucleus）：语调群里最后一个重读音节，语调的上升与下降均体现在调核上。有时调核会随着说话者想强调的信息而变化（本内容可参考本书第 21 课中句子重音中的语义重音）。

（2）调头（head）：语调群里第一个重读音节。

（3）前调头（pre-head）：调头前所有的非重读音节；若语调群中没有调头则指调核前所有的非重读音节。

（4）调体（body）：介于调头和调核之间的部分；有时语调群中也可以没有调体。

（5）调尾（tail）：包括所有出现在调核之后的音节。

I　ask　her to　help　me.*
P　H　　B　　N　　T

Ask　her to　help　me.
H　　B　　N　　T

She　helps　me!
B　　N　　T

Help　me!
N　　T

---

\* 注：N= nucleus；P= pre-head；H= head；B= body；T= tail.

## 第 6 单元　语调

Help!
N

以上例句表明，调核是句中不可或缺的部分，而其他成分有时可以不出现。调核作为最重要的成分，能随着说话人所要强调的信息变化而改变。例如：

a) <u>Has</u>　he　<u>bo</u> <u>rrowed a</u> <u>car</u>?（说话人所要强调的信息：car）
　　P　　　H　　B　　　N

b) <u>No</u>, he's <u>bo</u> <u>rrowed a</u> <u>bike</u>.（说话人所要强调的信息：bike）
　　N　P　H　　B　　　N

c) Has he <u>bo</u> <u>rrowed</u> a car?（说话人所要强调的信息：borrowed）
　　　　　P　　N　　T

d) <u>No</u>, he's <u>bought</u> a car.（说话人所要强调的信息：bought）
　　N　P　　N　　T

2. 语调成分的音高

语调成分的音高表示如下：

（1）调核（nucleus）：降调时其音高为句中最低。
（2）调头（head）：为整句最高音。
（3）前调头（pre-head）：声调保持低平。
（4）调体（body）：调体中的重读音节的音高以调头的音高为准，按顺序依次下降。
（5）调尾（tail）：句末使用降调的句子中，调尾声调低平，其音高和调核的音高一致；句末使用升调或降升调的句子中，调尾的声调依次上升。

All the students are reading aloud.

Who would like some chocolate?

Has the boss talked to you?

**你知道吗？**

在包含多个重读音节的长句中，如果仍然按照降调的规律逐个降低重读音节，会使整个句子读起来声音越来越低，听起来很单调，没有抑扬顿挫感。正确的方法是：根据场景，在每个语调群中选择重要的重读音节，再次提高其音高（以不超过调头的音高为准），重新开始递降过程。这种句中某个音节上升的现象称为句中上升，可用上升箭头"↑"表示。

例如：

I'm so happy | that you brought me | what I want most.

（重读音节逐个递降，声音越来越低，语调单一。）

I'm so ↑ happy | that you brought me | what I want most.

（出现一个句中上升，语调较生动。）

I'm so ↑ happy | that you ↑ brought me | what I want most.

（出现两个句中上升，语调生动，听起来抑扬顿挫。）

## 三、常见错误

### （一）调不达意

很多学生对语调的功能掌握不够，用英语交流时不能正确使用语调，也就不能理解语调变化引起的语义变化。在日常交流中，说话人可以根据自己的意思灵活变换语调，因此就会出现陈述句不用降调，或一般疑问句不用升调等情况。要想明白说者的真正意思，听者必须掌握好语调的功能才不会产生误解。例如：

Will you stop?

当说话人将此句以命令语气说出，意为"你住手！"时，该一般疑问句不应用升调，而应用降调。

Will you ↘ stop?　　√　　　　　Will you ↗ stop?　　×

**纠正办法**

通过多听、多读，注意英语的语调变化，模仿地道的语调，从而熟悉语调功能，并能在实际应用中灵活使用不同语调。

### （二）"中国腔"英语

所谓"中国腔"英语，即很多学生由于不了解或忽视语调成分的音高特点，导致朗读时按照汉语习惯，多用平调、降调，完全忽略英语中各个语调成分的不同音高。在朗读长句时，很多学生没有句中停顿，而是一口气读完或者随意停顿，也没有利用句中上升，句子语调显得过于单一。例如：

You've done a very good job so far.

朗读本句时，有些学生从头到尾全部读平调，忽略"ve-""good"和"job"这三个应该处于高音区的重读音节；有些学生则将所有音节全部重读，不区分处于低音区的非重读音节。这些都是错误的读法。

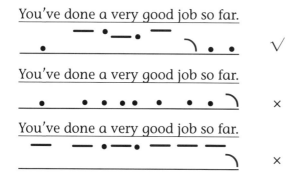

### 纠正办法

通过多听、多读，掌握语调成分的音高变化规律，注意摆脱汉语影响，逐步杜绝"中国腔"英语。

## 四、纠错训练

**（一）根据录音中的短对话回答问题。请注意说话人的语调。**

1. What does the woman think about Helen?
    A) She likes Helen.
    B) She doesn't like Helen.
    C) She thinks Helen is beautiful.
    D) She doesn't think Helen is beautiful.
2. What does the man mean?
    A) He wants to buy the same one.
    B) He likes the cell phone.
    C) He thinks the cell phone is expensive.
    D) He thinks the cell phone is cheap.
3. What does the woman mean?
    A) We shall stay in Sanya for a week.
    B) We shall leave Sanya earlier.

C) Shall we stay in Sanya for a week?

D) Shall we leave Sanya earlier?

4. What does the woman mean?

A) The man finished his report so quickly.

B) The man hasn't finished his report.

C) She knows nothing about his report.

D) She knows well about his report.

5. What does the woman mean?

A) She has ever been to Hong Kong.

B) She has never been to Hong Kong.

C) She is looking forward to going to Hong Kong.

D) She doesn't want to go to Hong Kong.

6. What does the woman mean?

A) She's very happy.

B) She's very angry.

C) She can't accept this.

D) She isn't interested in it.

(二) 根据例子，划出下列句子的语调单位，并模仿录音，注意各语调成分的音高。

例：My brother is the youngest.

P　H　　B　　N　　T

1. She wants some bread.

2. The boy is able to do it properly.

3. Can you show me where the theater is?

4. Nobody wants to buy it.

5. My mother will be angry.

6. Can you give me your name?

(三) 模仿录音，注意句中上升的音节。

1. I didn't realize ↑ how brave my father was ↑ until I became an adult.

2. I suppose it couldn't ↑ possibly happen again.

3. My father tried to catch the ↑ first bus into town.

4. Every time I ↑ follow your advice, I ↑ get into trouble.
5. My friends dislike ↑ me because I'm ↑ handsome and ↑ successful.
6. Now that ↑ everybody has come, let's ↑ begin our lecture.

## 五、专项训练

**（一）根据下列句子的不同答复，分别划出其调核，并标出其语调，然后根据录音，检查是否正确。**

例：— She is very pretty.
　　— Yes, but she is <u>odd</u> ↘ .
　　　　　　　　　　N

　　— She is very pretty.
　　— Yes, but her <u>sister</u> isn't ↘ .
　　　　　　　　　N

1. — Have you seen my book?
   — No, but it was here yesterday.

   — Have you seen my book?
   — No, but I saw Mary's.

   — Have you seen my book?
   — No, I haven't.

2. — My parents are driving to New York tomorrow.
   — Not today?

   — My parents are driving to New York tomorrow.
   — Not your grandparents?

   — My parents are driving to New York tomorrow.
   — Not to Baltimore?

3. — Were you at the airport on Monday?
   — No, I wasn't.

   — Were you at the airport on Monday?

— No, but my brother was.

— Were you at the airport on Monday?
— No, I was in the bank.

4. — He likes it.
— I'm glad.

— He likes it.
— He likes it?

— He likes it.
— Give him another one.

5. — Kate's arrived.
— But where's Harry?

— Kate's arrived.
— Isn't she ill?

— Kate's arrived.
— She is late.

**（二）模仿录音，注意句中的降升调及其含义。**

1. — I don't like the actress.
   — Well, she has a lovely voice. (Even if she can't act.)
2. — I must be off now.
   — You might wait for me. (Although it may be late.)
3. — It's $400!
   — You needn't pay. (Although it's expensive.)
4. — Who did the cleaning?
   — Who did? (Of course I did.)
5. — Did you break my cup?
   — Not I! (Although I was there.)
6. — It's gonna be a good game.
   — Should be good. (But the ending may be disappointing.)

## 第 6 单元　语调

**（三）英音视听说练习。**

以下是电影《国王的演讲》（*The King's Speech*）的片段，请欣赏视频，并标出画线部分的音高，标在所示的横线上。

Doctor Logue: They told me not to expect you.
　　　　　　　1. I'm sorry about your father.
　　　　　　　_____

Bertie: I don't wish to intrude.
Doctor Logue: 2. Not at all. Please, come in. Come in.
　　　　　　　_____

Bertie: I've been practicing. An hour a day, in spite of everything.
　　　　3. What's going on there?
　　　　_____

Doctor Logue: Oh, I was... Sorry. Mucking around with my kids.
　　　　　　　4. Do you feel like working today?
　　　　　　　_____

Bertie: Curtis biplane.
Doctor Logue: 5. I'll put on some hot milk.
　　　　　　　_____

Bertie: Logue. No. I'd kill for something stronger.
Doctor Logue: I wasn't there for my father's death. Still makes me sad.
I can imagine so.

Bertie: 6. What did your father do?
　　　　_____

Doctor Logue: He was a brewer. At least there was free beer. Here's to the memory of your father.

Bertie: I was informed, after the fact, that my father's... My father's last words were..., "Bertie has more guts than the rest of his brothers put together." Couldn't say that to my face. My brother...

Doctor Logue: 7. What about him? Try singing it.
　　　　　　　_____

Bertie: 8. I'm sorry?
　　　　_____

# 第26课 陈述句式的语调模式

### ● 考一考

请你和你的同伴轮流大声朗读下面短文：

The hostess apologized to her unexpected guest for serving an apple pie without any cheese. The little boy of the family left the room quietly for a moment and returned with a piece of cheese which he laid on the guest's plate. The visitor smiled, put the cheese into his mouth and then said: "You must have better eyes than your mother, sonny. Where did you find the cheese?" "In the rat-trap, sir," replied the boy.

请听录音，注意录音中的语调变化。短文中的句子都是陈述句式。你和你的同伴都读对了句子的语调吗？

### ● 导入

很多中国英语学习者误认为英语陈述句式的语调只有降调。导致该错误认识的主要原因包括：1）在英语学习初期，英语教师常常强调陈述句用降调，学习者因此将降调作为陈述句式的默认语调；2）在学习英语过程中，学习者常常忽略语境和场景，忽视说话者通过语调变化传达的感情和意图，坚持在陈述句式用降调。

在实际场景中，陈述句式的各种句型除了降调，还可用升调、降升调等来表达说话者的不同意图。如陈述句式中的简单句只有一个语调群，且说话者对事实持肯定态度时，句末用降调；如句中出现两个或两个以上的并列谓语，或说话者对说话内容表示疑问、讽刺、对比等态度时，这些简单句将不再一味使用降调。陈述句式中的并列句，句中也会随着两个分句的关系变化而出现语调变化。陈述句式的另一句型——复合句的语调更是灵活多变，需要英语学习者认真掌握其变化规律才能准确把握其语调特征。

## 一、学习目标

——了解陈述句式语调的基本模式
——掌握陈述句式语调的变化规律
——纠正陈述句式语调中的常见错误

## 二、学习内容

### （一）简单句的语调模式

1. 说话者陈述客观事实时通常用降调。例如：

    She gets angry with Lily at the meeting.

    The visitors will easily lose their ways.

2. 句中出现两个或两个以上的并列谓语，且语义上联系紧密时，前者用升调，后者用降调。例如：

    She is a good teacher at school and a kind mother at home.

    Jenny sat down by the window and read the letter.

3. 说话者对某情况表示疑问或要确认某种信息时通常用升调。例如：

    He is the President?

    This is your room?

4. 说话者表示对比、讽刺，或提出警告等包含强烈的感情色彩时，均可使用降升调。例如：

    He is very handsome.　　他可真够"帅"的。（表示讥讽）

    You will miss the flight.　　你会误机的。（提出警告，"再不快点，就赶不上飞机了。"）

5. 说话者列举多种事物时，前面的事物用升调，最后的事物用降调。例如：

    There is a book, a pen and a cup on the table.

    My dad brings me a cup, some nuts and some honey.

6. 句首出现较为重要的短语时，该短语以升调结尾，主句以降调结尾。例如：

    Turning the corner, I ran into my boss.

After going home, he'll take a shower.

## （二）并列句的语调模式

1. 若两者关系密切或进行对比时，前者用升调，后者用降调。例如：

   The red bag is yours | and the green one is mine.

   I left home early | so I could catch the bus.

2. 若两者关系不密切，或具有同等重要性，两者均用降调。例如：

   I study France and my brother studies English.

   Mother was ill and she was in hospital.

## （三）复合句的语调模式

1. 句中出现状语从句时，句子的语调为：从句在前面时，从句句末用升调，主句句末用降调；从句在后面时，从句和主句句末均用降调。例如：

   While she is watching TV, | the door bell rings.

   She was sleeping when the delivery came.

2. 句中出现定语从句时，句子的语调为：限制性定语从句和其先行词构成一个语调群，用降调；非限制性定语从句在句末时，主句和从句都用降调；非限定性定语从句在句中时，从句用升调，主句用降调。例如：

   Clock is a kind of instrument | which can tell people time.

   Then he met Mary, | who invited him to a party.

3. 句中出现表语从句时，若句中需要停顿，前面的系动词用升调，从句则用降调。例如：

   My problem is which car to choose.

Next Sunday is when we shall meet.

4. 句中出现同位语从句时，可单独作为一个语调群，多用降调。需注意：其引导词 that 与同位语从句在一个语调群。例如：

We heard the news | that our team had won.

The thought came to me | that maybe I should call John.

5. 句中出现宾语从句时，多用降调。例如：

He is wondering | why his mother made the decision.

Only the boss knows | who will be fired.

# 三、常见错误

## （一）不明其意

在陈述句式没有改变，但句末为升调或降升调时，许多学生不能领会说话者的真正意图。例如：

I don't think she is shy. (Whatever else she might be.)

说话人想表达的言外之意是"尽管她看上去很害羞，但据我了解她并不是这样的"，此时句末用降升调。如果句末用降调，就不能体现说话人暗含的意思。

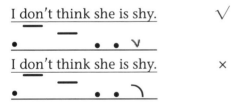

I don't think she is shy.　　√

I don't think she is shy.　　×

**纠正办法**

在听说练习或情景对话中，我们应根据实际场景来判断陈述句式的正确语调，这样才能领会说话人的真正意思，才能准确表达自己的意思。

## （二）长句中语调混乱

朗读长句时，许多学生因不熟悉语调规律，常常随意使用语调，或者按照汉语的习惯，都用降调。具体表现为：

1. 陈述句中出现两个或两个以上谓语部分，且意思联系紧密时，许多学生通常都以降调朗读句中的谓语部分，而正确语调为前升后降。例如：

   The old man felt very tired and went to bed early.

   本句中两个谓语部分语义联系紧密，其语调应是前升后降，即"tired"用升调，句末用降调。

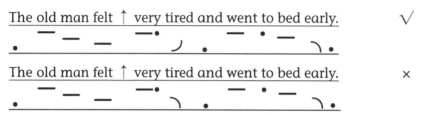

2. 许多学生在列举多个事物时没有语调变化，全部用降调，正确的语调应该是除了最后一个用降调以外，前面的事物均用升调。例如：

   A traditional breakfast includes milk, eggs, toast, bacon and juice.

   本句中，"milk""eggs""toast"和"ba-"几个重读音节均应用升调，"juice"用降调。

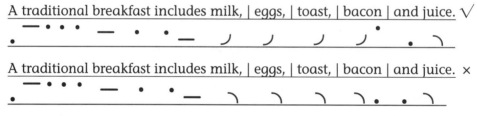

3. 在并列句的句型中，许多学生不能根据两个分句间的关系来判断其语调，通常将二者都读成降调。

   ① Because Christmas is approaching, many people are preparing gifts.

   ② The sun is shining and everything looks bright.

   Because Christmas is approaching, | many people are preparing gifts. √

   The sun is shining and everything looks bright. √

   ①句中，前后分句联系紧密，因此前面分句最后的重读音节"-proaching"用升调，后面分句最后的重读音节"gifts"用降调。②句中，前后分句语义独立，且具有同样

重要性，因此前面分句最后的重读音节"shining"和后面分句最后的重读音节"bright"均用降调。

4. 在复合句中，许多学生无论主句或从句均用降调，没有根据从句的位置来改变语调。

③ When she learned the news, she burst into tears.

④ We will have a bushwalking if it is fine.

When she learned the news, | she burst into tears.    ✓

We will have a bushwalking | if it is fine.    ✓

③句从句在前，因此从句最后的重读音节"news"应用升调，句末用降调。④句主句在前，主句、从句最后的重读音节"walking"和"fine"均用降调。

## 四、纠错训练

**（一）根据录音，判断下列句子中说话者对相关事实是否确定，并在括号里写"S"（Sure）或"NS"（Not Sure）。**

1. It is ten to eleven. (    )
2. He has his hair curled? (    )
3. They visited the Beijing Art Gallery. (    )
4. Nicole had a temperature as high as 40 degrees centigrade. (    )
5. Robert won the top prize in the essay competition? (    )

**（二）根据录音，给画线部分的音节标上语调，并模仿录音，注意句子中出现并列谓语时的语调变化。**

1. Mrs. Green went to the market (    ) and bought some vegetables.
2. May puts her hand into the bag (    ) and takes out a cell phone.
3. He finished his breakfast (    ) and went out of the house.
4. Suddenly, a young man ran into the thief (    ) and seized him.
5. Those women stood at the gate (    ) and chatted loudly.

**（三）根据录音，给画线部分的音节标上语调，并模仿录音，注意说话人列举事物时的语调变化。**

1. He turned off the light (    ), took his bag (    ), opened the door (    ) and went out.

2. I bought two pens (　　), three books (　　) and four rubbers (　　).
3. There is a cup (　　), a box (　　) and some bread (　　) on the table.
4. She has three brothers: John (　　), Mike (　　) and Henry (　　).
5. I like apples (　　), bananas (　　) and pears (　　).

（四）根据录音，给画线部分的音节标上语调，并模仿录音，注意并列句的语调变化。

1. She likes a red car (　　) but her husband likes a black one.
2. Tom is tall (　　) while his brother is short.
3. It is good (　　), yet it can be better.
4. She looks very young (　　), but she is already in her 50s.
5. The fisherman is poor (　　) but he always enjoys himself.

（五）根据录音，给画线部分的音节标上语调，并模仿录音，注意主句和从句的语调变化。

1. If it rains tomorrow (　　), the picnic will be cancelled.
2. We will be late (　　) if we don't hurry up.
3. After they eat dinner (　　), they watch TV for a while.
4. When she answered the phone (　　), her husband came back.
5. The manager didn't show (　　) up because he was ill.

# 五、专项训练

（一）听录音，选出正确答案，填在题号前的括号里。

(　　) 1. A. Sorry.　　　　　　　　B. Sorry?

(　　) 2. A. Yes.　　　　　　　　　B. Yes?

(　　) 3. A. He did.　　　　　　　　B. He did?

(　　) 4. A. His parents will call him once a day.
　　　　B. His parents will call him once a day?

(　　) 5. A. There will be 108 guests in the wedding.
　　　　B. There will be 108 guests in the wedding?

(　　) 6. A. The President promised to come.
　　　　B. The President promised to come?

( ) 7. A. It's ten o'clock.

　　　　B. It's ten o'clock?

( ) 8. A. Judy earned $400 by translating the essay.

　　　　B. Judy earned $400 by translating the essay?

( ) 9. A. The woman is the author of the novel.

　　　　B. The woman is the author of the novel?

( ) 10. A. I beg your pardon.

　　　　B. I beg your pardon?

**（二）模仿录音，并注意画线音节的语调。**

1. A: Mr. Johnson always plays soccer in the morning.

　 B: In the <u>morning</u>?

　 C: Mr. <u>Johnson</u>?

　 D: <u>Soccer</u>?

　 E: <u>Always</u>?

2. A: Laura drove the whole day and arrived at midnight yesterday.

　 B: <u>Laura</u>?

　 C: The <u>whole</u> day?

　 D: At <u>midnight</u>?

　 E: <u>Yesterday</u>?

3. A: Morgan has bought three cars this year.

　 B: <u>Morgan</u>?

　 C: <u>Three</u> cars?

　 D: <u>This</u> year?

4. A: I met Sam at the library this weekend.

　 B: <u>Sam</u>?

　 C: At the <u>library</u>?

　 D: This <u>weekend</u>?

5. A: He has put all the books in the closet and locked it.

　 B: <u>All</u> the books?

　 C: In the <u>closet</u>?

　 D: <u>Locked</u> it?

**（三）模仿录音，并为画线部分的音节标注语调，填在相应的括号里。**

1. In almost every country you will find <u>rice</u> (    ), po<u>ta</u>toes (    ), <u>eggs</u> (    ), <u>bread</u> (    ), <u>meat</u> (    ) and other basic foods. People just cook them <u>differently</u> (    ) in different countries.

2. Doctors recommend that old <u>people</u> (    ), or people of any age with <u>heart</u> (    ) or lung problems, get a flu vaccine every year. Because flu viruses change all the <u>time</u> (    ), a new vaccine must be prepared each year to protect against future attacks.

3. People like malls for many reasons. They feel <u>safe</u> (    ) because malls have private security <u>guards</u> (    ) and sometimes even police stations. Parking is usually <u>free</u> (    ), and the weather inside is always fine.

4. Ever since ancient <u>times</u> (    ), people have always loved a bargain. If they think they are getting a "good <u>deal</u> (    )" they will grab it <u>up</u> (    ), whatever it is.

5. Living with roommates in college <u>dorms</u> (    ), one is likely to have <u>problems</u> (    ) as well as suc<u>cess</u> (    ). Some students report more unhappy relationships with their roommates than they do the opposite.

**（四）英音视听说练习。**

以下是英国动画片《小鸡快跑》（*Chicken Run*）的片段，请欣赏视频，并标出画线部分的语调。

Nick: You <u>called</u> (    )? Nick and...

Fetcher: Fetcher.

Nick: At your service.

Ginger: Over here. We need some more things.

Nick: Right you are, Miss. How about this quality handcrafted tea set?

Ginger: Uh, no.

Fetcher: Or this lovely <u>necklace</u> (    ) and pendant.

Nick: Or this beautiful little number. All the rage in the fashionable chicken coops of Paree. Simply pop it on like so, and as the French hens say: "Voila!"

Fetcher: That is French.

Nick: That's two hats in one, Miss. For <u>parties</u> (    ). For weddings. Madame, this makes you look like a vision, like a dream.

Fetcher: Like a duck.

Ginger: No, thank you. We're making this. We need these things. Can you get them?

Nick: This is a big job, Miss. Bigger than the others. This is gonna cost.

Ginger: Same as always: One bag of seed.

Nick: You call this pay (　)?

Fetcher: It's chicken feed.

Ginger: What else could we give you?

Nick: Eggs.

Ginger: Eggs (　)?

Fetcher: Eggs.

Ginger: We can't give you our eggs. They're too valuable.

Nick: And so are we.

# 第27课 疑问句式的语调模式

### 考一考

请和你的同伴朗读下面的对话：

Amy: **Do you like jazz, Henry?**

Henry: No, not much. **Do you like it?**

Amy: Yes, I do. I'm crazy about Wynton Marsalis.

Henry: **He's a piano play, isn't he?**

Amy: No, he's a trumpet player. So, **what kind of music do you like?**

Henry: I like listening to rock.

请听录音，注意黑体句子的语调变化。这些句子都是疑问句式。你和你的同伴都读对其语调了吗？

### 导入

英语中的疑问句式有多种句型：一般疑问句、特殊疑问句、选择疑问句和反义疑问句。如同把降调作为陈述句式的默认语调一样，许多学生误以为疑问句式的各种句型也有既定语调，如一般疑问句用升调，特殊疑问句用降调。造成这种错误的原因也是类似的。他们记住了在英语学习初期老师所强调的这些句型的语调，却忽视了语境和场景对语调的影响。

本课将介绍疑问句式的常见语调，包括一般疑问句、特殊疑问句、选择疑问句以及反义疑问句。同时，本课也将详细解析很多学生在朗读这些句型时的常见语调错误。

## 一、学习目标

——了解疑问句式的基本语调模式

——掌握疑问句式语调的变化规律

——纠正疑问句式语调中的常见错误

## 二、学习内容

### （一）一般疑问句的语调模式

1. 句末通常用升调。例如：

   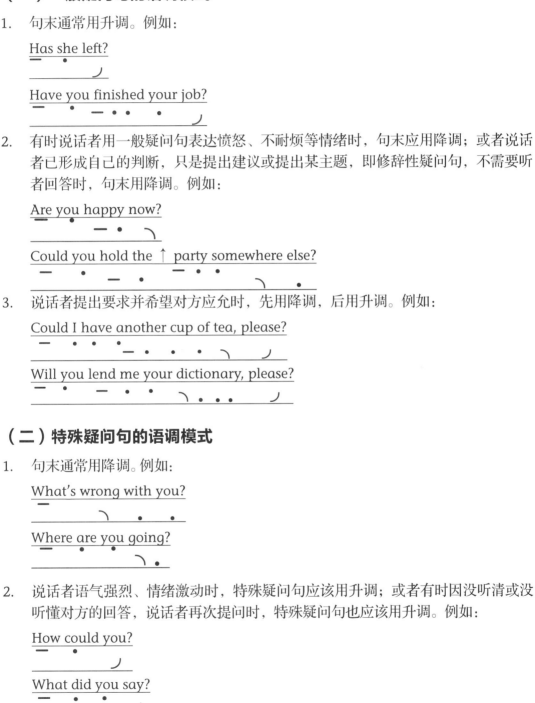

   Has she left?

   Have you finished your job?

2. 有时说话者用一般疑问句表达愤怒、不耐烦等情绪时，句末应用降调；或者说话者已形成自己的判断，只是提出建议或提出某主题，即修辞性疑问句，不需要听者回答时，句末用降调。例如：

   Are you happy now?

   Could you hold the ↑ party somewhere else?

3. 说话者提出要求并希望对方应允时，先用降调，后用升调。例如：

   Could I have another cup of tea, please?

   Will you lend me your dictionary, please?

### （二）特殊疑问句的语调模式

1. 句末通常用降调。例如：

   What's wrong with you?

   Where are you going?

2. 说话者语气强烈、情绪激动时，特殊疑问句应该用升调；或者有时因没听清或没听懂对方的回答，说话者再次提问时，特殊疑问句也应该用升调。例如：

   How could you?

   What did you say?

## （三）选择疑问句的语调模式

在选择疑问句中，前面的选择用升调，最后的选择用降调。例如：

Would you like veal or beef?

What color does he like best, white, black or red?

## （四）反义疑问句的语调模式

1. 当说话者对某种情况较有把握，只希望得到确认或允许时，句末通常用降调。例如：

Pro. Smith has gone back to America, hasn't he?

They won't come to the ceremony, will they?

2. 当说话者对某种情况毫无把握，希望对方给出答案时，句末通常用升调。例如：

You have passed the exam, haven't you?

The apartment hasn't been sold, has it?

# 三、常见错误

**老调常谈**

早在英语学习初期，中国英语学习者就被告知英语中常见问句的语调，如一般疑问句用升调，特殊疑问句和反义疑问句用降调。许多学生谨记这点，在朗读或情境交际中都遵照这一原则，完全忽略了在某些特殊情况下英语问句的特殊语调变化。

1. 许多学生遇到一般疑问句时，句末均用升调，忽视了当说话人表达特殊情绪时，不需听者回答的修辞性疑问句应用降调。例如：

Are you clear?

当说话者意欲表示警告的语气时，该句应用降调，而不是升调。

Are you clear?　　　√

Are you clear?　　　×

2. 许多学生遇到特殊疑问句时，句末均用降调，忽视了说话者情绪激动或需要确定某信息时的特殊疑问句应用升调。例如：

Where has she gone?

当说话者由于听不清对方的答复，想要确认"她去哪了"，该句应用升调，但很多学生仍片面地根据其特殊疑问句式用了降调。

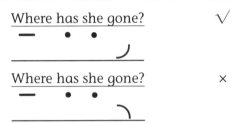

3. 许多学生遇到反义疑问句时，通常把尾句全部读升调或降调，没有区分说话人对事实很确定或不确定时的语调区别。例如：

Tom broke his arm in the football match, didn't he?

当说话者对此信息不确定，意为"汤姆在足球赛时摔断了胳膊吗"，句末应用升调；而当说话者对此信息较确定，意为"汤姆在足球赛时摔断了胳膊，是吧"，句末应用降调。

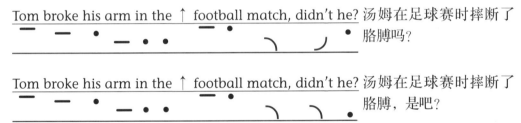

4. 许多学生遇到选择疑问句时，句末都错误地读成升调。例如：

Does your son like playing the guitar or the piano?

该句中的"guitar"应用升调，而"piano"应用降调，但相当多学生则习惯在句末的"piano"用升调。

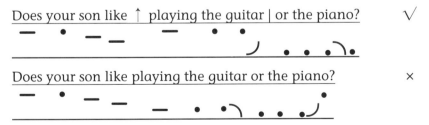

> **纠正办法**
>
> 熟悉疑问句式的语调变化规律；多听多读，注意纠正错误的语调习惯。

## 四、纠错训练

**（一）模仿录音，并在需要回答的句子前的括号里写"Y"（Yes），不需要回答的写"N"（No）。**

(     ) 1. Will you be patient?
(     ) 2. Was it perfect?
(     ) 3. Did you break my cup?
(     ) 4. Have you got your money?
(     ) 5. Wasn't Nancy a great singer?
(     ) 6. Haven't I made a mess of it?
(     ) 7. Will you come with me?
(     ) 8. Don't you know what he said?
(     ) 9. Will you stop acting this way?
(     )10. Isn't the woman lazy?

**（二）根据录音，判断下列句子中说话者对相关事实是否确定，并在括号里填"S"(Sure)或"NS"（Not Sure）。**

(     ) 1. They all speak Japanese, don't they?
(     ) 2. Professor Carl comes from Canada, doesn't he?
(     ) 3. He didn't show up, did he?
(     ) 4. You were invited to the conference, weren't you?
(     ) 5. There are some free tickets for the football match, aren't there?
(     ) 6. The house is old-fashioned, isn't it?
(     ) 7. She's never been abroad, hasn't she?
(     ) 8. The young man hasn't definitely refused, has he?
(     ) 9. They stayed at home playing cards, didn't they?
(     ) 10.The salesgirl looked very tired, didn't she?

## 第 6 单元　语调

## 五、专项训练

**（一）根据录音，给下列句子标上语调（降调用"＼"，升调用"／"），并模仿录音，和你的同伴朗读对话。**

1. At the table

    A: Steak? ( _____ )　　　　　　　B: What? ( _____ )

    A: Steak? ( _____ )　　　　　　　B: No. ( _____ )

    A: Why? ( _____ )　　　　　　　　B: Stomach. ( _____ )

    A: Stomach? ( _____ )　　　　　　B: Yes. ( _____ )

2. At the office

    A: Ready? ( _____ )　　　　　　　B: No. ( _____ )

    A: Why? ( _____ )　　　　　　　　B: Problems. ( _____ )

    A: Problems? ( _____ )　　　　　　B: Yes. ( _____ )

    A: What? ( _____ )　　　　　　　　B: Power failure. ( _____ )

3. At the front desk

    A: Name? ( _____ )　　　　　　　　B: Trigger. ( _____ )

    A: Tiger? ( _____ )　　　　　　　　B: No, Trigger. ( _____ )

    A: Trigger? ( _____ )　　　　　　　B: Yes. ( _____ )

    A: Room 1520 for you. ( _____ )　　B: Room 1520? ( _____ )

    A: Yes. ( _____ )

4. At the shoe store

    A: Some shoes? ( _____ )　　　　　B: Yes. ( _____ )

    A: The white ones? ( _____ )　　　B: No. ( _____ )

    A: The black ones? ( _____ )　　　B: No. ( _____ )

    A: The brown ones then? ( _____ )　B: No. Look at that! ( _____ )

    A: The red shoes? ( _____ )　　　　B: Yes, shiny red shoes! ( _____ )

5. Talking about a present

    A: He likes it? ( _____ )　　　　　　B: Yes. ( _____ )

    A: Give him another. ( _____ )　　　B: Give him another? ( _____ )

    A: Yes. ( _____ )　　　　　　　　　B: We have only one left. ( _____ )

    A: We can order more. ( _____ )　　B: Really? ( _____ )

    A: Yes. They are free. ( _____ )

**（二）听录音，在括号里标出画线部分音节的语调（降调用"＼"，升调用"／"），并模仿录音，和你的同伴朗读对话。**

**Dialogue One**

David: Nancy, what are you planning to do this <u>weekend</u>? 　　1. (　　)

Nancy: I haven't made any plans <u>yet</u>. You got any 　　2. (　　)

good <u>ideas</u>? 　　3. (　　)

David: I want to get away from the rat race of

life on campus for a while. How about <u>going</u> 　　4. (　　)

to the National <u>Park</u> 　　5. (　　)

on <u>Saturday</u>? 　　6. (　　)

We could invite <u>Laura</u>, 　　7. (　　)

<u>Tony</u>… 　　8. (　　)

Nancy: Sounds <u>great</u>! And what do you think we will 　　9. (　　)

do there? Maybe some <u>hiking</u>, and… 　　10. (　　)

David: Barbecue. We could roast hot <u>dogs</u> and 　　11. (　　)

hamburgers over a fire!

Nancy: Good <u>idea</u>! 　　12. (　　)

**Dialogue Two**

Laura: Dave, where are you off <u>to</u>? 　　1. (　　)

David: I'm heading for the library.

Laura: Hey, would you mind returning these <u>books</u> for me? 　　2. (　　)

They will be due in two days.

David: No problem. On my way <u>back</u>, I'll be stopping at 　　3. (　　)

the supermarket. You need <u>anything</u>? 　　4. (　　)

Laura: Yeah, could you get me some <u>chalk</u>? 　　5. (　　)

David: Sure.

**（三）英音视听说练习。**

以下是动画片《小鸡快跑》（*Chicken Run*）的节选片段，请欣赏视频，并标出画线部分的语调。

Ginger: So that's it. You're from the circus. You're on the run, aren't <u>you</u>
(　　)?

Rhodes: You wanna keep it down! I'm trying to lay low here.

| | |
|---|---|
| Ginger: | I should turn you in right now. |
| Rhodes: | You wouldn't. Would <u>you</u> (　)? |
| Ginger: | Give me one reason why I shouldn't. |
| Rhodes: | Because I'm <u>cute</u> (　)? Hey, hey. What kind of crazy chick are <u>you</u> (　)? Do you know what'll happen if he finds <u>me</u> (　)? |
| Ginger: | It's a cruel world. |
| Rhodes: | I've just decided I don't like you. |
| Ginger: | I've just decided I don't care. Show us how to fly. |
| Rhodes: | With this <u>wing</u> (　)? |
| Ginger: | Teach us, then. |
| Rhodes: | No. |
| Mrs. Tweedy: | He's valuable, you <u>say</u> (　)? |
| Man of the circus: | Sure. |
| Mrs. Tweedy: | Get the torch. |
| Rhodes: | Now, you listen here, sister. I'm not going back to that life. I'm a Lone Free-Ranger. Emphasis on "free". |
| Ginger: | And that's what we want, freedom. Fancy that, they're coming this way. |
| Rhodes: | Oh, no! They're onto me! |
| Ginger: | Teach us to fly. We'll hide you. |
| Rhodes: | And if I <u>don't</u> (　)? Was your father by any chance a <u>vulture</u> (　)? |
| Ginger: | Do we have a <u>deal</u> (　)? |

# 第 28 课 其他句式的语调模式

● **考一考**

请和你的同伴朗读下面的对话：

Peter: **Hi**, **Lucy**.

Lucy: **Hello**, **Peter**. How are you doing?

Peter: I'm just fine. **Thanks**.

Lucy: Well, **you see**, I'm planning to take Chemistry this semester. **Please tell me which professor to choose**.

Peter: John Smith, of course.

Lucy: Sorry, did you say Dr. John Smith?

Peter: Exactly. **They say he's a prominent professor in Chemistry**.

Lucy: **Wonderful**! I'll go and enroll his class. **Bye**!

请听录音，注意黑体部分的语调变化，其中包括祈使句、感叹句以及表示问候、告别、道谢和道歉的句子或表达。你和你的同伴都读对其语调了吗？

● **导入**

除了陈述句式和疑问句式，英语中祈使句、感叹句以及表示问候、告别、道谢和道歉的句子，其语调的变化也是非常灵活的。说话者会根据场景或自己的心情、暗含之意选择不同的语调，而大部分中国学生在使用这些句子时都用了降调。

本课将介绍英语中祈使句、感叹句以及表示问候、告别、道谢和道歉时使用的各种语调，同时解析很多学生在朗读这些句型时的常见语调错误。

## 一、学习目标

——了解祈使句、感叹句及其他句式的基本语调模式

——掌握祈使句、感叹句及其他句式的语调变化规律

——纠正祈使句、感叹句及其他句式语调中的常见错误

## 二、学习内容

### (一) 请求和命令的语调模式

1. 在表示请求的祈使句中,如说话者态度坚定,有时甚至暗含冷漠之意时,句末均用降调。例如:

   Turn off the radio, please.

   Put it there, please.

2. 说话者向对方发出指令,要求对方必须服从时,句末均使用降调。例如:

   Hands up!

   Go and find it out!

3. 部分祈使句中,调核使用升调或降升调时,表示语气友好、礼貌,暗含"建议"和"鼓励"之意。例如:

   Don't drop it!

   Mind your head.

### (二) 感叹句的语调模式

1. 感叹句最常用的语调是前调头在特高音区,调核在低音区,用降调,其他的重读音节均保持在声调高音区。例如:

   What a fast car!

   How marvelous!

2. 感叹句由单个词构成时,调核仍用降调。例如:

   God!

   Goodness!

3. 说话者别有用心，暗含嘲弄、得意时，感叹句句末可用升调或降升调。例如：

How nice!

Wonderful!

### （三）表示问候、告别、道谢和道歉的语调模式

1. 说话者客气地问候他人时用降调。例如：

   Good morning.

   How do you do.

2. 句末出现呼语的问候句，先用升调，后用降调。例如：

   Hello, Mr. Smith.

   Good morning, Mr. Bernard.

3. 熟人、朋友互相问候时，或说话者的语气轻快、活泼时，问候语可用升调。例如：

   Good morning.

   How do you do?

4. 双方告别时，一般用升调。例如：

   Good bye!

   See you!

5. 正式的道谢多用降调。例如：

   Thank you.

   Thanks a lot.

6. 朋友间较随意的道谢用升调。例如：

   Thank you.

   Thanks a lot.

7. 道歉可用降调或降升调。例如：

   Sorry.
   ⌒. 或 ˅

   I'm sorry.
   .. ⌒. 或 .. ˅

## （四）句首的副词或副词短语、插入语、同位语及报导短语的语调模式

1. 一些常用于句首的副词或副词短语常常用降调。例如：

   Surely, I've already told you.

   Of course, he should be punished.

2. 插入语出现在句首多用升调；在句中或句末时多用降调，且自成一个语调群，要有停顿。例如：

   You know, this is the best team in Europe.

   This is their best choice, I am sure.

3. 同位语在句中多用降调。需注意：当同位语被逗号隔开自成一个语调群时，要有停顿。例如：

   William, the pianist, will have a concert tonight.

   This is my wife, Jane Bennet.

4. 报导短语（即用来说明直接引语是谁说的用语，如：he said, I said）在句中不同位置用不同语调。出现在句首时，其意思常常是不完整的，故多用升调，且独自构成一个语调群；出现在句中或句末时，报导短语常常和前面引语构成一个语调群，被当作该语调群的调尾，多用降调。例如：

   Jane said, "I need your help."

"I am glad," said the man, "that you've called me."

## 三、常见错误

### 老调常谈

1. 许多学生错误地以为，表示提出请求或发出警告的祈使句都应用降调。实际上，当说话者语气轻快、活泼，尤其是对小朋友说话时，可以用降升调。例如：

   Come here.

   当说话人不是向对方发出指令、命令，而是表示鼓励、邀请时，句末应用降升调。

   Come here.　　　　　　　√

   Come here.　　　　　　　×

2. 许多学生忽略了感叹句用降升调的情况，认为感叹句句末均应用降调。例如：

   What a nice story!

   当说话者暗含嘲讽、调侃时，句末可用降升调，意指"这故事可真够差劲的"。

   What a nice story!　　　　√

   What a nice story!　　　　×

3. 如果问候语之后出现呼语时，许多学生在朗读或使用同类句子时，问候语仍然用降调。例如：

   Good night, Mike.

   当句末出现人名或称呼时，问候语应以升调或降升调结束。

   Good night, | Mike.　　　　√

   Good night, | Mike.　　　　√

   Good night, | Mike.　　　　×

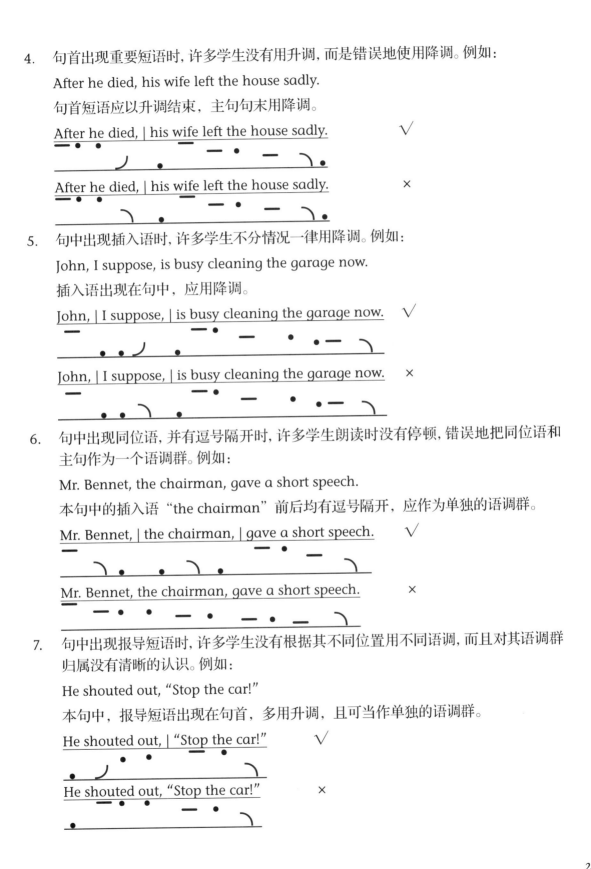

> **纠正办法**
> 
> 熟悉语调变化规律；多听多读，注意纠正错误的语调习惯。

## 四、纠错训练

### （一）模仿录音，注意句子的语调。

1. Come here.
2. Don't drive too fast.
3. Don't stay out too late.
4. Help yourself.
5. Open the door.

### （二）模仿录音，注意句子的语调。

1. Terrific!
2. What a pretty girl!
3. What a wonderful party!
4. How strange!
5. What nonsense!

### （三）模仿录音，注意比较句中出现呼语的语调变化。

1. A. Hello.                        B. Hello, Mike!
2. A. Hi!                           B. Hi, Jane!
3. A. Morning!                      B. Morning, Mr. Lee.
4. A. Good afternoon.               B. Good afternoon, Sister Nancy.
5. A. Good night.                   B. Good night, Dr. Ken.

### （四）根据录音，给画线部分的音节标上语调，并模仿录音，注意句首出现重要短语时的句子语调变化。

1. After the game (      ), they had some beer.
2. Despite his illness (      ), he came to the meeting on time.
3. From my point of view (      ), it's unfair.
4. Before going to the bed (      ), my father reads for a while.
5. Early in the morning (      ), the trash man begins his job.

**（五）模仿录音，注意句中插入语的语调变化。**

1. Strange to say, | he hasn't got my letter up to now.
2. I, | of course, | like a bicycle better.
3. True, | my apology would be too late.
4. Generally speaking, | he won't work on weekend.
5. This is all I have, | you know.

**（六）根据录音，给画线部分的音节标上语调，并模仿录音，注意句中报导短语的语调。**

1. Jim asked (    ), "What are those lights down there?"
2. "Maybe you are right," replied (    ) Bob.
3. "You've never been to the pub," David said (    ), "Come out with me tonight."
4. He suddenly shouted (    ) out, "That's my car!"
5. "I haven't met her for several days." said (    ) the client.

## 五、专项训练

**（一）听录音，根据句中画线部分的语调，判断说话者是给出建议还是发出命令。给出建议的，在横线上写"Suggestion"；发出命令的，在横线上写"Command"。**

1. Put the book in the case, Kim.  _____
2. Don't drink too much.  _____
3. Give me black coffee, Jack.  _____
4. Don't put too much salt.  _____
5. Answer the phone, Linda.  _____
6. Put the milk into the freezer.  _____
7. Don't drop the pot.  _____

8. Don't go to the wrong office. _____
9. Keep the change, boy. _____
10. Stop washing, Mrs. Blogs. _____

（二）朗读下列感叹句，并模仿例子，和你的同伴进行短对话操练。

> Oh my!   Oh dear!   Oh God!
> How awful!   How horrible!   How wonderful!

例：A: Gipson has won the prize.

　　B: How wonderful!

1. Andrew broke his arm in the match.
2. Sandy has had a car accident.
3. We'll go to Hong Kong for the holiday.
4. The terrorists attacked the airport last night.
5. The old man died alone in his house.
6. My little brother hurt his hand and he can't hold anything.
7. More than ten prisoners ran away from the prison yesterday.
8. Harry will come back for the Thanksgiving Day.
9. I've got a ticket for speeding this morning.
10. The pianist is going to visit our town this weekend.

（三）英音视听说练习。

以下是动画片《小鸡快跑》（*Chicken Run*）的节选片段，请欣赏视频，并标出画线部分的语调。

Ginger: I'm sorry (　　).

Rhodes: Is this your...? I'll get down.

Ginger: No, no, you just have it. Since you're here, there is something...

Rhodes: I'm glad you're here...

Ginger: I'm sorry. You go first.

Rhodes: You got it all.

Ginger: I just wanted to say, I may have been a bit harsh at first. Well, what I really mean is, thank you (　　), for saving my life. For saving our lives. You know (　　), I come up here every night and look out to that hill, and imagine what it must be like on the other side. It's funny. I've never actually felt grass beneath my feet. I'm sorry (   ). Here I'm rambling on about hills and grass, and you had something you wanted to say.

Rhodes: Well, yeah, it's just that..., you know (   ), life, as I've experienced it, you know (   ), out there lone free-ranging and stuff... It's full of disappointments.

Ginger: You mean grass isn't all it's cracked up to be?

Rhodes: Grass (   )! Exactly! Grass! It's always greener on the other side. And then you get there, and it's brown and prickly. You see what I'm trying to say? What I'm trying to say is... you're welcome.

Ginger: You know (   ), that hill is looking closer tonight than it ever has before. Well, good night (   ), Rocky.

Rhodes: Good night (   ).

# 附　　录

## 附录 1　英语国际音标总表

| | | | | | | | |
|---|---|---|---|---|---|---|---|
| 元音 | 前元音 | iː | ɪ | e | æ | | |
| | 后元音 | ɑː | ɒ | ɔː | ʊ | uː | |
| | 中元音 | ʌ | ɜː | ə | | | |
| | 合口双元音 | eɪ | aɪ | ɔɪ | əʊ | aʊ | |
| | 集中双元音 | ɪə | eə | ʊə | | | |
| 辅音 | 爆破音 | p | t | k | | | |
| | | b | d | g | | | |
| | 摩擦音 | f | θ | s | ʃ | h | |
| | | v | ð | z | ʒ | | |
| | 破擦音 | ts | tʃ | tr | | | |
| | | dz | dʒ | dr | | | |
| | 鼻音 | m | n | ŋ | | | |
| | 舌侧音 | l | | | | | |
| | 延续音 | w | r | j | | | |

## 附录 2　常用英语语音术语汉英对照表

| | |
|---|---|
| 元音 | vowel |
| 前元音 | front vowel |
| 中元音 | central vowel |
| 后元音 | back vowel |
| 合口双元音 | closing diphthong |
| 集中双元音 | centering diphthong |
| 辅音 | consonant |
| 清辅音 | voiceless consonant |
| 浊辅音 | voiced consonant |
| 爆破音 | plosive consonant |
| 双唇爆破音 | bilabial plosive consonant |

| | |
|---|---|
| 齿龈爆破音 | alveolar plosive consonant |
| 软腭爆破音 | velar plosive consonant |
| 摩擦音 | fricative consonant |
| 唇齿摩擦音 | labiodental fricative consonant |
| 齿间摩擦音 | dental fricative consonant |
| 齿龈摩擦音 | alveolar fricative consonant |
| 齿龈硬腭摩擦音 | alveolar-palatal fricative consonant |
| 声门摩擦音 | glottal fricative consonant |
| 破擦音 | affricate consonant |
| 齿龈硬腭破擦音 | alveolar-palatal affricate consonant |
| 齿龈后破擦音 | post-alveolar affricate consonant |
| 齿龈前破擦音 | fore-alveolar affricate consonant |
| 鼻音 | nasal consonant |
| 双唇鼻音 | bilabial nasal consonant |
| 齿龈鼻音 | alveolar nasal consonant |
| 软腭鼻音 | velar nasal consonant |
| 舌侧音 | lateral consonant |
| 半元音 | semi-vowel |
| 双唇半元音 | bilabial semi-vowel |
| 舌前硬腭半元音 | lingua-palatal semi-vowel |
| 舌前齿龈半元音 | lingua-alveolar semi-vowel |
| 音节 | syllable |
| 开音节 | open syllable |
| 闭音节 | closed syllable |
| 重读音节 | stressed syllable |
| 非重读音节 | unstressed syllable |
| 成音节 | syllabic consonant |
| -r/re 音节 | -r/re syllable |

| | |
|---|---|
| 字母组合 | letter combination |
| 元音字母组合 | vowel combination |
| 辅音字母组合 | consonant combination |
| 辅音连缀 | consonant cluster |
| 句子重音 | sentence stress |
| 语法重音 | syntactical stress |
| 语义重音 | semantical stress |
| 强读式 | strong form |
| 弱读式 | weak form |
| 连贯语流 | connected speech; speech flow |
| 音变 | pronunciation variation |
| 音姿 | gesture |
| 音姿交叠 | gesture overlap |
| 音姿目标 | target of gesture |
| 失去爆破 | loss of plosion |
| 不完全爆破 | incomplete plosion |
| 省音 | elision |
| 鼻腔爆破 | nasal plosion |
| 舌侧爆破 | lateral plosion |
| 中性元音 | schwa |
| 音的同化 | sound assimilation |
| 顺同化 | progressive assimilation |
| 逆同化 | regressive assimilation; anticipatory assimilation |
| 融合同化 | fusional assimilation; reciprocal assimilation |
| 语流 | speech stream |
| 连贯语流 | connected speech |
| 音节结构 | syllable structure |
| 滑读 | gliding |

| | |
|---|---|
| 拼读 | striking |
| 清晰 /l/ 音（明 /l/ 音） | clear /l/ |
| 浑浊 /l/ 音（暗 /l/ 音） | dark /l/ |
| 无擦通音 | approximant |
| 连音 /r/ | linking /r/ |
| 外加音 /r/ | intrusive /r/; extra /r/ |
| 外加音 /j/ | intrusive /j/; extra /j/ |
| 外加音 /w/ | intrusive /w/; extra /w/ |
| /h/ 不发音 | /h/ dropping |
| 缩略式 | contraction |
| 缩读 | contraction |
| 缩读符号 | apostrophe |
| 单词重音 | word stress |
| 单音节 | monosyllable |
| 双音节 | disyllable |
| 三音节 | trisyllable |
| 多音节 | polysyllable |
| 主重音（第一重音） | primary stress |
| 次重音（第二重音） | secondary stress |
| 零重音 | zero stress |
| 双重音（均重音） | double stress / even stress |
| 非均重音 | uneven stress |
| 节奏 | rhythm |
| 音步 | foot |
| 节奏群 | rhythmic group |
| 空拍 | silent beat |
| 节奏模式 | rhythmic pattern |
| 重音转移 | stress shift |

| | |
|---|---|
| 节奏型重音 | rhythmic stress |
| 停顿 | pause |
| 语调 | tone |
| 调核 | nuclear |
| 调头 | head |
| 前调头 | pre-head |
| 调体 | body |
| 调尾 | tail |

## 附录3　常用英语语音符号一览表

| | |
|---|---|
| 失去爆破 | - |
| 可省略的元音 | /ᵊ/（上移） |
| 连读符号 | ‿ |
| 意群符号 | \| |
| 省音符号 | ( ) |
| 缩读符号 | ' |
| 主重音符号 | ˈ |
| 次重音符号 | ˌ |
| 重读音节符号 | ● |
| 非重读音节符号 | • |
| 节奏群符号 | / |
| 空拍符号 | ? |